JEFFREY D. WILHELM

Deepening Comprehension
WITH
Action Strategies

Role Plays, Text-Structure Tableaux, Talking
Statues, and Other Enactment Techniques
That Engage Students With Text

NEW YORK • TORONTO • LONDON • AUCKLAND • SYDNEY
MEXICO CITY • NEW DELHI • HONG KONG • BUENOS AIRES

*"We cannot know through language what we cannot imagine...
Those who cannot imagine cannot read."* — Elliot Eisner

Dedication

To my friend, teacher, and student, Tanya N. Baker, and

*To my friends and fellow teachers at the Boise State Writing
Project, especially Jim Fredricksen, Rachel Bear,
Andrew Porter, Sarah Veigel, Sharon Hanson,
Emily Morgan, Jan Meeks, Kevin Thienes, Frank Dehoney,
Jerry Hendershot, Paula Uriarte, Yvonne Georgeson
and so many others!*

*Not to forget the Viking Kayak Crew: Ryan Mahan,
Cary James, Melissa Newell, and the "Commander" Bob White.*

*All of you help me negotiate the whitewaters
of life and teaching.*

Scholastic Inc. grants teachers permission to photocopy the reproducible pages from this book for classroom use.
Purchase of this book entitles use of reproducibles by one teacher for one classroom only. No other part of this
publication may be reproduced in whole or in part, or stored in a retrieval system, or transmitted in any form or
by any means, electronic, mechanical, photocopying, recording, or otherwise, without written permission of the
publisher. For information regarding permissions, write to Scholastic Inc., 557 Broadway, New York, NY 10012.

Cover and Interior Designer: Maria Lilja
Copy/Production Editor: Danny Miller
Cover photograph by Maria Lilja
Interior photographs by Michael C. York, Jamie Heans, and Seth Mitchell

Scholastic has made every effort to identify the correct source for work in this book. Any work not correctly
attributed will be attributed in future editions of this book.

ISBN: 978-0-545-21859-7

3 4 5 6 7 8 9 10   23   19 18

Contents

Acknowledgments

Special thanks to Sieta van der Hoeven at the University of South Australia and Charles Morgan at the Tasmanian Department of Education who helped arrange the visiting professorship to Australia, during which I wrote the first edition of this book. More extra special thanks to Erika Boas and to Rachel Bear, who provided considerable inspiration and help in the writing of this second edition through their creative, courageous, and contagious teaching, and their many ideas and responsiveness.

My heartfelt appreciation and thanks to my wife Peggy Jo Wilhelm, teacher extraordinaire and an inspiration in how to navigate life's challenges, and to Tanya Baker, another terrific teacher, for countless contributions: her own innovative work with drama/enactment, her involvement with the Maine Writing Project and now the national level of the National Writing Project, her work with student teachers, and for taking over my classes during my visiting professorship.

I have had the pleasure and privilege of working with some of the world's foremost experts on drama in education, and I am grateful for what I gained from their expertise. My participation in workshops led by David Booth, Cecilly O'Neill, Peter O'Connor, and Jonathan Neelands were inspirational and very useful to me.

Brian Edmiston, who had been my professor at the University of Wisconsin, spent several days in my seventh-grade classroom helping us all learn to use drama and enactment techniques in supportive and enjoyable ways. He also co-taught a summer institute with me at the University of Maine, where I learned a great deal.

I've enjoyed working with the arts educators at the Chicago Teachers Center and the teachers in many schools served by the Center. Karen Boran, Jackie Murphy, Mary Massie, David Flatley, and others have offered me the opportunity to both observe and participate in the best of arts-based education that supports reading and learning.

Thanks to the Viking entourage of teachers, especially Ryan Mahan and Averill Lovely, who are working tirelessly to help adolescent boys struggling with literacy through their own progressive and inventive teaching, and through the Maine Writing Project's Viking Summer Camp for Boys and Literacy. Thanks also to all of the Boise State Writing Project Fellows involved in various projects with me, particularly our Advanced Reading Institute, our Service Learning and Inquiry Institutes, and CCSS In-service work for your brave forays into using drama to teach content and processes and to develop, represent, and share understandings.

I am especially grateful to my many students over the years, those whom I have taught in fifth, seventh, tenth, and eleventh grades, and most recently in AP English classes, those with whom I have worked through pre-service methods classes in teaching English and Reading, and to the many teachers with whom I have worked through the Maine and Boise State Writing Projects, graduate courses, institutes, and in schools as co-teachers. You will see many ideas in this book created or adapted by these dedicated and innovative student teachers and practicing teachers.

I want to extend a special thanks in this regard to Nicole Gamblin, who did her senior project with me on using enactments to teach reading, and to Kate DeStefano, her student teaching partner, who also experimented early and often and consistently with drama strategies. Thanks too to Seth Mitchell for his use of process drama. Many of their ideas are used in this book.

Of course, I want to thank my large and lustrous group of family, friends, mentors, colleagues, and general supporters. Among these, I want to especially thank my editor and good friend Lois Bridges, who has carefully attended to and helped shape several of my books including the second editions of this line of Theory into Practice books, and Danny Miller, production editor extraordinaire.

Thanks are always due my friend and mentor Michael W. Smith, and my own high school English teachers Bill Strohm and James Blaser, who made me see that teaching literature was a powerful and worthwhile pursuit.

I thank Jeff Golub, a giant of generosity, for agreeing to write the foreword to this book. I also wish to thank my colleagues and the leadership at Boise State University for supporting what might at times seem to be somewhat unconventional work and research.

To my many colleagues and friends, I tip my hat and give a spontaneous, grateful and sincere salute. Thanks to all of the National Writing Project teachers from the Boise State Writing Project and the Maine Writing Project who experiment so bravely with their teaching. Here is a quick but in no way perfunctory thanks to special friends and teaching colleagues like Brian Ambrosius, Bill Anthony, Jim Artesani, Erv Barnes, Bill Bedford, Ed Brazee, Todd Fischer, Mike Ford, Paul Friedemann, Stuart Greene, Leon Holley Jr., Bruce Hunter, Jan Kristo, Craig Martin, Paula Moore, Bruce Nelson, Bruce Novak, Wayne Otto, Dale Reynolds, "One Armed" Willie Stewart, John Thorpe, Brian White, and Denny Wolfe. And, of course, extra thanks to my loving family, particularly my dad, Jack Wilhelm; my wife, Peggy Jo, and my two daughters, Fiona Luray and Jasmine Marie, who are very fine and smiling and wonderful human beings of whom I am very proud. They assist me every day and also assisted substantively in the writing of this second edition.

Author's Note: Action Strategies and the Common Core State Standards

In my opinion, the Common Core State Standards (CCSS) offer the best opportunity for progressive educational change that I have seen in more than 30 years as an educator. Using action strategies to promote more proficient reading, composing, and learning across topics, themes, and genres has never been more important. The CCSS represent a welcome and profound paradigm shift towards instruction that focuses on student expertise and the strategic tools that they need to excel across the disciplines.

Please note that these standards cannot be addressed, much less met, through business as usual. The standards call on every teacher to transform his or her teaching into a problem-oriented, meaning-making pursuit that develops effective strategic capacities. A robust body of research shows that developing strategic knowledge requires modeling, mentoring, and monitoring students' use of strategies in meaningful contexts—and how to do so is a major theme of the first few chapters of this book.

Look at the language of the CCSS: the standards use active production verbs such as *write, produce, research, argue,* and *persuade*. The later chapters of this book include engaging ideas for collaborative inquiry projects, opportunities for students to use technology and multimedia, and ways that you can draw on both formative and summative assessment to monitor and track your students' progress with Common Core and more (watch for the CCSS icons in the margins signaling a direct link). The comprehension and composition strategies I introduce in this book are useful in helping students to succeed as proficient, independent readers and composers of high quality, complex text.

Embracing the standards doesn't mean abandoning our smart, principled approach to informed teaching. What we know about time-tested research, best practices, and, particularly, those specific human beings who are our own students remains as critical as ever. Did you know that in a typical fourth-grade classroom, you're likely to find a reading span of seven grades—from a second-grade reading level all the way to ninth grade ability (Hargis, 2006)? Clearly, one size does not fit all. It makes sense, then, to provide our students with as many possible ways to access, comprehend, and converse with challenging texts of all kinds. Our struggling readers and writers, Limited Formal Schooling (LFS) students, and English Language Learners will succeed to the extent that we scaffold and differentiate our instruction.

Finally, the Common Core State Standards call for making our classrooms arenas of productivity and creativity (instead of consumption) where students may produce written work across genres, dramatic and theatrical performances, and create a wide range of artifacts from videos to museum exhibits. We need to move from places where kids only consume other people's meanings to places where they create their own.

This book will help you develop a productive repertoire of diverse teaching and learning strategies; what's more, you'll learn what contexts and strategies work best to assist students in becoming proficient readers and composers. Above all, you will promote a dynamic mindset (Dweck, 2009) of growth and potential in both your students and yourself that will lead to a lifetime of productive learning.

—Jeff Wilhelm
Boise, Idaho, July 2012

Introduction

I can't imagine teaching without drama, aka "action strategies"—and the fun, creativity, spontaneity, and very real joy that comes from doing them. While I write this, I am in Australia—just as I was nine years ago when I wrote the first edition of this book. Yesterday, I was asked to do some fishbowl teaching at The King's School outside of Sydney with some "Year 7s" and I readily agreed. The class was reading *Macbeth and Son*, a young adult novel that involves a modern-day protagonist, Luke, who dreams of Lulach, the son of the historical Macbeth—a figure who most historians agree was a good and peace-loving king. Luke becomes obsessed with the question: What is true? He struggles with the idea that history or other records like Shakespeare's play may be inaccurate and unfair to the characters involved.

The class had just finished reading the book on their own, and my class period was the first one devoted to exploring and responding to the reading. I began class by quickly explaining process drama and casting the class with the "mantle of the expert," in this case as dream analysts who had read the "case study" of our dreamer, Luke. To begin,

we did a ritual drama where everyone made a nameplate for their desk with the title: Dr. Miller, Dream Analyst or Psychoanalyst. We then introduced ourselves to each other. I played "teacher in role" as Der sehr geehrter Herr Professor Doktor Wilhelm from the Carl Jung Institute in Zurich. My role could also be considered "stranger in role" as I pretended to not have read the book—or "case study"—myself. This meant that all information about the book had to come from the class, and that they had to explain fine points and connections to me. Through the simple ritual activity, the class was already fully immersed in the drama.

In role, I had them write about a time in their own childhood when they had experienced a problem with discerning the truth. As we shared these stories, we explored different notions of the truth: the verifiable scientific kind of truth, "story truth" that resonates with or explains one's experiences, and "psychic truth" that seems to explain cultural or human experience more broadly. We discussed when different kinds of "truth" were important in our own stories, and promised to bring empathy to our case study.

We then broke into small groups whose job was to report out on the five most significant events from the "amaneusis" or "life history" of either Luke, his friend Megan, or Lulach. The groups reported out, then were asked to identify the most important event in each life and

Jeff plays the "stranger in role" as a Northerner asking the people of the Southern town of Strawberry what has happened there, as told in the book *Roll of Thunder, Hear My Cry.*

how this offered challenges to that person and eventually came to shape their personhood. Finally, each group identified the most important correspondences between Luke's life and his dreams about Lulach. We engaged in a "forum drama" as each group presented their findings and took questions from the rest of us. By the end of the hour, we were all highly motivated to continue our study of the book. We had summarized and reviewed major events and their importance and had already begun to search for patterns and make inferences about the text. It was a magical experience, and the class asked if I could please please PLEASE come back the next day, but unfortunately I was off to work with some teachers in the Aboriginal homelands in the far north of Australia. As I departed, one student shouted, "Good-bye, Professor! Safe travels to Zurich!" Another called out, "Your work has inspired our own!" A third, "I will reference you in my new book on dreams!" I had a good laugh—they were still in role even as the bell rang and we left the classroom.

Whenever I am asked to do a model lesson, I gravitate to drama/action strategies. If properly framed, this work always 1) proves to be great fun, 2) is active and engaging for everyone in the class, 3) leads to substantive learning, 4) is interactive, democratic, and a powerful form of joint productive activity as described by Vygotsky, 5) is able to model and teach practically any concept or strategy, 7) fosters imagination, creativity, and problem-solving that is rarely unleashed in schools, and 8) is practically foolproof. It works, and is so rarely used that the students and teacher observers are almost certain to see and experience much that is entirely new to them. The students become enthusiastic co-producers of curriculum and meaning, so the activity is spontaneous and energizing.

I've continued to work, almost daily it seems, with drama/action strategies in my own teaching—with students and people of all ages. Often the opportunity to use this repertoire of techniques comes up spontaneously. The techniques are just plain easy and FUN to use. They naturally fit into any classroom in any subject. Different techniques can be combined in

Denali, Stephanie, and Erin pay rapt attention to classmates providing expert testimony about the extinction of various animal species.

limitless ways. I love teaching with drama/action strategies, and my teaching would be greatly impoverished without this repertoire of teaching tools. Another benefit: when using drama, my students are engaged and construct substantive understandings, and they are accountable through their making, doing, and writing inside the drama. Using drama, I can't teach in a way that is mere transmission of information. The classroom becomes a workshop where we work together to mentor each other into deeper understanding. Action strategies are a great way to involve our students in developing knowledge through doing—and the planning and discussion that is involved in the application of knowledge.

Over the past decade, I've worked to help interns and practicing teachers use action strategies in all subject areas, with many different genres and data sets, with all kinds of kids (ELL, LFS or limited formal schooling/refugee students, struggling readers, AP English—the gamut!). As I've continued to work with and expand my repertoire of action strategies, I've become increasingly impressed with its multi-faceted applications and astonishing flexibility as a teaching tool.

I've been continually experimenting, as all good teachers do, with new variants of the technique. I've also combined the techniques with various technologies, used them as formative assessments, and used them as a teacher research tool.

This second edition is not only revised, but also includes several new sections on how to teach with action strategies. Action strategies can help students practice and master, *in real reading and learning contexts*, all the general processes of reading (activating background knowledge, decoding, visualizing/experiencing text, predicting, summarizing, questioning, monitoring) as well as higher order interpretive operations such as those that comprise genre-specific and task-specific strategies.

It's worth noting that the next generation of standards (including the Common Core State Standards—or CCSS—in the states and provincial standards in Canada) and assessments (like Smarter Balance and PARCC) require this kind of higher-order strategic work with narrative, informational, and argument texts. These standards also require short and extended research projects and inquiries. It's also worth noting that these standards are not *standardized*, but encourage—in fact, require—teacher autonomy and creativity. It's up to us to choose materials and implement methods that will best help our students to meet these standards.

To meet the letter and spirit of these standards, students need to engage, over time, with compelling problems that require literate behaviors to address: ways of framing events, seeing multiple perspectives, finding alternatives, collaborating, analyzing and synthesizing, problem-solving, constructing identities, and practicing one's agency. All of these activities are required by action/drama strategies and by inquiry itself. Therefore, this second edition also focuses on how action strategies help foster new ways of understanding inquiry-oriented teaching.

I'll also provide some of the most popular FAQs (Frequently-Asked Questions)—and answers to them, too, of course—that have come up in my drama workshops, classes, and email exchanges with teachers about the techniques.

For your convenience, the text in the following chapters is coded with icons referring you to particular examples from the DVD.

I am very pleased that this second edition has a section on how to use technology to promote and extend the action strategy repertoire, and that it is being released with a DVD, filmed during the National Writing Project's "Camp Reading Rocks" for kids—many of whom are English Language Learners (ELL), Limited Formal Schooling (LFS), or struggling readers. What you will see on the DVD are real teachers using drama strategies for the first time with real kids. The DVD will show you how you can reasonably introduce the technique to your students to various ends. Where you will take the technique next is anybody's guess. This repertoire is so powerful and flexible that I'm constantly amazed with how teachers and students come up with new techniques and transform existing ones for their own purposes. Action strategies truly are learning and problem-solving strategies made visible. For your convenience, the text is coded with icons referring you to particular examples from the DVD.

If you'd like to see more video clips of me explaining a range of comprehension strategies and learning theory, check out the Curriculum Services of Canada (CSC): http://curriculum.org/content/about-csc. Type "Jeff Wilhelm" into the search line and a complete offering of my archived webcasts will pop up; it's all free—download and enjoy.

How This Book Is Organized

Chapter 1 answers the most pressing and frequently-asked questions I've received over the years regarding action strategies: "What are they, Jeff, and why do you believe so passionately in their ability to foster learning in the classroom?" Chapter 2 reviews the learning theory that informs all of my books and that aptly supports using enactment. Chapter 3 shows you how to use various before-reading enactment strategies to motivate and equip students with the knowledge they will need to approach and deeply comprehend a new text. Chapters 5, 6, 7, 9, 10, and 11 divide the enactment strategies into "families." Sometimes strategies fit more than one family type, and my assignment of a strategy to a particular family is done for the purpose of introducing you to the technique with coherence and clarity. In other words, as you become expert at using enactments, you'll find yourself blending the "families" together; adapting and combining them as you wish. Again, for the sake of clarity, I've chosen a single core text for this book—a short story called "The Fan Club" through which I model and explain various enactments. I encourage you to read and become familiar with the story, as it will help you take in all of the myriad renditions and curricular uses of action strategies that I'll be throwing your way in these pages. New chapters to the second edition, besides Chapter 1, include Chapter 4, which spotlights drama, Chapter 8, which centers on technology, and Chapter 12, which explains the role of drama/action strategies as both summative and particularly formative assessment.

CHAPTER I

FREQUENTLY-ASKED QUESTIONS ABOUT ENACTMENTS

What They Are and Why They Work

Rachel Bear divides her AP English Students into small groups and then casts each group as a character from *Candide*. One group becomes Dr. Pangloss, another Candide, and so on. The last group takes on the role of the author, Voltaire. She then asks each group to brainstorm questions that a talk show audience would want to pose to their assigned character and to rehearse possible answers. The groups intently get to work on posing open-ended questions of interest. They know that one of them will soon be on the spot! A few minutes later, Rachel chooses one student from each group to be on a talk show panel. The home group will get to ask the first two questions to their "character" and will then play the "lifeline," helping their "hot-seated" group member field challenging questions that come up from the rest of the class.

Before sharing Ronald Wallace's poem, "Grandmother Grace," with a group of seventh graders, Kylene Beers cuts up lines from the poem and gives one to each student. For ten minutes they walk around, share their lines, and try to stitch together an idea of what the poem may be about. Their voices rise with their building curiosity. Kylene smiles. She's got them hooked. She then asks them to sit down and imagine they are one of the characters in the poem and to talk about their feelings about what may happen to them. Finally, Kylene hands out the complete poem and begins to read it aloud.

In my own class, I invite my students to identify themselves as either a New England Patriots football team fan or as a fan of the archrival New York Jets, and go to opposite sides of the room. I tell the two groups that I want them to interact as if they are meeting each other on the way to the championship game. They can make signs, taunt each other, whatever, but they have to prepare quickly. In a few minutes, they are ready. "You're going down!" "Your team is lunch meat!" they exclaim. One girl holds a sign: "Don't Bet on the Jets. They'll Be Grounded!"

I ask them to add gestures. They do. Then I suggest they bite their thumbs at one another, explaining that it's an old-fashioned way of showing your disapproval. They do one last go-round of good-natured taunts, and bite their thumbs.

With the students' energy high, I tell them that now, one group is to be Capulets and the other Montagues. *Ahh, we get it*, their expressions tell me. Having spent five minutes acting out a contemporary rivalry that they understand, students can now connect personal experience to the feud introduced in the first scene of Shakespeare's *Romeo and Juliet*.

What's the common thread linking all these vignettes? Action strategies—also known as *enactment strategies* or *drama strategies*. For the purposes of this book, I will regularly refer to them as enactments, since even the word "drama" can understandably produce full-blown stage fright in many of us. And just so you know from the get-go: enactments are not theater, and do not require props, stages, rehearsals, or acting skills.

Enactment: A Definition

Enactment is, quite simply, creating situations in which we "imagine to learn" (Wilhelm and Edmiston, 1998). As a teacher, I invite students to imagine together, actively depicting characters, forces, or ideas, and to interact in these roles. An enactment may be cast in the past, the present, or the future, but always happens in the "now of time." In other words, the time of reference may be past or futuristic, fictional or historical, it may be the year 1776 or 3076, but the action unfolds as if that time is now. Enactments can be used in any curricular area or disciplinary study. Through enactments, you can highlight and teach strategies of reading and learning, and help students create interpretations of text and data sets that reverberate with artistic, aesthetic, and metaphorical meanings.

The Benefits of Enactment Strategies

As I trust is palpable from the teaching scenarios described above, students take to these strategies like squirrels to acorns and trees; enactments enliven and engage students, and get them interacting with texts in profoundly different ways than when students sit at desks and answer questions about a book. Enactment strategies are the most powerful strategies I use, so much so that I cannot imagine teaching without them. Curiously—as educator David Booth once told me—they are the most underused strategies in the American teaching repertoire. I hope this book will give them a higher profile, as my own teaching and research has shown me how effective they are for motivating and assisting students—particularly at-risk and reluctant students—to become more engaged and competent readers and learners (Wilhelm, 1997/2008; Wilhelm and Edmiston, 1998; Wilhelm, Baker, and Dube, 2001; Smith and Wilhelm, 2002; 2006; 2009; Wilhelm and Novak, 2011). The findings in my own studies are abetted by a wide research base that has shown how these strategies can help all students, particularly those whose ways of learning and knowing are not privileged, in traditional classrooms. (See Wagner, 1998, for a research review. See Smith and Wilhelm, 2002, for a data-driven explanation of why enactment strategies engage and assist students.)

I have adapted many of the enactment strategies in this book from the field of drama in education; many others I have developed in collaboration with colleagues and students. Here, I will outline enactment's nine chief benefits.

1. Enactments Make Both Teaching and Reading Transformative Experiences

Re-enactment Drama: Entering the Story World

Enactment strategies give students new entry points into text—and yes, many of them are active, requiring students to move physically—but the goal of enactments is to get students' minds to move to new places, to be transformed. *Think about it:* When we teach anything, but particularly when we teach something like reading or literature, we are actually involved in a more significant pursuit—transformative teaching. Transformative teaching is the flip side of transformative learning, which Valde and Kornetsky define as "learning experiences that alter one's understanding of oneself, one's notion of the nature of knowledge or the meaning of knowing, one's ethical sense or world view, one's sense of self and one's place in the world, and/or one's life or vocational trajectory" (2002, p. 5). I know that I love reading and teaching literature because stories and other kinds of texts provide me with a unique way of knowing, giving me new lenses for seeing myself and the world in different ways. Reading transforms me and helps me see and try out new possibilities. Since I want the same experience for my students, I give them the tools and strategies necessary for transformative experiences with texts. Enactments assist students in internalizing these kinds of strategies.

2. Enactments Can Be Used Flexibly

Enactments can be engaged individually, silently, in writing, through pair work, or in large groups. They can be used spontaneously, with little preparation, for as short a time as 30 seconds or for extended periods. Enactments can be used in combination with other strategies to form a *story drama* (a series of enactments that get students using certain reading strategies to support their comprehension and engagement in extended ways as they work throughout a whole text) or a *process drama* (where one dramatic activity helps students spontaneously plan and shape another activity). However, when you are first using these strategies, you'll probably feel most comfortable with shorter, single strategies. You will soon learn to combine them in more sophisticated and extended ways. My friend and colleague Michael W. Smith has these rules for enactments: they should be short, spontaneous, scriptless, and used often because they can teach any concept or process in the curriculum!

3. Enactments Assist Students Before, During, and After Reading

To quote educator Margaret Meek, enactment strategies "make public the secret things that expert readers know and do" so that these usually invisible strategies will be made physical, external and concrete. This is powerful, as the noted Russian psychologist Lev Vygotsky (1978) argued that all learning must proceed from the concrete to the abstract, from the external to the internal, from the "near to home," if you will, to understandings and ways of doing things that are "further" from home—meaning more foreign, specialized, and distant from students' lived experience.

Enactment strategies can be used by a teacher or fellow students to model expert reading strategies and to work through the strategies together, through each of the three phases of reading: *before reading, during reading,* and *after reading.*

Before reading, enactments help students to

- activate their prior knowledge and relevant background experiences.
- connect a text to related texts, in terms of content, structure, genre, required strategies and interpretive operations, or all of these combined.
- build the schematic knowledge/content background necessary to comprehend the text.
- set purposes for reading.
- build motivation to read.
- prepare emotionally and cognitively for the reading experience.

During reading, enactments help students to

- evoke the textual world.
- build and sustain their belief in the textual world.
- use appropriate reading strategies and develop facility with new necessary strategies.
- enliven their reading and be motivated to continue reading.
- feel their way through a reading by emotionally navigating it and training their emotional responses towards compassion and understanding.
- intensely visualize places, situations, actions, and people.
- enter into varying perspectives; help students become characters, ideas, or forces acting upon the characters.
- infer—to see and make meaning of simple and complex implied relationships.
- connect the text to their lives and/or larger issues of social significance; to elaborate on the textual world.
- engage their ethical imagination, helping them to ask: "What if?" "What do we believe?" "What should we do as a result?"
- assist other's reading performance through modeling, sharing, and collaborative work.

Anchor Standards for Reading, 1–3

After reading, enactments help students to

- negotiate and reflect on meaning.
- discern, discuss, and evaluate the author's visions, meaning his or her generalizations, themes, and main ideas.
- reflect on text structure and how this affects meaning.
- reflect on their own interpretation and response, rehearsing what do and work on in future readings and how to act in analogous real-life situations.
- consider alternatives and elaborations, going beyond what is directly stated to other possibilities—or pursue inquiry into questions raised by the text.
- consider how to apply what's been learned in the text to their own lives (asking questions like "So what?" and "Now what?").

Anchor Standards for Reading, 4–9

Later, you will see how many of these readerly strategies get practiced in a 90-minute period, working with the short story "The Fan Club."

4. Enactments Harness the Power of the Social Nature of Learning

Vygotsky (1978) posited that all learning is social. Enactments give teachers a way to "socialize" meaningfully with students—engaging, confronting, and challenging them, so they will outgrow their current selves and learn new strategies, stances, conceptual knowledge, and ways of being. Enactments give students a means of learning together in the following ways:

Enactments are action-oriented and participatory. They

- require students to work together, express their opinions, listen to each other, and create meaning together.
- require active involvement by all parties.
- provide a variety of roles and ways to participate.
- begin with and are driven by student interests, by what they already know and find significant, by their feelings and problems and emotional charges, through sharing of all of this, and by what is socially relevant to them.
- develop new interests in students.

Enactments are socio-constructivist and democratic. They

- enable students and teachers to construct meaning and new understandings together.
- give everyone a voice, and those voices must all be attended to.

5. Enactments Invite Students to Think and Feel and Imagine

As you will see throughout this book, enactments take students' thinking and imagining to new heights. They bracket emotions and can harness and train them for positive ends. They create situations where feeling and creativity are at the center of learning, fueling it in ways supported by current cognitive science and neuroscience (e.g., see Doidge, 2006; Begley, 2008), instead of being placed on the periphery. They powerfully combine feeling, creativity, divergent thinking, and the embodiment of lived-through experience with rigorous, reasoned thinking. They flex students' intellects, emotions, and imaginations in the following ways:

They are liminal.

An enactment exists on the threshold between what is real and what is imaginary. Things can be said, done, or manipulated in ways that are experimental, and yet the situation will have the power of reality (O'Neill, 1982).

They are substantive.

In an enactment, reasoning must be made visible, and knowledge made accountable (cf. Mercer, 1995). What is created during an enactment must fit what we know from the text and the world. Enactments make hidden processes of reading and learning visible and open to evaluation and revision.

They promote inquiry.

Enactments require us to go beyond facts to their causes, meaning, and ramifications, and to what could be different. Students will observe others (ethnographic research), live through and experience new positions and perspectives (phenomenological research), and can experiment with the possibilities and consequences of different courses of action (action research) (Edmiston and Wilhelm, 1998).

6. Enactments Are Motivating

This sixth chief benefit may be the most potent benefit of all: motivation. An enactment is playful, fun, and emotionally engaging. Various theorists and researchers studying the brain, learning, and human potential have demonstrated that learning is most powerful when the participants are having fun (Bloom, 1976; Csikszentmihalyi, 1990; Csikszentmihalyi, Rathunde, and Whalen, 1993; Hillocks, 1995; Heath and McLaughlin, 1993; Vygotsky, 1978, see also Doidge, 2006; Begley, 2008).

Attending to how kids learn and whether they are enjoying something is essential. As Vygotsky (1978) argues, people can only learn in their zone of proximal development— a zone in which they can do (or feel or be) with help what they cannot do (or feel or be) independently. When people enter into their cognitive zone of proximal development (ZPD), where learning occurs, they must first have moved through their motivational ZPD (Coles, 1998). They need to have a reason to learn, a purpose for learning, and a belief that they will be successful. Enactments fulfill all these needs, and are motivating because they

- provide a meaningful context and applicable situation for learning.
- highlight human purposes and experience.
- connect reading to the world and to social action.
- frame the learning, supporting and assisting students to use new strategies and ways of knowing.
- make use of a variety of student strengths and literacies by using various kinds of movement, gestures, visuals, oral language, and so forth, to create meaning with text. In so doing, they provide students with alternative ways to work through and think about texts. This is particularly motivating for those students considered at-risk or unsuccessful in normal school settings (Wilhelm, 1997/2008; Smith and Wilhelm, 2002, 2006; Wilhelm and Edmiston, 1998; Yaffe, 1989).

Enactment is "a major force in boosting a child's self-concept and desire to be an active part of a learning community" (McMaster, 1998), and the success students experience in enactments can lead to increased motivation for reading, which in turn leads to further success (Bordan, 1970).

7. Enactments Help Students Achieve a State of "Flow"

My recent research with Michael Smith on the role of literacy in the lives of boys and young men demonstrates that students are engaged by learning situations in which the conditions of "flow" (optimal experience) are present (Smith and Wilhelm, 2002, 2006; cf. Csikszentmihalyi, 1990). These conditions include

- choice and control.
- social interaction and involvement.
- a sense of developing competence.

Using Enactments Throughout the Reading Process

An Example Using *The Great Gatsby*

So, what might it look like to weave enactment strategies into your teaching repertoire? Just how do they support students throughout the reading process? I invited teacher Tanya Baker to share how she does this. She says, "I'm planning my unit on *The Great Gatsby*. In the past, this novel has given my students trouble in several places, and I think drama can help them over those humps."

With Tanya's comment, you see, when planning a unit, one aim might be to anticipate things students might struggle with, and build your enactment activities around them.

Tanya continues. "After they read Chapter 1, I want students to concentrate on making connections to the characters. I know that the setting (the time and the wealth, for example) is foreign to them, but they should still be able to think about what sort of people these characters are. I'll have them work in groups for support and use the text to make sense of the characters. They

will write questions to ask a character and practice answering them. They will also make a list of questions they'd ask other characters. When they are ready, I'll put students 'in the hotseat' to take turns answering questions from their peers as if they are the characters.

"After the first four chapters, I will have students work together on teams as private detectives in a 'mantle of the expert' strategy. Their job will be to determine an answer to their client's question: Who is Jay Gatsby? They will make a list of what they've heard about Gatsby, using things that Gatsby and other characters have said. The students will decide which things on the list they believe and which they don't, and they will also have to give their reasons for believing or disbelieving. Student groups will write up a report to be delivered to their clients. This will help them see the complex implied relationships that the text asks them to see.

"During Chapter 5, I'm planning to do 'tableaux/ silent movie.' Students are always confused by the silent scene at the end of Chapter 5. So here, I'll have students form acting companies that will perform a 'silent movie' version of what Gatsby sees through

- active assistance to meet new challenges.
- a connection to high levels of personal relevance and social significance.

These conditions abound in the kinds of enactment activities this book will explore. Interestingly, the boys in our study often cited drama—by which they generally meant role playing—to be a favorite part of school because it gave them the chance to be active, to work with others, and to make and express meaning. The strategies in this book will assist teachers in helping students do all those things, but will also go well beyond traditional notions of role playing or acting out a dramatic script.

the window on the night of the accident. Each company will have a director, a reader, and two actors. As the reader goes over the paragraph phrase by phrase, the director will 'direct' the actors playing Tom and Daisy. Ultimately, each acting company has to decide what Gatsby witnesses between Tom and Daisy that night. Each company's actors will present the scene as the reader reads. In a 'director's cut,' the director will explain why she 'shot' the scene in this way. Students will discuss the scenes and any discrepancies, and reach a consensus on what Tom and Daisy discuss and decide on that night.

"After the silent movies we'll do 'whispers,' with one student playing Gatsby. I'll give the other students a chance to come up to him as he sits alone to give him advice about what he should do. Because of 'silent movie,' students will be quite involved in making sense of what Tom and Daisy are doing to ruin Gatsby's plans, so they should be more than willing to tell what Gatsby ought to do next. Also, I think it is a point in the story at which, although the narrator still has mixed feelings about Gatsby, he feels compassion for him. I want my students to think about the mess that Gatsby is in and try to express their feelings about that to the character.

"At the end of the book, few people come to pay their respects to Jay Gatsby. And although both Nick and Gatsby's father seem to love Gatsby, they don't talk to each other much. I'll divide the class into two groups, and we will imagine that it is a month after the funeral. Group A will take on the role of Mr. Gatz, group B will play the role of Nick Carraway. Each student will write from his or her assigned character's point of view to the other character about what they know and what they wish to know about Gatsby. Individuals in groups A and B will exchange letters, and each person will underline a particularly apt, moving, or poignant line. Students will then work in their groups to prepare a choral montage of the letters." (See Chapter 9 for details.)

8. Enactments Are Embodied, Deeply Experienced, and Felt

Action strategies provide imaginative and lived-through experiences. There is an engagement of the whole person through "body, mind, and soul." There is a privileging of emotion and an exploration, consideration, and even training in feeling and using emotional experiences more positively for one's own benefit, for others' and the environment's benefit. Powerful emotions can be explored in safe and contained ways as the drama work is bracketed, and can be stopped and stepped back from for more objective consideration at any time or interval.

9. Enactments Promote Character, Social Imagination, and Ethical Imagination

No matter what we teach, and no matter whether we are aware of it or not, we are always teaching students how to be in the world, how to deal with problems, collaborate, value, see other perspectives (or not), care, and deal with moral dilemmas. Enactments make this process visible and into an object of study and reflection.

More on Boys and Literacy

The boys in our study complained about the lack of action-oriented learning activities in school. As Michael Smith and I began to analyze the data, it became clear why enactment strategies would be so attractive to them. The boys expressed a desire for:

A challenge that requires skill

- including assistance to meet challenges.

Clear goals and feedback, which was supported by the chance to

- make or do something.
- apply or use what has been learned.
- name what they learned and how they could use it.

A sense of control, which was abetted by the opportunity to

- make choices.
- develop and display competence.
- express their own opinion.
- construct, share, and use their own understandings.

Social activity, such as

- working together on something meaningful.
- the chance to share who they are and what they have learned.

Fun and humor, including

- laughter.
- losing themselves in the immediate task.

(Smith and Wilhelm, 2002)

Frequently-Asked Questions About Enactments

Over the years, I've received numerous queries about enactments—what they are and why they work. In addition to discussing their great benefits for all teachers and students, I'd also like to answer some frequently-asked questions and reassure my readers that anyone can use enactments in the classroom; they are easy to implement and make a huge difference for all students.

Why do you love action strategies so much?

They are fun and active for both the teacher and students. They encourage and actually require all students to be engaged and involved. Every time I use an action strategy it turns out differently, so I don't get bored. The students, the teacher, and the material work together to dynamically co-produce meaning. There is sure to be laughter, flashes of surprising insight, and astounding creativity. Action strategies make use of creative imagination and problem-solving. Did I mention how engaging and fun action strategies are? When I use one with a class, they invariably beg me to plan another time to use that strategy again.

How do action/drama strategies differ from theater or theater-in-education strategies?

Drama-in-education strategies and theater–in-education are often used interchangeably, but drama is more spontaneous, short, and unscripted. Drama does not require costumes, a stage, or rehearsal. You can use an action or drama strategy at any point in a class where it might be useful, without a lot of prior planning and preparation. My friend Michael Smith says his rules for drama are: short, spontaneous, scriptless, and not seldom! Theater is typically more pre-planned, scripted, and rehearsed. As a classroom teacher, I prefer drama/action strategy. I can see an opportunity to use one to fill a current need and a few seconds later we are "imagining to learn." (See Wilhelm and Edmiston, 1998, for a series of studies on the power of using classroom drama for various ends.)

What "good" are action strategies? What can you teach through them?

Anchor Standards for Reading, 1–10

Speaking and Listening, 1–5

You can use drama/action strategies to provide a meaningful context for learning, to model almost any strategy for students, and then to assist them on how use that strategy in a meaningful context. Action strategies are great for dealing with difficult and complicated processes required by the Common Core State Standards (CCSS), like determining central ideas or themes and analyzing their development; and analyzing how and WHY individuals, events, and ideas develop and interact over the course of a text. Action strategies activate the human, the contextual, and the emotional elements of what is being learned. I strongly believe that we must attend more to emotional affect if we want our students to be engaged learners who come to understand deeply.

Action strategies make use of multi-modalities, which allow students to "know" and "understand" through what is known as *transmediation* —the capacity to explore and express understandings in various forms.

One way in which the CCSS differ from previous state standards is that they have a specific focus on 21st Century literacies like the use of multi-modalities. Both the reading and writing standards include specific directions to read and compose in "diverse formats." The importance of 21st Century literacy is clear from the inclusion of standards for speaking and listening; for example, speaking and listening Anchor Standard Number 3 requires students to be able to "make strategic use of digital media and visual displays of data to express information and enhance understanding of presentations." The CCSS are vertically aligned through the grade levels, e.g., in order or to meet this standard, Grade 6 students should be able to "interpret information presented in diverse media and formats and explain how it contributes to a topic, text, or issue under study" while Grade 11-12 students should be able to "integrate multiple sources of information presented in diverse formats and media in order to make informed decisions and solve problems, evaluating the credibility and accuracy of each source and noting any discrepancies among the data." The multi-modal action strategies, like documentaries, how-to videos, Facebook newsfeeds, etc., are engaging and effective ways to meet these standards at all levels and can be adapted for the increasing text complexity called for as students move into the higher grade levels.

Nate, dressed up as the protagonist of *Deathwatch*, tells other adventurers how he survived his ordeal. Fiona, in the role of Death, comments on how Nate cheated her of his life to help the class explore the thematic implications of the book for our survival study.

Action strategies are what Santayana calls "imaginative rehearsals for living" so that students are thinking about how they might enact their knowledge, or what they might do in similar situations. Action strategies, when used in the context of an inquiry unit, lead toward deep, felt, humane, embodied, and enacted understanding—essential, according to current neuroscience, to laying down new neural pathways in the brain (see Damasio, 2008). Action strategies naturally prepare students and lead them to creating culminating projects involving drama, interactive presentations, video and filmmaking, and much more.

I would also argue that we must attend to the quality of our students' lived-through experience each day. We need to leverage the unique social capacities of the classroom and do things together that cannot be done alone. We need to have fun each day with our students, and they need to have fun as well. *Learning is fun!* It may be challenging fun, but becoming more competent and developing new aspects of ourselves in terms of interest and ability is just plain fun! Indeed, it is our professional responsibility to engage in such activities and conversations and to endlessly strive to outgrow *our* current teaching selves.

Anchor Standard for Reading, 10:

Text Complexity Standards

It is also our responsibility to induct students into the grand conversations (Peterson & Eeds, 2007) of humankind, so well exemplified by literature, so that they can continually outgrow *their* current selves. As we do so, we need to consciously cultivate some often ignored aspects of our students' learning repertoires: imagination, empathy, taking on different perspectives, establishing identity and agency, relating and belonging, civic engagement, and the willingness and ability to serve others and ideas bigger than oneself. If one cannot imagine, then one cannot entertain or take on other perspectives. Without imagination and the capacity to take on other perspectives, one cannot create a meaningful identity, sense of agency, or cultivate empathy. Without empathy, one cannot live a moral and morally satisfying life in relationship with others.

I often challenge the teachers and student teachers with whom I work to consider how they can teach in such a way so that we—as teachers—and our students can all develop towards becoming our best possible selves. Drama is one such way to achieve this.

Don't action strategies interrupt the reading process?

I often use action strategies at the beginning of class as a way to review, explore, and respond to the previous day's reading. I sometimes use them at the end of an excerpt or at the end of class to consider more deeply a character's dilemma or another issue that has come up. These kinds of teaching moves do not interrupt reading. But sometimes a question will come up or an issue will present itself and we decide to stop and explore this through drama during a reading. Sometimes I use "story drama" where action strategies are inserted throughout a reading. This does interrupt a reading—but there are huge payoffs—all readers who use the drama/action strategies in such situations *placehold* their comprehension, deepen their response, are alerted to implied patterns of meaning they must continue to attend to, develop deeper metacognitive awareness, and enhance their engagement with characters, situations, and ideas. Furthermore, the CCSS requires *all* students, including ELL, LFS, and students who struggle with reading to independently and proficiently read the range, quality, and complexity of texts described in Reading Standard 10. In order to do this, students will need clear and explicit instruction in the reading strategies that take place with such complex texts and interrupting reading with comprehension and interpretation drama strategies is a powerful way to assist students toward independent reading of such texts.

Action strategies meet the "correspondence concept" of helping student readers to do what experts do—and in a way that is safe, exploratory, and fun. Action strategies meet the *real reader test, the real writer test*, the *real and humane democratic citizen test*. They are toolish, not schoolish. They use imagination in such a way that develops real world functions and capacities.

When would you use action strategies? How often?

I probably use drama/action strategies more than any other technique in my repertoire. I use short drama techniques, often lasting only two or three minutes, each and every day. Sometimes I do more extended drama work. Opportune times to use dramas include: when students ask a question that drama can help answer, where characters are faced with dilemmas, in dense sections of text where ideas must be clarified or reinforced, or when we need to reflect and consolidate our learning or textual experience—such as after an emotionally intense episode or an ambiguous or challenging segment of text.

Each different technique works to meet different purposes and promote different strategies, stances, moves, and perspectives. The more you use these techniques, the more you will see the "work" they get done, and the invitations within the text for using certain strategies for particular ends. We will explore this idea throughout the book.

Process dramas and story dramas are sequences of linked drama strategies that navigate students through the reading of a longer excerpt of text, or even through a whole problem, genre structure, problem-solving process, or inquiry unit. In such work, teachers create a coherent drama world and continually use the opportunities that arise to plug in appropriate strategies to get that work done. This can be a very spontaneous, "seat of the pants" kind of activity in which the teacher proactively exploits every opportunity and invitation to use drama to make meaning in the context of a reading or inquiry.

I'm still experiencing some trepidation. How can I be sure I'll be successful when I use these strategies?

No strategy is guaranteed to run like a Cuisinart. But I've found that when drama is successfully framed, it always works—maybe not exactly the way I was hoping it would—but it works. I "frame" drama work by making sure every student knows the *purpose* of the activity, the *process* of the activity (including their role and what they are being asked to do), and the *deliverable* for the activity—what they must produce or be able to report out on at the end. I keep drama activities short and make sure there is accountability—artifacts and ideas that must be composed and shared. I call this PPD—Purpose, Process, Deliverable.

I would advise those new to drama to use one short version of a technique to start. Then try another short drama episode sometime later. Embed a

single strategy when you read aloud to students. Do lots of quick hits and you will soon feel more comfortable doing more extended work or work that connects the use of one drama strategy to another strategy.

Douglas acts as Nick's Inner Voice or Alter Ego, explaining what he is really thinking after he responds to questions from students in their roles as Nick's parents and teachers.

I'm sold, but how can I convince and help colleagues to use drama/action strategies and other creative strategies?

Teachers need exactly what students need –purposeful and meaningful work, situated practice, and assistance over time. In sum, teachers need a clear vision of what they are doing and why they are doing it. They also need to understand how these strategies fit and work towards achieving the goals that they value. Often, that is conceptual understanding—but research clearly demonstrates that you can't develop the conceptual separate from the procedural/strategic. You learn the WHAT through doing the HOW. Having a book study group or lesson planning group is a great way to try out new ideas. Having a peer coach is kind of like having a training partner—somebody you commit to helping and being helped by as you try new ideas. Vygotsky indicated that "play is the most natural form of learning" and anybody who has been around small children knows this is true. BJ Wagner has found that the older you get, the more uncomfortable you become using drama. But old dogs *can* learn new tricks if they see the purpose and what can be achieved. So we have to try to get over our own reluctance and give it a try. If you commit to trying drama just a few times, you will be sold. Learning new techniques and finding new powerful ways to teach is empowering and fun!

How do you persuade students to use action strategies?

It's not hard. Kids want to be active and they want to be competent; they want to be assisted into expertise. They want to engage in social activity. They want to do and learn things that are transferable and exportable— that can be used in new situations, shared, and talked about. In my studies on boys and literacy (Smith and Wilhelm, 2002; 2006), I found that kids check out and give up when they have nothing meaningful to do, when they think they can't do something, or when they know they aren't going to get the help that they need. If the competence being developed is assisted through techniques like action strategies, and if the competence is in service of knowing and doing something important (e.g., working towards understanding and completing culminating projects in inquiry contexts) then, in my experience, even very reluctant students can be brought to the point where they embrace drama with enthusiasm.

For the few students who might still resist, I always have some non-role-playing roles for them to take: observers and secretaries, camerapeople and notetakers. If a kid doesn't want to be involved, I say, "Excellent! I need a secretary to keep track of what this group is saying and doing." Or, "I need a cameraperson to film this group." This can often become a role in itself that can be incorporated into the drama work, but more often the student playing this role sees what fun we are having and changes his or her mind about joining in.

If a whole class seems resistant, I begin with non-role playing activities—like in-role writing, Facebooking in role, and other correspondence dramas that don't involve "acting." If this is in service of understanding a riveting inquiry topic and then being able to know and do something in the world, that is highly motivating. It "de-schools" the learning process and makes it real. Such activities typically are great "frontloading" into a sequence of more active action strategies later on down the road.

The author and main characters of *The Giver* answer questions from reporters during a press conference.

What about standardized tests and student achievement on them?

Anchor Standards for Reading, 1–6

When kids learn how to comprehend, monitor comprehension, solve problems, metacognate, and reflect; when they can see implied relationships between ideas (required by the CCSS standards for reading in all disciplines) and between their experience, the text/material, and the world, then they do better on the tests. There's a huge amount of research that shows this (see *Engaging Readers and Writers with Inquiry* for a full discussion). So even if you are under pressure for kids to perform well on standardized tests, action strategies are your friend. Plus, with action strategies, kids focus and engage and are on-point. In this way, everything becomes easier for the teacher—most importantly, it's easier to help the kids achieve actual understanding. Finally, what I have seen from the new CCSS assessments indicates that inquiry and problem-solving tools are going to be hugely rewarded by these assessments. Factual recall is not going to be rewarded. Reflection and metacognition are required by process analyses of how tasks were performed. So drama will be a tool that will help students with the new generation of CCSS assessments.

What support do you need to teach with action strategies?

This book is a great support. So is the accompanying DVD that provides models of real teachers trying out the techniques for the first time—in ways that you can emulate and adapt. Like the Nike commercials, I'd say: *Just do it* and learn from doing it, making adjustments and improvements every time you use one. It is helpful to work together with peer teachers and coaches. So is enlisting your students and being willing to follow their lead.

But the real key is just to try the techniques and to keep trying them. There's a huge amount of research that shows teachers improve by trying new things, and then sticking with those new techniques to improve them. Doing something once isn't really trying it. Doing something unreflectively isn't really trying it. When teachers honestly try new ways of teaching, it's been shown that their theories and other practices begin to evolve in powerful ways. People don't change their theories and then change their practice. They change their practice and that changes their theories and that feeds further improvement and development.

What about assessing action strategies?

Action strategies work because they are experimental, involve trying stuff out, practicing, having fun, engaging in bricolage, and playing around. I think it's unethical to teach in ways that are not fun and engaging and that don't cultivate imagination—not to emphasize the fun of learning and the joy of the process and the freedom to try stuff out and re-do it and try it again (see Jensen, 2009, and Wilhelm & Novak, 2011). I also think it is unethical to grade students on something you haven't taught them and helped them to know how to do over time. I regard action strategies as rehearsals and as practice in using a new sophisticated strategy and in dealing with new and difficult concepts. Recent research in cognition has shown how important both multi-modality and repeated practice are to mastering and consolidating new kinds of learning. I might flexibly and supportively assess students' use of some action strategies on completion of the deliverable, on effort, or on improvement. Action strategies can provide excellent formative assessments but these really shouldn't be graded on quality, since the kids are in the process of learning. Of course, action strategies can evolve into final projects and presentations, and then I would grade the students rigorously on pre-negotiated criteria that I had helped them to prepare to meet. (More on this in Chapter 12.)

What Does It Mean to Be a Teacher Who Motivates?

Now that I've made a case for why enactments are supportive of deep experiential learning *and* motivating for students—and answered the most frequently asked questions about enactments—let's step back and take a more general look at ourselves as teachers who motivate. In other words, beyond deciding to try enactments, it's important to reflect on our teaching as a whole—and to define what it really means to be an effective, inspiring teacher. This reflection exercise will provide you with a good "lens" through which to read the rest of this book.

To motivate, as my long-time team-teaching partner Paul Friedemann asserts, is to bring out the best in people and to celebrate both their current achievement and future potential. When you enjoy helping others excel, grow, and discover, you are motivating them. Motivating others must always, by its very nature, be positive—though it must also be challenging. Papert (1996) asserts that the best learning is "hard fun"—a challenge that is compelling but that we feel able to meet. This is because self-efficacy—the belief that one will be successful with a challenge—is essential to learning (Pajares, 1996).

As teachers, we choose whether to focus on students' strengths or weaknesses. What is the best way to be successful? Undoubtedly, it is to focus on and build from their strengths. What's your focus as a teacher? Use the checklist provided to reflect upon this.

How Good a Motivator Am I?
A Self-Reflection Checklist

(based on current motivation research: Bandura, 1998; Csikszentmihalyi, 1990;
Pajares, 1996; Smith and Wilhelm, 2002; 2006)

Usually = 4 points	Sometimes = 2 points	Never = 0 points

____ **1.** I believe my students are trustworthy and communicate this to them.

____ **2.** I believe a teacher should care about students and express this caring.

____ **3.** I believe my students are competent and can become more competent with proper assistance. I embrace the notion of a dynamic mindset vs. a fixed mindset, i.e. I believe all children can learn and develop with proper assistance.

____ **4.** I attend to student interests and provide some level of choice.

____ **5.** I help students to do things, to know how to do things and to talk about how to do things.

____ **6.** I avoid labeling students.

____ **7.** I send explicit invitations to succeed, both to my students as a group and individually.

____ **8.** I listen to what my students really say; I noodle around trying to get to know them.

____ **9.** I make good use of student experts in my class—getting kids to teach each other and share their expertise.

____ **10.** I use heterogeneous groups and interest groups to build interdependence and to highlight and use different students' strengths.

____ **11.** I avoid overemphasis on competition, rewards, and winning—though I may foster a fun, gamelike atmosphere where every one can win and succeed.

____ **12.** I help students to evaluate themselves; to build, articulate, and apply their own critical standards.

____ **13.** I communicate high expectations to all my students.

____ **14.** I focus on future success vs. past failure.

____ **15.** I name what students can do, focusing on their abilities and achievement; I celebrate student expertise.

____ **16.** I negotiate, help set, and communicate clear goals as I highlight focus and higher purpose to the work that we do.

____ **17.** I provide continuous feedback to students about how they are doing and create learning situations that provide immediate feedback.

____ **18.** I frontload unit work by starting with what students already know, activating background, and building interest and a sense of purpose.

____ **19.** I foster connections to students' current life concerns.

____ **20.** I encourage the reading of a variety of different kinds of texts.

____ **21.** I encourage fun, humor, and laughter in the classroom, including the reading of humorous texts.

____ **22.** I use artifacts and concrete objects in my teaching, and ask students to design artifacts and concrete objects that make knowledge visible and reasoning accountable.

____ **23.** I welcome and encourage multiple responses to class questions and projects.

____ **24.** I model the behaviors that I value for students (e.g. I read; I am pleasant).

____ **25.** I am passionate about reading and about ideas, and I model and communicate this passion.

____ **26.** I teach my students for who they are and who they might be RIGHT NOW in the present moment (not for who I think they should be and be able to do sometime in the far off future).

____ **27.** In my classroom, we read texts that can be related to real world situations and activity.

____ **28.** The activities in my classroom allow students to identify and use their expertise.

Total:

100 and up = You are a most excellent motivator!	88–100 = Good
78–87 = Fair	>77 Try something different!

SHOW ME, HELP ME, LET ME
Assisting Readers to Higher Levels of Comprehension

A sk any colleague of mine, "What's Jeff's main mantra?" They would say something along the lines of: *The most powerful teaching is grounded in a theoretical perspective that informs how we practice our teaching craft.* As I said at the end of the last chapter, it's important to take the time to reflect on who we are as teachers, on our beliefs about teaching and learning. I invited you to ponder: How motivating am I? In this chapter, the question we'll explore is: What is the theory behind enactment strategies?

I'll begin by sharing a conversation with a colleague, Tanya Baker, that illustrates how theoretical understanding is most powerful for a teacher not when it's learned in isolation from a book, but when it's discovered *in concert with* teacher practice.

Tanya used to be my doctoral student and she taught at a school in the Professional Development Network where I worked. The tables are now turned as she serves as a director of the National Writing Project and supervises many of the projects that my Boise State Writing Project teachers and myself work on each year. We have collaborated closely for years. One afternoon, we were sipping coffee, discussing our teaching, when she said, "You know that drama saved my career. I wouldn't have continued in my teaching career if I hadn't discovered it."

I thought she was being hyperbolic and I laughed, but she persisted. "I'm serious. I was ready to quit. I'd been teaching for a while and I was really struggling. I thought teaching was transmitting information and my kids didn't understand the information I taught. So it was clear: one of us has to be fixed. Either I'm not doing a good job or they aren't. And I couldn't see how to fix either of us."

"When I started using enactment strategies I became happier with my teaching and had more fun with my kids. But it was much, much bigger than that. I realized through using the drama strategies that it wasn't me or the kids who were deficient. The enactments made me see that I'd been working with a deficient *theoretical model* of teaching. I realized I shouldn't be delivering information or letting kids do whatever they want. I should be explicitly guiding them to do new things, and creating situations that encouraged and assisted them to think and feel and *be* in new ways. The enactment work showed me how to use the sociocultural model of teaching and learning—though I didn't know what that was at the time. Later, I made the connection to Vygotsky—and that made me see that no one was broken; if the kids can't do something, teach them. And teach them in a context in which teacher and students can play, build, and learn together. In that realm, anything the kids don't know how to do I can help them do. Enactment provided me with a way to help them. It made me see that learning happens between me and the students and that there is always something a teacher can do that teaches and transforms the situation, herself, and the students. That's how drama saved my career—by helping me rethink the theory behind what I do."

Tanya's anecdote shows how discovering a new set of strategies—enactment—changed not only her teaching, but her theoretical understanding of her teaching. (If her story makes you want to flip ahead to the next chapter, dive right in to the new strategies, and read the theory later, go right ahead! But do come back to the theory later!)

Teaching as a Process of Lending Expertise to Students

In this series' first book, *Improving Comprehension With Think-Aloud Strategies,* I introduced the idea that teaching is composed of actively guiding and explicitly assisting students to more competent performances (versus providing them with information or allowing them to discover things "naturally"). I used the theoretical perspective of Russian psychologist Lev Vygotsky that this kind of assistance consists of the conscious lending of expertise from the teacher to the student, so that the student can do with help what she could not yet do alone. That theoretical perspective informs the uses of enactment that will be explored in this book. This theory is explored even more deeply in *Strategic Reading* (2001) and the next books in this series on visualization (2004/2012) and inquiry (2007).

The following steps illustrate the process of giving over expertise to students through the learner's zone of proximal development (ZPD), that cognitive area where students can do something with the appropriate assistance that they cannot yet do on their own.

1 Goal Setting: Teacher Purposefully Identifies a Strategy to Teach
Teacher perceives a strategy that students currently need and a real context in which to teach and use it.

2 Modeling: Teacher Uses the Strategy, Student Observes
Students learn to recognize the strategy and identify what it is, why and when it is used, and how it is useful in real contexts by watching the teacher model its use.

3 Teacher-Led Collaboration (Mentoring): Teacher Uses the Strategy, Cues Students; Students Help

Students begin recognizing textual cues that invite them to use the strategy. They then start to use the strategy when appropriate and explain its use. They also begin to be apprenticed to take on the strategy with less assistance.

4 Student-Led Collaboration (Mentoring): Students Use Strategy Together, Teacher Helps as Needed

Students use the strategy in small groups with peer assistance and move toward independence.

5 Student Independence (Mentoring): Each Student Uses the Strategy on His Own, Teacher Observes and Assesses

Students use the strategy and self-assess to monitor their comprehension and engagement, and to adjust strategy use. Teacher uses assessment to inform future teaching. If a student does not use the strategy to the fullest potential, the teacher will want to provide more guidance and assisted practice. If the student has mastered the strategy, the teacher will consider how to introduce new and more complex situations in which it can be used, or how to move on to teaching a new strategy.

As you try enactment strategies with your students, refer back to these five steps to help guide you. I think you'll find the steps come naturally—teacher assistance, peer assistance, and independent use can all occur seamlessly and interchangeably during an enactment strategy. Another way to think about the process of moving students to independence is: *show me, help me, let me.* And another: doing the strategy *for* students, *with* students and then having students do it *by* themselves in groups and individually: *for, with, by.*

Helping Students Enter the Community of Expert Readers

Cognitive research shows that people who become competent in a particular domain make use of shared social practices to complete important tasks, to create and communicate knowledge, and to participate in and identify themselves as competent members in that field's particular community of practice.

In *Improving Comprehension With Think-Aloud Strategies,* I described how canoeists and kayakers maintain their boats, use specialized equipment and practice special techniques, speak with specific vocabulary, and interact in certain ways to mark and maintain a sense of competence and membership in the whitewater fraternity. The same disciplinary or community-specific processes are exhibited by teachers, librarians, tailors, waitresses, architects, butchers, civil engineers, and all other communities of practice. Lave and Wenger (1991) argue that good teaching is the inducting and apprenticing of learners into a community of expert practice. Such teaching requires overt sharing and providing structured support in the development of expert strategies—in this case, apprenticing students to use the strategies of expert readers and the strategies of the field reflected in the text's content, that of the scientist, the historian, and so forth. Lave and Wenger write that, "Learning... is a process of becoming a member of a sustained community of practice. Developing an identity as a member of the community and becoming knowledgeably skillful are part of the same process" (p. 65).

To induct students into such a community, we must involve them as novices in the actual work of the expert, what the philosopher John Dewey (1916) called "the healthy work of the present," instead of the decontextualized practice of skills that often occurs in schools. Providing this kind of apprenticeship puts new expectations on teachers, as explained by Brown, Collins, and DuGuid (1989) in their work on situated cognition:

Recent investigations of learning challenge the separating of what is learned from how it is learned and used. The activity in which knowledge is developed and deployed is not separable from or ancillary to learning and cognition, nor is it neutral. Rather, it is an integral part of what is learned. Situations might be said to co-produce knowledge through activity. Learning and cognition are fundamentally situated. (p. 32)

Addressing Reservations to Enactment Strategies

Given the proven power of using enactment strategies, why do so few American teachers use the technique? I think it is important to address teachers' reservations, which I have observed both in schools and in the research base (Morgan and Saxton, 1987).

Reservation 1: "My students will be hesitant to use such strategies."

I have found this to be decidedly untrue. I have used enactment strategies with groups from kindergarten age to senior citizen homes and they have worked wonderfully. I have also observed hundreds of other pre-service and in-service teachers make successful use of these strategies on their first attempt.

When I work with elementary schools, the students uniformly and immediately embrace the work. In middle schools and high schools, where I do most of my teaching, I may initially have some limited reluctance on the part of a few students. In response, I allow reluctant students to watch the enactment work and be recorders, or to take some kind of role outside of the major activity. The same thing always results: those kids see that everyone else is being active, having fun, and undertaking interesting challenges, and they want to be involved, too.

Reservation 2: "But I can't act."

Don't worry—you are not there to act or entertain your students. You are using enactments to shape a learning environment and support particular learning activities. Though much of the shaping and guiding occurs inside an enactment, most of it can be done outside an enactment as well. Your role is director and co-participant, as it is in any teaching situation.

Reservation 3: "I may lose control of the class."

I am more in control during enactments than during other class activities. After all, during enactment everyone is engaged in the same or similar activities. What they are doing or not doing is obvious to me. I am shaping and guiding their work quite actively from inside or outside of the enactment. During normal classroom activities, kids could be goofing off or daydreaming and I would be less likely to notice.

Reservation 4: "What if things take a direction that I don't like?"

One of the reasons that you are always in control during an enactment is that you can end or interrupt an enactment at any time. I use special clap sequences or hand signals for doing so, and often just say, "We are leaving the drama world now." We can discuss the direction of the work and see if it makes sense and fits the facts offered by the text we are reading. Plus, there are ground rules for enactment: We will respect each other at all times; We will remember that if we are exploring tensions between different positions, we are doing so in role, not with each other. We will act in ways consistent with the evidence offered through the texts and learning materials that serve as the basis of our enactment; We won't use offensive language. (And so on. You will certainly come up with guidelines and rules of your own.)

If these rules are not being met, or if I feel uncomfortable with the direction things are taking, I stop the work. We discuss what is happening and reflect on it outside of the enactment. I can then always work with my students to rearrange or recalibrate, and then enter the enactment again.

Enactments can also be stopped for a variety of pedagogical purposes, even when they are going well. For instance, you might "stop and sum up" when you feel it is time to change directions or introduce new information or tensions, to reflect on and evaluate what has happened and to name what has been learned, or to go back and try it again but with a different twist to see how that makes a difference. You might also pause if the activity and the enjoyment of it are not serving the teaching goals, or when you are not sure what is happening. Besides, most enactment episodes are short and provide you with natural breaks for reframing and reflecting on the work.

Reservation 5: "I have so many other things to cover and do. How does this fit the curriculum?"

Curricular mandates almost always emphasize the information to be covered. (though this is changing with the next generation of standards and their emphasis on procedural knowledge). Enactments provide a means for developing procedures for reading and learning content, and a situation for engaging deeply with that content. Enactment is the *how*, and can work with any *what*. As many researchers and theorists have pointed out: Enactment is a way of teaching curricular content where the relationship between human beings is important, or where the relationship of human purposes, needs, ideas, and issues to the content is important. Personally, I can't imagine that we would think anything worthy of teaching does not fit this definition and cannot be taught through enactment. My own research and that of many others has shown that enactment results in powerful learning of content as well as new strategic procedures (Wilhelm and Edmiston, 1998). If you do decide to include extended process enactment work, the deep learning that will be achieved will be well worth the time spent, especially if you compare such deep learning to the research about how ineffective and transitory are the results of rushed coverage, lecturing, and information presentation.

Reservation 6: "But this is too much fun for school."

Ironically, some teachers actually have this reservation toward enactments. We have already seen how important fun is to learning. In fact, Csikszentmihalyi's research (1990) shows that when students engage in challenging activities, their three major reasons for doing so include: It is fun, I enjoy it, and I enjoy using what I have learned. Further research from neuroscience to cognitive science shows that the more fun we have, the more, and more deeply, we learn.

Voices From the Field

In this email, teacher Julie Hosum shares what she found out when she started working with enactments.

Jeff:

You know, doing drama work is so parallel to reading. It's like it turns reading inside out so the kids can do together what they should be doing inside their heads when they read. The drama shows the kids what they should be doing when they read, and helps them do it.

The kids see that they have to meet another perspective, unravel what the text is telling them, and create a dramatic world out of it. It is so cool! It's helping even my reluctant readers become part of the classroom activity, and it helps the better readers not just understand what they are reading, but how to understand it. It helps them make inferences and use their background knowledge. I think it really shows them what reading really is about. And surprisingly, that's something I don't think many of the kids really know. Too many years of phonics and worksheets, I guess! And the drama work helps me help them because I can see what they understand and don't understand. Anyway, we are having lots of fun along with lots of learning. You should hear them laugh but then get right back on track. There's a real purposefulness to some of the kids that I've not seen before.

— Julie

CHAPTER 3

MAKING THE CONNECTION
Enactments to Use
Before Reading

I t happens all the time. I am teaching my student-teaching seminar and one of my student teachers will come in and say: "I tried that think-aloud technique you recommended. It didn't work." Then I ask: "How did you frontload the activity? What did you do to activate your students' background knowledge and prepare them for success?" And the student teacher will slap herself on the forehead or some equivalent of this. Even though we've been over and over the importance of frontloading (see Wilhelm, Baker and Dube, 2001 for a full discussion of the theory and research behind this practice), and how the most important time to teach is *before* you try a new activity, begin a new reading, or start on a composition—even though I require frontloading for all units and lessons—my student teachers always seem to plunge right in without laying the necessary groundwork for success.

Frontloading is meant to set purposes for learning, set a meaningful context for that learning, connect students personally to what will be learned, activate the background knowledge that they need, and provide an organizing structure to assist the learning. There are times when students just don't have enough background to activate. In this case, frontloading can build the background that is needed, and drama/action strategies are a powerful means to do so. A few years ago I was teaching a social studies unit on colonization. To frontload, I began by asking my students to brainstorm what they knew about colonies, hoping to soon move on to the issues raised by this practice. The only student who contributed talked about his ant colony, so he wasn't all that much help! I realized that the students did not know enough about the topic to comprehend, much less care about and see the importance of the texts we would read. So I asked them to brainstorm issues that arise between teens and parents. We listed issues like wanting more freedom, chores, family vs. personal schedules and needs, curfews, control, driving the car, computer and cell phone use, dress, and so forth. They had no trouble generating this list.

We then role-played several situations between parents and teenagers around these issues, enacting, for example, an argument between a girl who wants to stay out past her curfew and her parents who insist she cannot. Another one was about assigned chores and a child's responsibility to the family. I then asked the students to think about how these situations paralleled the relationship between Great Britain and the thirteen colonies prior to and during the Revolution. In this way, I introduced them to the practice of colonization and the issues it raises. Because they knew about living in a family, the kids quickly noted differences, too, for example that a family lives together but a colony is usually physically separate.

Later in the year, we were preparing to start a unit on the Depression. Again, the kids knew virtually nothing about it. One student thought the Depression took place during the sixties and meant that people were depressed. He wasn't sure why people were depressed but he thought it had to do with "a war somewhere."

This time I handed out series of photographs from the WPA (Works Progress Administration) to small groups of students. I asked them to imagine they were relatives who had found these family photos in the attic. Their job was to reconstruct what life had been like for the family members in the photos and to give an oral report on this to the "historical society," which would meet during our next class.

After the unit, Jen wrote this in her reflective journal:

> Doing the activity with the photographs before we read about the Depression really helped. I guess I didn't think how it really was back then and how it affected real people. I guess pretending they were family photos made me think of what it would have been like for me living through the Depression and that really changed how I read the stuff later on. I thought it was a good activity and really helped make it all real to me.

The famous educational philosopher Jerome Bruner has called a teacher who can create significant learning experiences a "drama-creating personality." There's no time when it's more important to make use of this ability than when you are preparing students to read a new text, (or engage in a new problem-solving process like writing a new genre of composition), especially one where they deal with new content, are faced with a new genre, and/or must use new reading or composing strategies. The findings from various research studies (Wilhelm, 1996, and Wilhelm, Baker, and Dube, 2001) compel me to assert that *the most important and powerful time to teach is **before** students read—or undertake any new learning challenge.*

In light of this, the importance of frontloading your units, and planning and framing your enactments cannot be overemphasized. The use of enactments are also a powerful way to highlight purpose and provide background experiences that can prepare students to learn new content, read an unfamiliar text, or compose something new. Like any good teaching, the teacher must know where she is going, what she wants the students to learn, where she wants the students to end up, and how she plans to get them there through the guidance of her instruction. Enactments can help on many levels throughout the entirety of this process.

Framing the Enactment

Whenever I have had an enactment strategy fall flat, it was always because of inadequate framing. Framing simply means that the students understand how the work will proceed and what is expected of them. In other words, proper framing requires that students know

- what they are learning about and why (Purpose)
- what set of circumstances or context (the drama world) will motivate and support the learning (Process)
- who the students (and teacher) will be in the enactment (Process)
- the viewpoints or roles they will take, and most of all (Process)
- what is expected of them—what they need to achieve in the time allotted and how they will know they are done. (Deliverable)

Generally speaking, you frame the enactment by providing a purpose, a process—including the situation and roles (for yourself and the students), and by focusing on accountability through a deliverable—requiring students to find out, establish, or make something during the enactment that they can share afterwards. I call this process PPD = Purpose, Process, Deliverable.

Framing highlights the purpose of the work. I usually have a *macro-frame* and a *micro-frame* in my enactment work. The macro-frame is the purpose of the current inquiry unit, such as an essential or existential question: What makes and breaks relationships? What are civil rights and how can we promote and protect them? How does the metric system work in actual problem-solving situations? This said, I also have micro-frames for particular drama strategies that are much more specific, but that help us develop the knowledge or skills to address the larger issue. This micro-frame should provide a viewpoint from which students will work, and should create tension—for example family counselors helping characters agree about how to deal with a family crisis, civil rights activists planning a social-action campaign, museum workers who have a civil rights exhibit to finish with limited

Max, Denali, and Mark use a map to plan a way to fight "The Great Fire."

resources, a client who has a legal problem, the President and his advisors facing a crisis, builders who must put up an emergency bridge by translating English measurement to metric, NASA engineers correcting calculations mistakenly done in the English system so that a space probe will actually land on Mars. Notice that, as part of the frame, you highlight the purpose, citing a goal to be attained or problem to be solved. You also emphasize action that must be pursued or deliverables that we are accountable for creating. All of this serves to grab your students' attention and get them going.

Framing: An Example Using "The Fan Club"

As you read this book, you'll discover I refer to the short story "The Fan Club" by Rona Maynard in each chapter as I explain how various enactments work. (I recommend that you take the time to read the story now, which can be found on pages 43–47, so my discussion of it will make sense.) I will present variations of each enactment technique, often exploring how I or other teachers have used it with other books often used in the classroom. In this way, you can see how different techniques operate to deepen comprehension and interpretation in the context of one story, and how these techniques can be adapted for various purposes, with different texts and data sets to cultivate different reading strategies.

"The Fan Club" appeared in *Read* magazine several years ago. It's a provocative story, and I have used it in grades 6 to 10 as part of units studying the nature of good relationships, friendship, and even civil rights. In these cases my organizing macro-frame throughout the unit was an essential question, such as *What makes a good relationship? What is essential to real friendship? What are our civil rights and how can we promote and protect them?* I always use such questions for everything I teach. Here are some guideposts to help you formulate your own essential or unit-organizing questions (see Wilhelm, 2007 or Wilhelm and Boas, 2008 for chapter-length discussions of essential questions and how to compose them).

- The questions are personally relevant and compelling to my students *right now*.
- Students' prior knowledge allows them to contribute experiences and perspectives that can be shaped and changed.
- The questions are socially significant to our culture and to democratic living and invite a wide variety of perspectives.
- The question will lead to significant learning and enduring understandings from my discipline.
- The question is contended: I do not know the answers to the questions, though I have views on these subjects.

Anchor Standards for Writing, 7–10

This last criterion, *I don't have the answers*, is worth underscoring. In other words, reading a variety of texts like "The Fan Club" that explore various perspectives around the theme will invite honest inquiry and exploration, instead of the fake research we often do in schools that involves playing "guess what the teacher already knows." This kind of false inquiry leads to student cynicism, a lack of engagement, and sloppy behaviors, like copying notes out of reference works, plagiarism, and regurgitation of facts without comprehending them. What are the best ways to secure civil rights? I have some ideas but this is an ongoing cultural conversation with no clear or single answer. What does make the best relationship? No one knows, but it is worth trying to figure out. Any really important question is debatable and worthy of continued debate in just this way.

Anchor Standards for Reading, 1–6

My micro-framing of particular enactment strategies during our reading of "The Fan Club" involves focusing on a concept, cognitive skill, and/or reading strategy important both to the reading of the story and the pursuit of the inquiry. I use enactment with this story to focus on developing a variety of strategies: visualizing settings, situations, and characters; developing a sense of text structure; supporting the ability to infer, fill textual gaps, and elaborate; helping students to see from multiple perspectives; and assisting them to converse with an author about the central focus/thematic generalization of a story. Finally, the enactment work can help students decide whether they embrace that authorial vision regarding relationships or civil rights or prefer to adapt or reject it, and how to translate this decision into social behavior and action.

The Fan Club

Adapted from the story written by Rona Maynard
Note: Numbers in the story correlate to numbers in the lesson plan beginning on page 48.

1.

It was Monday again. Rain splattered the cover of *Algebra I* as Laura heaved her books higher on her arm and sighed. School was such a bore.

Before her, the high school building loomed massive and dark against the stormy March sky. In a few minutes she would have to face *them*—again. Laura closed her eyes trying to block out the memory of Diane Goddard's sleek blond hair and Terri Pierce's hot-pink fingernails. And Carol and Steve and Bill and Nancy.

But it was no good. She heard again their laughter, smothered at first, then outright loud as Laura had struggled to think of the right answer in algebra class. That was Friday. Now it was Monday, another damp, cold day in a school filled with too many Dianes and Terris and Steves.

They sat at the back in Algebra and in English class, passing notes and whispering to one another. Laura thought of their latest-fashion clothes and their identical outlooks and their superior stares as they passed her in the corridors. They were clods, the whole gang of them.

Laura shoved her way through the main door of the building. Upperclassmen thronged the hall, streamed in and out of doors, and passed bulletin boards covered with red and yellow posters advertising the latest rock concert. Reluctantly, Laura submerged herself in the stream.

Down the hall a short way were Diane and Terri and Steve, standing in a tight little circle, as always, in front of their lockers. They were laughing, as always.

As Laura opened her locker, she heard Diane squeal, "It'll be a riot! Can't wait to see her face when she catches on." Laura flushed painfully, hiding behind her open locker door so the three would not see her. "What do you think she'll do?" Steve said. "Run out of the room probably," said Terri. Again Laura closed her eyes. Her mind went back to the previous Friday.

2.

She was standing alone in front of the class, unable to multiply or divide or factor, unable even to think—just feeling the room heat up like a hot-air balloon ready to explode.

"Don't you know the answer, Laura?" asked Mr. Knowles. His voice was hollow, distant, an echo behind the sound of rustling papers and hushed whispers. Laura stared at her half-finished home-work and the scribbled flowers in the margins. On the cover of her notebook was a sketch of a guitar she had drawn that morning in class.

"Well, Laura?"

She really had tried to memorize the theorems the night before. But then she had pushed the textbook aside to scratch into her notebook the lyrics to a new song she was writing. She could multiply and divide those words and rhythms better than she ever could the lifeless numbers in

Algebra I. Besides, what did it matter? One day she would be a musician and live in New York City or L.A. And everyone would accept her, and there would be no more algebra.

Snickers from the back of the room filled the silence. They swelled into mocking giggles that rang in her ears. "You can sit down now, Laura," said Mr. Knowles, not trying to hide his exasperation....

3.

"Laura!"

She looked up startled. It was Rachel who was calling her and who stood beside her now at the locker. She was wearing a floral blouse and a corduroy skirt that billowed over the heavy columns of her legs. Laura glanced sideways at Diane and Terri and Steve. They were fumbling with little yellow index cards, passing them out among the circle of freshmen guys and girls who had gathered around. Then Diane looked up, directly at Laura, and she laughed out loud. Laura closed her locker and turned away.

"Why didn't you come over this weekend like you said you were going to?" Rachel said.

Rachel stood there, her mouth half open, her pale, moonlike face strangely urgent. Shapeless black curls ringed her forehead. Laura shrugged. "I had to study."

Rachel shrugged too, forgiving the broken promise. The two girls started walking down the hall, away from the exclusive circle. "So did you watch *World of Nature* last night," Rachel asked, "on channel 11?"

"No, Rachel. I almost never watch that kind of program."

"You used to."

Rachel was her old friend. In grade school, everyone had called her "Horton," a friendly nick-name for Hortensky. Her father was Jacob Hortensky, the tailor. He ran a greasy little shop where Laura could always smell the cooked cabbage from the back rooms where the family lived. Laura hadn't been there since the two girls had started high school last September. As freshmen they shared only one class, English. No one called Rachel "Horton" anymore.

"It was a really good documentary. It was all about monarch butterflies and how far they can travel." Rachel was smiling, flapping her hands as she talked. "Remember when we found a monarch chrysalis and kept it at my house until it hatched? Remember how beautiful it was? We let its wings dry off and took it outside so it could fly away to Mexico. And then waved good-bye. That really was exciting!"

Once they had shared a deep interest in science and insects. Now, even if you still liked that stuff, you should have enough sense not to show it.

"That was a pretty good poem you wrote for English class last week," Rachel said.

"You think so?" said Laura. "I mean, not many people like poetry."

"Your stuff is good, though. I wish I could write like you."

Laura turned. "I have to go."

"Why don't you come over after school today? You can stay for dinner. My parents would really like that—they ask about you all the time. They wonder what happened to you."

Laura remembered the narrow, dirty street and the tattered awning in front of the tailor shop. Once, none of that had mattered. "OK," Laura said, faking enthusiasm. "I'll see you later."

4.

In homeroom, Laura spread her notecards over her desk, reviewing one last time her speech for English class. "We will now have the national anthem," said the voice on the loudspeaker. Like the others, Laura stood. She shifted her weight from one foot to the other. It was so false, so pointless. How could they sing of the land of the free when there was still so much that was unfair going on in the world?

That thought was the theme of her oral report. Laura imagined herself standing in front of the class, in front of that exclusive little circle led by Diane and Terri and Steve and Bill, and her throat went dry. Just be confident, she told herself.

The steel sound of the bell shattered the silence. Amid scraping chairs and cries of "Hey, wait!" Laura escaped homeroom and started for English class. She moved down the hall with the crowd, a thronging jostling mass. Laura felt someone nudge her. It was Bill. "Now there's a good-looking girl." Smiling, he pointed to the other side of the hall.

The gaudy flowers on Rachel's blouse stood out garishly, too summery for gray March. What a lumpish, awkward creature Rachel had become! Did she have to dress like that? Laura thought. Didn't she see how her stockings wrinkled around her heavy ankles? Laura turned to say something to Bill, but he had gone ahead into the room. Rachel went in behind him, and just then her books tumbled from her arms onto the floor.

Laura was behind her, still in the hall, but she heard the laughter.

The bell rang. Students ambled to their seats. Laura saw Diane and Terri exchange eager last-minute whispers. "Steve doesn't have his," Diane said.

"Don't put it on until it's time," said Terri.

After 20 minutes of reviewing last night's homework, Miss Merrill pushed aside *Adventures in Literature* and beamed at the class as if they were in for a real treat. "All right, people, get out your notecards. Today we start our oral reports. Laura, will you begin, please?"

At once, Laura's throat clamped tight like a hinged lid. It was as if she had eyes in the back of her head, so clearly could she see Diane and Terri and Steve grinning at her, waiting for her to make a fool of herself again.

Careful, careful, she thought as she stood and walked to the front of the room. Look confident. Before her, the room was large and still; 25 round, blurred faces stared back at her. Was that Diane's muffled laughter already? Laura folded her hands over her notecards and looked at the rear wall, strangely distant now, its brown paint cracked and peeling. A dusty portrait of Robert Frost, a card with the seven rules for better paragraphs, last year's calendar…and the hollow ticking of the clock.

"Well," Laura cleared her throat. "My report is on civil rights." A chorus of snickers rose from the back of the room.

"Most people," Laura began, then began again, "most people don't care enough about others, but we are all responsible for those people who haven't had the same advantages as we." Even as she repeated the words she had practiced all weekend, Laura wondered if anyone was really listening.

"A lot of people think prejudice is limited to ethnic groups. But most of us are prejudiced—whether we know it or not—in other quiet ways. It's not just that we don't give people who are different a chance; we don't give ourselves a chance either." She looked past the rows of blank, empty faces, past the bored stares of Diane and Terri. All they cared about were concerts and parties.

"One person's misfortune is every person's responsibility," she recited. She wondered if Diane or Terri or Steve knew what it was like to be unwanted and unaccepted. What misfortunes did they have? None.

"Most of us are proud that we live in a free country. But is it really true? Can we call the United States a free country when millions of people face prejudice and discrimination every day?" Laura looked at Rachel, who was staring at her with deep attention.

Laura took a breath, ready for the big finish. "Only when Americans learn to respect the dignity of all people can we truly call our country free."

5.

The room was silent. "Very nice, Laura." Miss Merrill looked briskly around the room. Laura returned to her seat, and the other students waited in dread to see who would be next. "Rachel Hortensky," Miss Merrill announced. There was a ripple of dry, humorless laughter—almost, Laura thought, like the sound of a rattlesnake. Rachel stood before the class now, her face red, her heavy arms piled with shoeboxes.

"Shoes?" whispered Steve. "She's going to talk about shoes?"

Diane giggled, tossed her hair back, and winked at Steve.

Rachel's smile twitched at the corners, and Laura knew that her old friend Horton, who had never been afraid of mice, or garter snakes, or spiders was frightened now. Rachel set her stacked boxes on the desk without paying much attention to how they were balanced. Immediately they collapsed to the floor with a ringing clatter. Now everyone, not just Diane, was giggling.

"Hurry and pick them up, Rachel," Miss Merrill said sharply.

Rachel crouched on her knees and began very clumsily to gather her scattered treasures. Some of the boxes had broken open, spilling their contents. Her index cards had fallen, too, and she shuffled them together quickly. At last she stood. "My report is on shells," she said.

A cold and stony silence settled upon the room.

"People might collect shells simply because they're kind of pretty. They might find them on the beach."

"Well, whaddaya know!" It was Steve's voice sounding a mock amazement. Laura jabbed her notebook with her pencil. Why was he so cruel?

"This one," said Rachel, opening the first shoebox, "is one of the best." Off came the layers of paper and there, at last, smooth and pearly and shimmering, was the shell. Rachel turned it over lovingly in her hands. "It has white, fluted sides like the close-curled petals of a flower and a scrolled coral back," she said.

Laura held her breath. It was beautiful, really beautiful, but from the back of the room the snickers had started again. "I bet she bought it at Woolworth's," said Diane. "It might make a nice ashtray," said Steve.

6.

Rachel seemed not to hear. The shells were something she knew about and loved. She held out another, a small, drab, brownish thing. "This is the common snail shell," said Rachel. "It is a different kind of pretty…. "

Just as Rachel finished, the bell sounded. Suddenly, chairs were shoved aside at the back of the room, and there was the sound of many voices whispering. They were standing, the whole row of them, their faces grinning with delight. Choked giggles, shuffling their feet, and then applause—wild, sarcastic, malicious applause.

Laura turned and stared at them. They were all wearing the little yellow index cards that Diane and Terri had passed out earlier that morning. Drawn in the center was a fat, frizzy-haired figure. Printed in big red block letters above and below it was HORTENSKY FAN CLUB.

Then Laura understood. It was what all the snickering had been about that morning at the lockers. She had been wrong. Diane and Terri and Steve weren't out to get her after all. It was Rachel they were after.

Rachel stared in frozen confusion, looking at the applauders in the back of the room. Her hand holding the brown shell began to tremble, and she dropped it. As it shattered on the floor, the sound was drowned out by the laughter and clapping.

Diane slid forward. "Here, Laura," she said, holding out a yellow index card. "Here's one for you."

For a moment Laura stared at the card. It was pierced with a safety pin. They must have planned the joke over the weekend and brought the pins to school with them. Laura looked at Diane's mocking smile. She heard the pulsing, frenzied rhythm of the claps and the stamping, faster and faster.

Laura reached out slowly and took the card from Diane. She pinned it to her sweater. As she turned back, she saw Rachel's stricken face.

"She's such a nerd, isn't she?"

Diane's voice was soft and intimate.

And Laura began to clap.

7 and 8.

Rona Maynard was a 15-year-old student when she wrote this story.

Planning Lessons for "The Fan Club"

With my framing nailed down, and my major goals articulated, my next step is to plan how I will use enactments to support students in applying the strategies necessary to explore this short story, and apply what they come to understand to future reading and future problem-solving. Below you will find an outline of strategies which provides an overview of the many teaching possibilities one could draw from when exploring a story or a book with students. Each of the strategies is mentioned in "shorthand," as I will explain them fully in later chapters. I want to stress that this is a deluxe plan; I would never use all of these strategies for one story. I would use those that seem to help students engage with the story and practice the strategies with which they need help. I might insert or adapt other strategies based on students' prior responses during the enactment. This is an important point: Have a plan, but use only the strategies that will assist students to engage with substantive ideas or cultivate important strategies. Enactment strategies are teaching techniques that should be used at the point of need and to develop significant learning.

Basic Lesson Plan for "The Fan Club"

Strategies to Use Before Reading: Preparing for Success, Building High Expectations

1. **Frontloading through:** Continuum Dramas, Brainstorming from Different Perspectives, Trigger Letters (explained in next section).

    Students articulate past experiences and pre-existing values, theorize about the issues to be read about so that they have resources to help them comprehend, enliven, and converse with the reading.

    Reading strategies practiced: activating and building background, setting purposes, motivating story entry

    Reflection and sharing: *How might a story about harassment help us with our inquiries? What are our current personal stances on the issues the story will address: How do we define friendship, bullying, harassment, betrayal, and the protection of civil rights in school? Write about a time someone you know was bullied—what happened, why, how could this have been avoided? How might such violations be best redressed?* Share and discuss. Create an anchor chart listing student civil rights, threats to these rights, and ways to protect these rights.

Strategies to Use While Reading the Story, After Each Break, Evoking the Textual Experience and Connecting, Seeing Patterns

2. **Revolving Role-Play #1:** Students take on perspectives of all main characters as they share points of view and address problems.

Anchor Standards for Reading, 1–3

Reading strategies practiced: entering character perspective, topic and problem definition, connecting life to literature

Student A is Laura

Student B is a friend who is enjoying school

Have Student B start the conversation by exploring Laura's recent experience in school. How is she feeling about school compared to her friend? What accounts for the difference?

Reflection and sharing: Teacher in-role plays role of parent of a friend of Laura in a forum drama—addresses all students as if they were friends who have conversed with Laura. *What did each of you find out from Laura about her experience in school? What accounts for this experience and her feelings about it?* (Note that different friends might have found out different things).

2a. **Flashback Drama:** Students imagine and represent what happened before a story or scene, identifying possible causes, context, and background.

Reading strategies practiced: inferring the pre-text, building contexts and story worlds

Have students imagine and represent the scene when Laura first began to dislike school in a short role-play or tableaux.

2b. **Laura's Doodling:** Students draw a character's inner feelings and then interpret the doodling in the role of guidance counselors.

Reading strategies practiced: in-role visualization, attending to and interpreting significant details

3. **Revolving Role-Play #2**

Reading strategies practiced: entering character perspective, making predictions, exploring possibilities, acting as character agent

Student A is Mr. Knowles

Student B is Laura's mother or father

Have student B start the conversation. You're at a parent-teacher conference exploring Laura's experience in math class. What is on your mind? What can be done to improve things?

Reflection and sharing: *Why do some kids not engage in school?* (*Who is interested in this question?* Chance to use a Mantle-of-the-Expert strategy. Students could take on role of guidance counselors, psychologists, or family counselors.) *What was challenging about responding as a parent?* (Enactment allows students the chance to see from real-life perspectives they may not understand or may often resist.)

Anchor Standards for Reading, 1–7

4. **Hotseat/Inner Voice With Laura and Guidance Counselor:** Students interview from role and are interviewed in role. They may take on roles of experts who have the knowledge and power to help address the problems at hand.

   Reading strategies practiced: inferring character, taking differing perspectives, seeing complex implied relationships, filling gaps, reading the subtext.

   Inner voice explores: *What is the character really trying to say?*

4a. **Postcards from the Past:** Students create a postcard about an earlier time that is important to the current situation.

   Reading strategies practiced: inferring past action, visualization, emotional engagement, and response

   They illustrate a scene from the past and a character's feelings about it. Postcard may be addressed to someone the character thinks will understand.

4b. **Missing Scene Drama:** Students notice a missing scene, infer, and fill this textual gap.

   Reading strategies practiced: inferring past action, visualization, emotional engagement, response

   Ask: *What significant experiences have occurred between Laura and the "in crowd"? Between Laura and Rachel? Why have Laura's feelings toward these characters developed as they have?*

5. **Talk Radio Show:** Students respond to story issue or dilemma as radio talk show hosts and callers in role to express their opinions.

   Reading strategies practiced: evaluating significance, conversing with an author, identifying main ideas, expressing acceptance, adaptation, rejection of authorial vision

   Talk show host asks: *What do you think of the point of Laura's speech? Are we all prejudiced in quiet ways?*

5a. **Vote With Your Feet:** Students place themselves along a physical continuum to stake their position on an issue or dilemma raised in the story.

   Reading strategies practiced: identifying directly stated main ideas, judging a character's and author's vision, taking a personal stand on the explored issues

   Ask: *What do you think of Laura's assertion that all people are prejudiced?*

6. **Whispers/Good Angel:** Students decide what a character needs to know, be reminded of, be advised on, and then decide how to present the information.

   Reading strategies practiced: connecting life to literature and literature to life, acting as an agent for character, considering social action based on issue in reading

   Student A is Rachel

Student B is her guardian angel

Ask: *What kind of encouragement or advice does Rachel need right now? What does she need to hear that will help her?*

Strategies to Use After Reading, to Reflect, Extend and Apply Understandings

Anchor Standards for Reading, 1–9

7. **Choral Montage of Lines from Notes Between Rachel and Laura:** Students write notes between characters and cull lines from them to write a poem about the characters' experience at this point in the story.

    Reading strategies practiced: composing a shared response, interpreting meaning, understanding text structure and its contribution to textual meaning

7a. **Hotseat:** Character Interview or Press Conference. Groups of students are interviewed about their experiences.

    Reading strategies practiced: inferring character and character relationships, evaluating character, identifying theme and main idea, considering author's vision, conversing with an author

7b. **Tableaux:** Students create visual pictures with their bodies, emphasizing key details and relationships. Have them create a slide show of key scenes.

    Reading strategies practiced: identifying key details and relationship to main idea, understanding text structure, visualization

7c. **Statue:** Students create a statue with their bodies that highlights and commemorates the story's meaning.

    Reading strategies practiced: identifying, justifying, and expressing theme/main idea, representing ideas, transmediation of ideas into multimodal formats

7d. **Scene After the Story:** Students imagine and represent an elaborated scene that captures consequences, changes in behavior, future action, and so forth.

    Reading strategies practiced: elaborating, extending, inferring story meaning, considering how text can shape future understanding, behavior, and social action, inferring, seeing and extending complex implied relationships

8. **Mantle-of-the-Expert:** Follow-Up on Issues Raised. Students take on roles that address issues that have been raised, inquire into appropriate action, and propose such action.

    Reading strategies practiced: connecting literature to life and life to literature, using reading to inform inquiry and behavior, application of learning to life

    Have students interview a lawyer (in role) or panel of figures from the history of civil rights: *What are civil rights? Were Rachel's civil rights violated? What are the most effective methods for redressing civil rights violations? How can we learn from mistakes and issues to best protect and promote civil rights? What has worked and not worked in analogous historical situations?* Research and follow up on a subsequent day of class.

Social action project: How can we protect and promote civil rights and social justice in our own school and community?

Frontloading: Introductory Activities That Activate and Build Prior Knowledge

Using research data from schema theory, cognitive science, psychology, and reading research, I have shown that the majority of comprehension problems can be addressed by activating and/or building students' background knowledge (the schematic knowledge/prior experience necessary to understanding the text), building genre knowledge (knowledge of how the text works), and/or setting a purpose prior to reading. (See Wilhelm, Baker, and Dube, 2001.)

This kind of frontloading work helps students access or develop the knowledge they need to read a particular text successfully. If students do not possess the requisite knowledge, frontloading builds it so that they can successfully prepare to approach the task. Frontloading helps the students use what they already know (the "near to home") so that they can build on this to move "further from home," learning new concepts and strategies. In other words, knowledge in the ZAD (zone of actual development) is activated and then built upon in order to move through the ZPD (zone of proximal development). Research demonstrates that direct experience is the most important resource for successful reading, and that experiences from enactments can be a powerful alternative resource when students do not have the requisite personal experience (May, 1990). All learning is metaphoric: we must connect the already known to something new to perceive, understand, and achieve new understandings and capacities. In other words, the only resource we have to help students learn something new is what they already care about and know. These resources must be activated or we will have no resources to learn what is new.

Frontloading Activities for "The Fan Club"

The subject and material of "The Fan Club" is close to student experiences, making it a good text to use early in a unit on civil rights—or friendship, relationships, fairness, or other issues (a rich text always has multiple topics, uses, and inquiry connections). Connections can be made between the text, experiences close to students, and experiences further away (like the 1960s civil rights struggle, or women's and children's rights in the Third World). In this way, the story reading itself frontloads future reading about civil rights issues the students have not personally experienced. Nonetheless, while reading "The Fan Club," students need help to see from the various perspectives of Rachel, Laura, the members of the fan club, parents, and teachers to understand the story. To do this, they must start with what they know and build from there. Eighth-grade language arts teacher Chris Prickitt uses a Trigger Letter to activate students' background knowledge about peer issues at school.

Chris Prickitt's Trigger Letter for "The Fan Club"

(Notice how Chris organically models formal letter writing, a skill that can be used later in the enactment and in the students' lives.)

1955 Elm Street
Sweepsville, Missouri
Date

Office of the Principal
Sweepsville Middle School
Sweepsville, Missouri

Dear Mrs. Harrigan,

I've been wondering why Lucille, my eighth-grade daughter, has been so unhappy lately. After much cautious, but persistent, questioning by her father and me, she has begun to talk. Finally, the reasons have begun to emerge.

It seems she has been the victim of a lot of teasing in school, some of it quite hurtful. The reasons? Mostly, it seems she is given a hard time just because she does her schoolwork well, is polite and respectful to teachers and other students, dresses neatly, plays sports, and basically behaves responsibly! For these choices, she is ostracized, called a "prep" and a "suck up," and made to feel "corny and uncool."

I'm worried. I'm afraid Lucille will eventually give in to the peer pressure to conform to the behaviors and choices of those who, for one reason or another, would rather disrupt, coast, fail, victimize others, or worse, who want to "fit in" rather than think for themselves.

I know it is a tough task, but please do what you can to instigate a change in the attitude of your students. We must not despair. Society seems to be spiraling downward, but that does not need to be so. I believe that schools and teachers like you can help to change things for the better, and to transform the misguided youths who are causing Lucille problems and pain.

Thank you for listening and let me know how you plan to proceed.

Sincerely,
Phyllis Goldberg

Frontloading With Trigger Letters

Before Reading a Story, Hand Out the Letter to Students. Chris's letter requires students to respond via a form of dramatic play. Chris asks his students to read the letter and imagine how they would react if they found it.

He poses: *What would they want to say about this letter to their friends?* Then, he and the students brainstorm ideas:

> Do kids get made fun of for being good students? For being "good"? For being different in some way? Why else do kids get made fun of?
>
> What parts of the story are not told in the letter? What might be the rest of the story?
>
> What might Mrs. Goldberg not know? What other issues might be at play?
>
> When does teasing become harassment?
>
> Where is the line between good natured fun/hurtful teasing and bullying? How do you tell the difference?
>
> What is peer pressure? In what circumstances is it used? When can this become bullying?
>
> Is this pressure always negative? How do adults and society use peer pressure? In positive and negative ways?

Guide Students to Work in Groups to Discuss Class-Generated Questions. Next, Chris asks groups to form and imagine that they are at their lunchroom table discussing the letter and the questions.

Conclude Activity—Sum Up With a Report Out. Chris calls the activity to a close and has students "report out" by sharing the most interesting ideas explored in their group.

Pose a Question That Sets Up a Follow-Up Activity. Chris then asks: *What kinds of people would be interested in discussing this issue and possible ways of dealing with it?* His class brainstorms this list: Lucille, Mrs. Goldberg, Mrs. Harrigan, the assistant principal, a kid who teases and harasses others, a sympathetic student, a friend of Lucille, a guidance counselor, a psychologist, a schoolyard proctor or police officer, a movie or TV show producer, an artist, teachers, a newspaper reporter, God, the Dalai Lama, and several others. Their list identifies people who would have vested interests and knowledge of the situation, and the capacity for commenting on and dealing with it in some way.

Engage in Mantle-of-the-Expert Writing. Each of Chris's students chooses one role from the list of people they generated and writes a monologue about the situation, including their feelings about it and their ideas for addressing the issue. After 10 minutes, Chris invites volunteers to stand, tell the class "who they are" (in-role) and to read an important excerpt from their writing. As they go around the class, their readings form a choral montage of different perspectives on the issues raised, and though Chris does not require participation, he told me later that four out of five of his students stood to read an excerpt—a level of participation he considers phenomenal. When he then told his students they would now read a short story that dealt with these issues, they were extremely enthusiastic.

Frontloading With a Trigger Letter and Role-Play

I also use a Trigger Letter to frontload my students' reading of "The Fan Club." But I move them directly to role-play—to imagining they are someone else. I ask my students to imagine that they are students in another school. I give them the following letter and ask them to read it, explaining that in their role-play they have found it on the classroom floor. Next, I ask students to pair up and discuss what they think of it. To practice inferencing and prepare for story entry, they are given three minutes to figure out to whom the letter was written and who wrote it, why this copy was lying around, what situation is being referred to, what they should do with the letter, how this person's situation is similar and different from their own and others they know about, and what the writer might suggest they do.

> Dear Counselor,
>
> This place is a nightmare! Do you not know that there are people out here who are being harassed and hounded and no one is doing anything about it?!
>
> There are people who make other people miserable and no one stops them. In fact, they get rewarded and admired! This happens in front of adults, who should be protecting someone like me from getting hurt, and I mean HURT in every sense of the word.
>
> Isn't there something you can do? I mean, isn't it your job to make sure all of us are safe? Open your eyes and do your job!

Frontloading With Tableaux

Teacher Donna Dachs took a different tack because she felt her students did not need conceptual front-loading but did need procedural preparation to use new reading strategies. Donna felt that the biggest issue facing her students in comprehending "The Fan Club" was understanding the ironic disjuncture between the usual kind of "fan club" and the one in the story. To prepare her students to notice and interpret this irony, she frontloaded her students' reading with a simple brainstorming activity, asking her students to define "fan club," identify fan clubs they had heard of or belonged to (officially and unofficially), and name a fan club they would belong to now if they could. Donna followed up this discussion with short tableaux activities, asking different groups to create frozen pictures with their bodies of a meeting between a fan club and a famous athlete, pop star, or movie star. Students were instructed to pose in such a way that reflected their feelings about the celebrity and their desires to get close to, honor, or get an autograph from that person. She then asked students to create an ironic version of their tableaux by adding an unexpected detail that would radically change the expected meaning of the encounter. The students discussed the use and meaning of irony, how irony works to express a more subtle meaning, and concluded by brainstorming clues that a scene might be ironic and how they might be alert to this during their reading.

How These Activities Are Rich With Strategic Teaching

These three variations of frontloading for "The Fan Club" illustrate how the wise use of such techniques not only helps students activate and build the conceptual knowledge necessary for successful reading comprehension, but can also assist them in developing procedural knowledge, such as how to understand diverse perspectives and irony. The letters, for example, helped students make inferences (an important strategy for reading the story) and motivated their willingness to read the story, as they could now see it as dealing with a real issue that affects people they know. The brainstorming and tableaux activities helped activate background knowledge that will alert them to the irony used during the story that requires understanding the disjuncture between a real fan club and the kind described in the story. Remember to *strategically choose and strategically use*; the techniques should be matched and adapted to the needs of your students at any given point of time to help them transact more meaningfully with the material at hand.

More Enactment Techniques to Use Before Reading

Response to Pictures

Anchor Standards for Reading, 1–3, 7, 9

Photographs can build background necessary for a successful reading and help students practice strategies like inferring the setting, situation, characterization, author's purpose, and how all of this is related to the information and presentation of the photograph. (See Smith and Wilhelm, 2010 for more ideas about teaching setting, character, perspective and theme.) Family portraits or famous paintings can be used in much the same way, and this is a great way to introduce students to famous paintings like Renoir's *La Loge* (in which a man in a box at the opera is looking at another woman while his wife watches the performance). This depiction of a love triangle requires and prepares students to infer character and character relationships. Munch's *The Scream* (the famous hallucinatory painting of a man screaming on a long bridge) would be great for frontloading a story exploring oppression, harassment, fear, or mental illness.

As I mentioned earlier, I've opened a unit on the Depression by passing out WPA photographs, such as those by Dorothea Lange. I might ask the students to view the photos and make inferences: Who might Dorothea Lange be? Why did she take such photographs? How are her concerns similar and different from our own? What can we learn from the photographs? What did she hope to accomplish?

Students could then take on the Mantle of the Expert, pretending they are historians trying to reconstruct what life must have been like during the Depression and how that experience compares to life today. Or they could be invited to role-play people in the photographs and respond to questions like: What is your biggest problem right now? What is causing this problem? What do you fear most? regret most? want most? What other people are most like you (from history, for example)? What do you want from the future? How do you plan to achieve this? (Cecily O'Neill uses photographs and artifacts to great effect in her process dramas; see O'Neill and Lambert, 1982.)

Precious Object

Before reading a text that contains symbolism, students are introduced to the concept of symbolic meanings, how these accrue to an object through association and experience, and how to notice and interpret such a symbol. (Teaching how to read and interpret symbolism is covered more thoroughly in *Improving Comprehension With Think-Alouds*.) A powerful way to do this is to have your students bring in or imagine objects that are precious to them. Then ask them to describe the object and why it is precious. What kind of functional or sentimental value does it have? As a variation, you could have them choose a precious object from the point of view of an historical figure or a story character.

Anchor Standards
for Reading, 1–6

When my students read the story "Human Frailty" by Alex Xlebnikov, which involves two people on a special mission in outer space, I tell them they are going to play these roles and ask them to pack a bag (the story and the story drama lesson appear in Wilhelm and Novak, 2011). What things will they take and why? They are also allowed to take one sentimental object. What will it be and why? Similarly, as Cecily O'Neill often does in her dramas like "The

The Precious Object technique in action. Students in role describe the importance of their chosen object.

Way West" (O'Neill and Lambert, 1982), students can be asked to imagine they are pioneers heading off across the Great Plains. What object have they brought or saved from their past life that is of great sentimental or functional value? Why have they brought it? This activity builds belief in the story world and helps students pay attention to significant objects and other key details in a text and what these might mean. The Precious Object activity is great for teaching *key detail, symbolism, setting,* and *characterization* and leads to a consideration of *perspective* and *theme.* Any story involving a trip or journey, stories about the orphan trains, for example, could easily make use of this technique, and it can be adapted to prepare students to explore character, details, and event in any other kind of story, too.

Presents/Gifts

After brainstorming basic information about an historical time period or situation, students imagine that they are a person living during the Holocaust (before reading *Number the Stars*), during the Depression (before reading *Roll of Thunder, Hear My Cry*), during the Korean War (before reading *Year of Impossible Goodbyes*), or during the Civil Rights Movement or some other time of great tension and momentousness. Students can then come up with a present they would most want if they were a character involved in these events, or what present they would want to give to an involved character if they could, which may or may not be a conventional kind of gift. This is a nice entrance into reading about characters in these situations. Alternatively, the teacher could provide a present and ask students to role-play their reaction to receiving it, their future use of the gift, or the context in which it would be meaningful and useful, etc.

Storytelling About an Object

Any photograph or object could be the stimulus for Storytelling in Character's Role, an activity in which students recount the importance of the object. The student can describe it from her own point of view or from the point of view of a relative or friend who lived during the era—or the situation/issue—you're studying. Students could also play the role of detective, historian, or archaeologist interpreting the object's importance. If you find that students remain sketchy about background information, introduce more objects, artifacts, and photographs to get their imaginations flowing about the topic. Students can also interview adults or experts in person or on-line, or Google to find background information associated with the object.

Maps

Maps, aerial views, building or floor plans, or other schematics can provide useful background knowledge about the setting of a story. You might share one and ask your students to predict the significance of that setting to the text they will read. Or students could surmise the challenges or concerns a character might have as he tries to complete the journey outlined on the map. Students could also use a map to solve a problem. For example, before reading *The Great Fire* by Jim Murphy, I wanted my students to consider how they might use the map I'd given them to try to plan evacuation routes or work to stop the fire. Before and during reading *Deathwatch* by Robb White, I asked students to brainstorm how they might advise the protagonist to prepare for surviving his journey—and later, how to escape. Maps and schematics can also be created by students as they read a story to help them visualize and situate themselves in the story world.

Primary Sources, Videos, and Incident Reports

Another great frontloading tool is a primary source document or a video that is relevant to the reading students are about to do. For instance, when studying the American Revolution, I gave groups of students a facsimile of the Declaration of Independence. I asked them to assume the role of the colonists and figure out what this new document would mean to them. What dangers and possibilities did they now face? What would happen to them if they were caught with the document by the British troops or Tory sympathizers? This enactment gave them a reason for reading the Declaration and a context in which to appreciate it. It also frontloaded readings like Howard Fast's *April Morning* and the Colliers' *My Brother Sam Is Dead*.

Likewise, during my civil rights unit, I often have students view video clips from documentaries or movies like *The Cradle Will Rock* and then write Incident Reports, in role as police or newspaper reporters, or in-role letters describing what has happened and the issues and questions the incidents raise.

Character Quotations

I learned this strategy from Doug Buehl, whose *Interactive Strategies for Reading* (2001/2009) is full of great activities for support before, during, and after reading. Many can be adapted as enactment strategies, as I have done here.

In Character Quotations, the teacher previews the text and pulls out important quotations that reveal a character's problem, personality and nature, and values, or that reveal important information about the main issue at hand. Students are given different quotations and work together as detectives in small groups to figure out: Who is this person? What is his problem? How is this person like me? What might happen to him? Through this work, students practice making inferences, predictions, and personal connections.

During my civil rights unit, I choose quotations from Chief Joseph, Frederick Douglass, Martin Luther King, Jr., Elizabeth Cady Stanton, the Dalai Lama, and others, but without identifying the author. I have students work in small groups, providing each group with quotations from a different civil rights leader. Once they have made and justified inferences about their person, students "jigsaw" to other groups and attempt to figure out what the individuals quoted have in common. One variation is to have students *become* the quoted characters (obviously, they'll have to figure out who they are first!), and jigsaw with other characters in a kind of "Meeting of the Minds", brainstorming what their common problems are, what they might do about them, how they might learn from each other or be helpful to each other. Even if all inferences are not correct, students are alerted to key quotations, key situations, and the issues faced by all, which will be read about during the unit. They are

CCSS

Anchor Standards
for Reading,
1–4, 6, 9

alerted to searching for patterns of meaning across texts and situations, which is the basis of all deep understanding.

Tea Party

A similar technique, which I learned from Kylene Beers, involves passing a different line from a single poem or story to each member of the class, and then asking students to mingle and make predictions about the topic, characters, relationships, problems, and events that will take place in that text. I've adapted this technique by giving one different quotation from the same character to each student in a group of five or six students. The students then share their quotations to figure out who the character is or what the story or poem will be about. Likewise, students can be given a list of quotations from a character and asked to assume the role of that character, walking around the room and visiting other characters from different groups, figuring out each other's concerns, how they might agree or disagree with each other, and how they might work together. This works nicely if students have read different books in literature circles or reciprocal reading groups, but it also works if students have all read or will read the same texts.

Rituals as Triggers

Anchor Standards for Reading, 1–4, 6,7

Rituals can also activate the sharing of information and perspectives that are important to the reading of a text. These techniques can be used in small groups or with the whole class. Some rituals I have used during enactments include:

Naming Ceremonies. In an extended drama about Columbus, created by Brian Edmiston, we begin by imagining we are the native Tainos before the arrival of Columbus. (See Wilhelm and Edmiston, 1998.) We pass an imaginary baby around the group, suggesting a name and the significance of the name. (As another example, when doing our dream analysis drama described in the introduction to this book, we began by making nametags for ourselves as "Dream Analyst Jones" or "Psychology Professor Smith" and then introducing ourselves and our particular specialization and interests to each other in that role.)

Wishing/Bestowing/Bequeathing. We then bestow upon or bequeath the child (though this could be any character before a challenge or quest) something of cultural importance to us, by assigning him a totem or making a wish for his future. Since the Tainos left no records (though contemporary archaeologists offer some provocative ideas about what their culture was like), these activities help us to imagine the values of the natives before Columbus arrived. They also help us build knowledge about what might have happened when this culture met Columbus.

After reading Michael Dorris's *Morning Girl*, we undertake a repeated ceremony, this time actually deciding on a name. After reading translations of documents about Columbus' time on Hispaniola, we perform the ceremony as Spaniards so we can contrast the values of the natives and the explorers, and by extension, of the two different cultures.

Swearing/Oath Taking. Imagining an oath or pledge one might have had to take to enter into the group or society or undertaking a challenge we will read about is another knowledge-building ritual. For instance, my students have imagined the oath of a Templar Knight before reading Catherine Jinks's *Pagan's Crusade* and have also imagined the oath taken by Danes to resist the Nazis before reading Lois Lowry's *Number the Stars*. Of course, like most strategies, this one can also be done—or done again—*after* a reading, so that students can incorporate what they have learned into their oath. Comparing before and after oaths help students to see how their knowledge and understanding has developed throughout a reading and gives "visible signs of accomplishment" so important to motivation and a feeling of competence (Smith and Wilhelm, 2002; 2006).

Processions. Students participate in a procession celebrating, commemorating, making offerings, and so forth. Processions can also be used during or after a reading. For example, after reading *Number the Stars*, my sixth graders imagined we were Danes parading through the streets. Each of us in turn made a promise to future generations, recalled a friend or memory we would not let die out, and so forth. This kind of work can easily be made into a choral montage.

Gauntlets. Students run a gauntlet by walking between two lines of students who whisper or tell them things as they walk by. For instance, before reading Mildred Taylor's *Roll of Thunder, Hear My Cry,* I asked students to imagine what it would be like for an African-American trying to achieve equal rights and fair treatment during the Depression. We brainstormed what we knew about this from our experience. Then as each student walked the gauntlet, those students on their right offered encouragement and support to their cause while those on the left offered discouragement and mentioned obstacles. In this way, the students brainstormed together about what life would be like for the people struggling for social justice during this time, what their resources and challenges would be. Likewise, students could first run a gauntlet of negativity that highlighted obstacles and challenges, then a gauntlet of encouragement. The experiences could be compared and students could consider how words are powerful in influencing people negatively and positively, consider how to usefully phrase encouragement, how to know when people need to understand challenges, and when they need to be encouraged.

Passwords. With this technique, students are asked to imagine that they will become part of a secret society or a group of characters and that they must make up passwords that will summarize their calling. For instance, when reading *Number the Stars*, I had students imagine themselves in the Resistance and to adopt passwords for different situations they would imagine themselves in; when reading *Roll of Thunder, Hear My Cry*, students imagine themselves becoming part of a civil rights group and making up passwords for imagined challenges and situations.

Rumors/Gossip (Predictions). Before reading a text about a topic, students are given a hint about the general subject or conflict they will encounter. They then pass around "rumors" or "gossip"—predictions about what they believe might be involved or what might happen.

Departures (for example, farewell send-offs), **Arrivals** (passing through immigration), **Celebrations** (anniversaries, acknowledging achievements, toasting someone, a banquet), **Dedications** (initiations or contracts, acknowledgements of past help and indebtedness), **Affirmations** (swearing allegiance, giving praise), and **Procedures** (calling roll, taking an inventory, running a meeting) are all kinds of ritual enactments that can be used to build belief and express or share knowledge before, during, and even after a reading.

Motivating Students to Embrace the Unfamiliar: Effective Frontloading Techniques

Anchor Standards
for Reading,
1–2, 4, 6, 7, 9
Anchor Standards
for Writing, 1–7

It is not enough to have interesting material for students to read. We must create a context that will motivate students to read, help them set purposes and ask relevant questions, and encourage them to create and enter into story worlds. They must engage with the characters and ideas expressed there, think about the meaning of the situations, actions, and consequences that occur, and apply these reflectively to their own lives.

A central finding about motivation, as well as cognition, is that these processes are "situated" or "context-dependent," i.e., they exist in particular contexts and are enabled, made possible, and supported by the conditions of those contexts. We often regard "motivation," for example, as an individual quality as in, "He is a highly motivated person." In fact, any individual is both motivated and unmotivated every day and this is explained by the situations that person finds herself in. For example, I am highly motivated to Nordic ski in winter when I am on the ski trails. I am likewise highly unmotivated when there is a boring faculty meeting at the end of the day. However, I could be motivated by a faculty meeting if the conditions were changed; if, for example, we had substantive work to do and were given decision-making power to enact that work. This is very good news for teachers, but also a challenge. If students are unmotivated, it is within our power to change the conditions of the situation that will lead to their motivation. (See Smith and Wilhelm 2002; 2006 for a full discussion of these conditions.)

An excellent presentation at a recent NCTE conference explored how enactment techniques can create situations that help students set purposes for reading and cultivate concern for characters or real people who are different than the students. Betsy Ver Wys, Jennifer Haberling, and Brian White (2000) demonstrated that if characters or situations are too distant from student concerns, then students may dismiss the characters and the issues they represent. Teachers must bridge the gap before reading by assisting students to see how they share the concerns and issues faced and how the characters are worthy of their attention.

Value Cards

To introduce the Washington Irving story, "The Devil and Tom Walker," about a deal with the devil, these teachers handed each student a set of three cards that signified different values. These values could include ideas like health, respect, friendship, wealth, competence, love, family, political power, fame, the willingness to serve and help others, artistic talent, athleticism, a close relationship with God, and many others. The students discussed how we make many trade-offs in life; by pursuing one value we often do not have the time nor energy to pursue other values or develop other talents and possibilities. They were then asked to engage in dramatic play and walk around the classroom making trades to accumulate the cards with those values they most wanted. After about 10 minutes of trading, the enactment was called to an end. The students then wrote about one trade that they never would have made if it had been real life and one trade that they actually would have. Students were thereby introduced to the story.

These teachers had found that previous students tended to dismiss Tom Walker and the story as "off point" and "stupid," but this activity helped them experience how we all make such trade-offs on a daily basis, how decisions about what to do and not do all involve a trade-off. This allowed student to see their commonality with Tom Walker, the issues he faced, and the underlying reality and meaning of the story.

Of course, there are many other examples from literature about trade-offs. I have recently used this technique to frontload the reading of books like Lois Lowry's *The Giver*. This activity, of course, can also be done in the role of literary or historical characters during or after a reading. Character values and the effects of these values, how values influence decision making and trade-offs, and how characters change in their values are always very closely tied to the thematic meanings of literature and this activity is excellent at exploring these character values.

Fate Cards

My friend Janett Jackson recently used a similar technique to frontload a health unit on smoking. She had her students write down their life goals, both personal and professional. Then, each of them received a smoking card describing on one side how smoking (their own habit, second-hand smoke, or the smoking of a loved one) had affected their life, and on the other side statistics about the prevalence of this effect. Some students received cards that indicated they were short of breath, had smelly clothes, had lost a family member to premature death, or were at a greater risk of heart disease. They were the lucky ones. The rest had cards indicating they would suffer from various cancers and diseases, amputations, and the like as a result of smoking. All students then had to write about how their condition would affect their life goals. Later in the unit students studied the various health consequences of smoking. They were engaged in "imagining to learn" as they prepared to learn even more.

"What If?" Questions

These questions stimulate imagination in the form of dramatic play. What if students could live in a future where they had fewer freedoms but their health and peace were guaranteed? (*The Giver*) What if your property was going to be taken by a more powerful person? What if you had the chance to destroy your property before it was stolen? (*Roll of Thunder, Hear*

My Cry) What if you were accused of being an accessory to murder and you had no way to prove your innocence? (Walter Dean Myers' *Monster*) These questions can be directed to the students as themselves, and then they can be asked to imagine historical, popular culture, or literary characters who would have similar or differing answers. Students can also be asked to imagine contexts in which their answers would change.

Thematic Scenarios

Another idea presented by Ver Wys and colleagues comes from Smagorinsky, McCann, and Kern (1987) and is used to stimulate Dramatic Play, Mantle of the Expert, or Role-Playing. Before a unit on discrimination, the teachers developed several written scenarios that described different kinds of discrimination. Students were asked to respond to the scenarios as if they had happened in their community. They were to consider how the character felt, what caused the discrimination, and what the character and community could do to address it. They moved from closer to further from home by starting with scenes that had happened in their community: teenagers being falsely accused of shoplifting in a store, a devoutly Christian teenager denied a job because he refuses to work on Sundays. They then moved to scenes that were further from their students' experiences and that had occurred elsewhere: a woman denied a promotion because she may become pregnant, a family that is not sold a house because they are of a different ethnic background, and so on. Students role-play the dilemma, discuss it in-role as experts, and rehearse possibilities that would extend or work towards resolving the conflict.

Such scenarios should capture moments of tension and consequence that parallel those that will be read about. Scenarios that point out complexity, surprise, contrast, and different perspectives are very stimulating and can pull students into a story that uses similar issues or techniques.

Review Board

A variation I've used is to write the scenarios as letters of complaint to a board of experts, such as a local civil rights board. The students, in role as a civil rights oversight committee, must rank the complaints in order of urgency and merit and decide what to do about each one. In this way, they enter into the reality of each situation, articulate their own beliefs, and can then examine their own prejudices or "pre-judgments."

Scene Extensions

Another option is to have students create written scenes or to role-play the scenes that would have followed the scenario descriptions, such as what happens as the teens in the store are told they are suspected of shoplifting and must be searched. What happens afterward? All of these activities require the students to draw on their personal experience to adopt the experience and identity of a character.

Character Coat of Arms

When Ver Wys, Haberling, and White frontloaded a unit on identity (What makes me me?), they wanted their students to consider how we define ourselves, how we are defined by others, and how we define others who are different from us. This unit not only established conceptual knowledge about identity and different belief systems, but also built procedural knowledge on inferring character, character values, and thus the ability to infer a central focus or authorial generalization. This unit, in turn, functioned as the frontloading for other units on discrimination and civil rights.

The unit opened with students creating a four-panel coat of arms as a visual depiction of their identity and values. The different panels can be matched to different aspects of character important to explore in a text or unit. Throughout the unit, this activity served as a template as students discussed what kind of coats of arms various characters would create for themselves. Students could also be asked to create these shields in role as a character and to justify how the activities described in the texts demonstrate these values and sense of identity. Shields can be created early in a story and at the end, then compared to explore character change and how that relates to the thematic generalization of the story.

Character Manifesto and Creed

A similar activity that I have used starts a unit by asking students to write a personal creed. To prepare, we sometimes read short models of various creeds, such as the Dalai Lama's, the Nicene Creed, Edward Guest's poetic "My Creed," "the Slacker's Creed," "the Ranger's Creed," Desiderata, and even popular music creeds like "Let It Be" (all easy to find on the Internet). These examples are short, and students can grasp the meaning after several examples. I then ask students to write their own creed and to make sure it covers the following: What do you believe in? What is important to you? What do you want to achieve? How do you want to live each day? What is worth working for? What is the ultimate goal of your life? What is your desired legacy?

I have students compose creeds in various ways: as a written creed, as poetry, as a web site, as a Barbara Walters interview, as a rap song called "What I Believe," as a one- to two-minute video documentary called "What Is Jake's Creed?" This is great frontloading for a book where characters face challenges to their beliefs. Students can compare their beliefs to characters and evaluate what might make people forsake, change, or strengthen their beliefs. Later, students can write a creed in role as a character.

Simulations

I have used the simulation "Desert Survival" before reading Robb White's *Deathwatch*, and "Moon Survival" before reading the short story of survival "Human Frailty." (See Wilhelm and Novak, 2011, for the complete story drama of "Human Frailty;" and Wilhelm, Smith, and Fredricksen, 2012, for how such rankings can lead to composing with various informational text structures.) Versions of these simulations were found on the Internet. In both simulations, students rank the importance of various actions, equipment, and provisions to their survival. They get points for how closely their rankings match those of survival experts. Their point totals show whether they would survive, survive after great suffering, or die. Needless to say, most students would perish and therefore learn through the simulation a great deal about the difficulty of surviving in harsh environments and how to do it. This knowledge can then be applied to our readings. I also have used a simulation of Puritan life, available from the company Interact, prior to reading about the Puritans, Elizabeth George Speare's *The Witch of Blackbird Pond*, or Arthur Miller's *The Crucible*. The simulation helps students see what it would be like to have lived under Puritan religion, schooling, and law. This provides them with background that helps them to engage with texts "distant from home" and to make more constructive meaning with such texts.

The end goal of all enactment is for students to internalize content and strategic knowledge, including that of using the enactment techniques themselves as ways to approach and solve problems. I know I am getting somewhere when students have difficulty with a text and suggest using an enactment to address that problem.

Voices From the Field

Dear Jeff:

Warning! This is going to be a somewhat philosophical e-mail.

I used some of the enactment techniques to frontload readings over the past few weeks. I thought the effects were profound. The techniques somehow helped connect our reading to more authentic "being." I mean that the students were more "present" to the characters and the story, took it all more seriously, connected things more carefully to their own lives. It was as if the dramas helped enact a rite of passage and transformation in how they read and how they were affected by their reading.

Truly, I had students responding in ways that I would have previously thought impossible. This drama is powerful stuff. An elixir for educationists. More later (another warning of sorts!).

—Chris

CHAPTER 4

DRAMA AS INQUIRY

Engagement, Joy, Imagination, Agency, Identity, and Wisdom

I want to emphasize that drama/action/enactment strategies are the most powerful set of strategies in my teaching repertoire. This is because drama is a natural form of substantive inquiry that engages the whole being: the mind, the imagination, the body, and the emotions. Drama requires creativity, activity, proactivity, and reflective reactivity. Drama also leads to an exploration of ethical imagination and ethical identities, and towards wisdom in action (see Wilhelm and Novak, 2011). As Vygotsky has claimed: play is the most natural form of learning. Children imagine and role-play constantly in order to learn and rehearse for living.

But there is more. Drama, like all forms of play, is exploratory in a fun, empowering, and joyful way. I see my students pursuing drama with great engagement and often exuberant joy. True learning is always fun. We miss this point at great peril to our students (and ourselves). When an experience is deadening and does not involve us, we are not likely to learn what is important from it.

In *Play: How It Shapes the Brain, Opens the Imagination, and Invigorates the Soul* (2009), Stuart Brown documents the neurological and ethological research showing how play is the central complex of human behaviors evolutionarily developed to facilitate social bonding and learning among mammals. Social imagination and deep understanding are facilitated through participants' sportive, artful, innovative participation within loosely rule-governed frameworks lying comfortably between the extremes of total anarchy and total standardization. There is actual evolutionary truth to the saying "all work and no play makes Jack a dull boy" (and, of course, Jill a dull girl)!

Many of the issues surrounding effective curriculum instruction, standards, and assessment could be resolved by seeing how the most important learning of all occurs when people come into serious concept-driven play with one another!

Drama as Inquiry

Drama promotes and can constitute rigorous forms of inquiry because it is active and embodied, involves action, and leads to future action. Drama can be the framing device for any curricular unit, setting it up as a problem to be solved and providing roles, such as "mantle of the expert," that lead to pursuing understandings and solutions. Drama can promote inquiry at the global curricular level as well as the local lesson or activity level.

Drama is also a form of "design": a way of negotiating, representing, and sharing carefully constructed meanings that may include processes of understanding and problem-solving as well as justifications and representations of particular understandings. Drama can lead to the culminating projects that inquiry works toward; it offers a way into all kinds of materials and texts, ways of interpreting these texts, and the opportunity to create a "performance of understanding" (Blythe, T., et al, 1998), in which the performance itself is a knowledge artifact, an intervention, and/or a proposal or solution to a problem, as well as a way to demonstrate literacy and problem-solving repertoires.

The variety of mutually supportive action strategies explored in this book have the potential to transform classrooms into liminal spaces for literacy learning and inquiry. These are spaces that create nearly limitless possibilities for composing and interpreting texts (easily expanded into the kinds of critical inquiries that develop student agency and identities) teach students HOW to learn, HOW to read and write, and that lead towards ethical understandings, wisdom, and application of understandings. And I must ask: If we are not teaching for understanding and wisdom, then what is it that we are teaching for?

Here is the challenge laid down recently by Dorothy Heathcote, our foremost pioneer and practitioner of drama-in-education:

> The big shift is [for teachers] to move from holding the information and doling it out like charity to creating the circumstances where it is imperative to inquire, search out, and interrogate the information we locate. If at present it isn't possible to merge the work of adults and

the work of students because we don't value the contribution young children can bring to cultural development of the world's good, we can rely on proven drama systems to create 'the mirror to nature' and harness, through identification and empathy, the life knowledge which children will bring generously to meet us half-way.

—Dorothy Heathcote (2006, p. xii)

Dramatic Inquiry as a "Third Space"

The "third space" capacity of drama (i.e., its position between different realities such as home and community or academic knowledge and real world knowledge; a place for the meeting of different cultures or perspectives in order to co-generate new ones, for moving from "what is" toward "what could be") is essential to its power as an inquiry tool. Drama situates learning and provides an immediate context that lends purpose to and assists that learning. The use of drama can connect all readings and the larger classroom projects to real-life experiences.

Cognitive scientists have long argued for the necessity of "situations" or "spaces" to promote and understand learning. No text, data, activity, outcomes, behaviors, emotions, or decisions can be enacted or understood except "in context." This is an essential insight and one that demonstrates why "decontextualized" instruction of anything from phonemes to math facts to literary themes does not lead to understanding or use. One of the most powerful recommendations for using action strategies is that it provides an immediate simulated context for learning, understanding, and application.

In dramatized inquiry contexts, students learn in meaningful situations how to use language, actions, interactions, interventions, and other concrete tools to create abstract symbolic meaning for thinking, for reflecting, and for rehearsing future action. As the famed anthropologist Jacob Bronowski proclaimed in *The Ascent of Man*, "there is nothing in the head that was not first in the hand." In other words, we proceed in understanding from the concretely experienced to the abstract. Further, abstractions are always situated in particular concrete situations. *Abstract concepts and processes cannot be taught or learned separate from contextualized use.*

In inquiry, students are assisted over time to deep understanding. There is a tremendous amount of information, data, concepts and strategies to be learned. But these are best taught at the point of need, when they can be used. In drama, teachers can provide data and assist students to use new strategies for immediate dramatic social purposes that are tied to social action in the world.

"Understanding" requires that students see multiple perspectives on an issue and make an informed and justified choice that can be defended according to disciplinary procedures and standards. It is therefore important to depart from information transmission and teacher proselytizing of students ("Just believe me—this is the way it is!"). Teachers must instead engage students into disciplinary debates: get them to engage in various points of view, and work to encourage students to entertain perspectives and ideas that they resist or don't understand. Drama is particularly suited to this kind of work, because in drama you are not yourself and can easily imagine and take on differing perspectives as someone else, at least tentatively entertaining new and foreign points of view.

Drama is not only useful for contextualizing and pursuing understandings, but also for representing and sharing these. In my classes, students have demonstrated understanding through various kinds of culminating drama projects: how-to dramas, tableaux slide shows, dances, museum exhibits, wax museums, museum kiosks, debates, in-role presentations of various written artifacts like arguments, extended definitions, artist statements, guidebooks, newspapers, action plans, proposals, songs, phrase books, picture books for reading buddies, and much more. The creation of such artifacts gives students the opportunity to compose, edit, and read—often in role, taking on "the mantle of the expert" of editors, proofreaders, graphic artists, experts in the field, interested or oppositional citizens, and so on.

Drama as Real Research

When Brian Edmiston and I pursued our research into using drama as a way of promoting students as inquirers (Wilhelm and Edmiston, 1998; Edmiston and Wilhelm, 1998), we identified three salient research traditions promoted by drama.

Phenomenological research: In phenomenology, we "live through" the experience of people who are different from us in time, place, or situation in an attempt to understand them and their contexts. Dorothy Heathcote stressed the ubiquity and easy access of dramatic phenomenological research: "the ability of humans to 'become somebody else', to 'see how it feels' … to 'put yourself in my shoes' [is a capacity that] humans employ naturally and intuitively all their lives" (1969, p. 54). This is certainly a capacity that we want to cultivate in all our students as it is essential to democratic living, to all relationships, and to all problem solving. It is the capacity to exercise sociological imagination, so necessary to moral development and problem solving.

Ethnographic research: In ethnography, we become participant-observers in new situations so that we can understand the qualities of living in different cultures or situations from the "inside" or "emic" perspective. In forum dramas, fishbowls, and even as participants in-role, we can be both an internal audience for the drama work we are experiencing, and play a role of external audience members observing and responding to what is happening. We can take on both the participant and the spectator stance.

Action research: In action research, we attempt some kind of action or "intervention" to assist a person or persons, or to change the qualities of a situation, or the results and consequences that may follow. Drama affords many possibilities for "rewinding the tape" and trying something over in various ways; and many opportunities to play the role of "agent" trying to advise or help another sentient being or to improve a situation.

Working Toward Ethical Imagination and Identities

I now want to quickly argue for the importance of imagination, identity work, and the cultivation of wisdom in our educational endeavors. I argue these points much more thoroughly in some of my other recent work (see Wilhelm and Novak, 2011), but since dramatic inquiry is particularly powerful for promoting these often neglected but essential elements of the human experience, they are worth touching on here.

Throughout the nearly fifty years of my career as a student and teacher, I feel that schools have become less creative, energetic, and fun places to be. I would argue that we have moved further and further from the role of imagination in learning as we have moved more toward standardization and testable facts. We have moved away from powerful and transferable concepts and processes and towards inert sets of information. Given the challenges facing individuals, our culture, humanity, and the world, this kind of move is not what we need. We need to move toward more imagination, more creativity, more 'outside the box' thinking. Schools should be in the business of developing imagination and of cultivating the capacity to explore alternatives—to apply imagination to problems.

All inquiry involves the imagination. To inquire we have to ask: Why is this a problem? What if it were otherwise? What are possible solutions? How can I use what I am learning? What if X or Y were different? Inquiry involves translating imagined actions, theories, and models into real action where they can be tested and refined (see Smith and Wilhelm, 2010). In dramatic inquiry, we can explore our identities and our capacity for agency and action. I'm grateful to my colleague Brian Edmiston for his work on drama and identity (see Edmiston, 2008; Beach, Edmiston, et al, 2010).

In schools, agency—the capacity to try things out, to act, to think for oneself—is rarely cultivated. As one boy told me during my studies on boys and literacy (Smith and Wilhelm, 2002; 2006), "In school, all you do is play 'Guess what the teacher already knows!'" Or as another boy maintained: "If you try to climb out of the box, the teachers will throw you back in and nail it shut." Many researchers have maintained that students learn exactly what they have the opportunity to learn (see Eisner, 1999). *If we want students to be empathic, active, problem-solving agents in the world, then we must provide the opportunity for them to develop these skill sets.*

When we act with personal agency, we are trying on new identities, or at least new facets of identity. Dramatic inquiry can create spaces where student agency is confronted by actions and voices coming from opposing or complicating viewpoints they had not previously considered. This deepens understanding, and offers alternative actions, identities, or ways of being in the world.

As Edmiston (2010) has found, the understanding created in exchanges like these is more "dialogic"—more aware of how one's point of view and identity exists in a network of other possibilities—for students who entered various perspectives and considered action from various viewpoints (Bakhtin, 1981).

When people play, they can try out new kinds of actions and take on new identities, trying out new "possible selves"—different ways of behaving and being. Through techniques such as "mantle of the expert," they can also try out new community identities, seeing what it is like to be an editor or a scientist or a person in authority. They can learn about and take on what can be called the "epistemic frame"—the perspective and way of knowing—of the expert's community of practice—taking on the affiliations and commitments of that community (Edmiston, 2010).

In this kind of work, it is easy to transform learning from passive reception into active learning and the promotion of social justice. Why? Because in such work you experience how knowledge can be made, interpreted, and applied differently. You realize that knowledge is a human construction open to critique and revision, which can be extended and networked in many new ways beyond the conventional. Imagination is essential to agency, and agency to identity. *The takeaway: We need to consciously cultivate some often ignored aspects of knowing and being: imagination, empathy, identity and agency, relationships and belonging, civic engagement, and the willingness and ability to serve others and ideas bigger than oneself.* If one cannot imagine, then one cannot entertain or take on other perspectives. Without imagination and the capacity to take on other perspectives, one cannot create a meaningful identity, sense of agency, or cultivate empathy. Without empathy, one cannot live a moral and morally satisfying life in relationship with others.

> Imagining things being otherwise may be a first step toward acting on the belief that they can be changed... an imaginative ability is required if the becoming different that learning involves is actually to take place.
>
> —Maxine Greene (1995, p. 22–23)

Dramatic Inquiry and Wisdom

When Brian Edmiston and I undertook the research for our book *Imagining to Learn* (1998), we did not yet have access to the research from neuroscience that shows that "imagining" exercises the brain's "neuroplasticity" in powerful ways that not only change how we think, expanding our repertoire for problem-solving and feeling, but also change the actual structures and activity of the brain. I've read widely around the topic of neuroplasticity due not only to my interest as an educator but because my wife has a rare blood disorder which causes severe bleeding and injuries to her brain.

The news from the research community is astonishingly hopeful: the brain is very good at growing around injuries, of recruiting other parts of the brain to do new kinds of work, of essentially healing and outgrowing itself. The news for teachers and learners is also very powerful: we can change our brains and our modus operandi by training our minds. The latest research indicates that we can teach in ways that will actually change our own and students' ways of thinking, change ways of being and behaving, change the very components and capacities of the brain (see e.g. Damasio, 2008). Such teaching must be active, must be emotionally compelling, must entertain kindness and compassion and the acceptance—at least provisionally—of multiple perspectives. The activities need to be repeated over time and become habitual to make the desired changes. Drama/action strategies fit on all counts. Why would we NOT teach in such a way and toward such a goal?

But here is a caveat: boring instruction that requires passive reception will also change the brain and ways of being—but not in ways that I would endorse or that serve democratic living. Neuroplasticity is a powerful and double-edged sword.

Teaching Toward Wisdom

What is it that I want for my students? If I do not aim to help them develop their wisdom and wisdom-in-action in the world, then I am aiming too low. I work around the considerable constraints of my everyday teaching by keeping my eyes on the true prize. I consider how "standards" and other mandates can be leveraged towards working for wisdom, instead of submitting only to a lower aim such as preparing students to pass the test or enter the workplace.

But What Is Wisdom?

Here's a tentative stab based on my current work: wisdom is becoming increasingly more conscious of interconnectedness (between people, between groups, and between people and creation); developing a profound respect for others and other perspectives; cultivating compassion; being guided by a greater good than materialism, status, and image; valuing stillness and reflection—and seeking guidance from an inner versus outer locus of control; developing inner awareness of one's own identity, perceptions, motivation and possibilities; and a commitment to agency: to service and social action for a communitarian good.

It strikes me that all of these aspects of wisdom involve the interpenetration of "I" and "you" into the "us" of a new and new kind of community. Wisdom, that is, involves creating "third spaces" of possibility. And, of course, one of our most powerful tools for inquiring, for understanding each other, for building and deepening conceptual and procedural understandings, and becoming a community, is the process of respectful dialogic conversation, the essence of dramatic inquiry. *Why would we not teach in such a way?*

CHAPTER 5

GETTING IN ROLE
Reading and Learning From Various Points of View

My favorite stories about the naturally engaging power of role-playing come from my family. Throughout their lives, my daughters have "imagined to learn." On vacations they play the roles of Helga the irritating tour guide and Meany the irritating tourist. They are now college students and their current schtick is role-playing musical gangstas who bring their bling and gangsta ways to common pursuits like making raps while cooking, giving gang signals to cheat while playing cards, or tagging grocery bags.

Introducing Role-Play

In keeping with the Vygotskian notion of moving from the easiest and safest roles to those that are more complex and "further from home," I often prepare students for role-play by brainstorming information that the character in question would know and considering how they would feel, or by asking students to write a diary entry from the perspective of a character. But so natural is the ability to imagine, that students will usually be able to role-play very successfully with some very simple framing, brainstorming, and warm-ups. Following are several such activities to try.

Dramatic Play

In this simplest form of the role-play strategy, the student plays himself faced with an imaginary situation. For example, I have on occasion begun the "The Fan Club" drama by asking students: *How would you respond if you were interviewed by a local newspaper reporter and asked whether there is harassment in our school?* I might even have the students to do a Vote With Your Feet enactment by physically placing themselves on a scale from "would totally disagree" to "would totally agree" in response to statements about harassment and its prevalence.

In a science class, I could use the problem of dwindling water supplies to frame dramatic playing (cf. Morgan and Saxton, 1987). For example, I could say, "As you all know by now, when we turned on our taps this morning and tried to take showers, there was no water. It turns out that there is no more water in our town's holding ponds or water tower, and the wells outside of town have been condemned. What are we going to do?"

These forms of dramatic play derive their power from their connection to reality and to the students' lived experience. Spontaneous dramatic play highlights that students must bring their own "funds of knowledge" to bear on a situation that will be paralleled in the reading and inquiry. It is also very easy to build from dramatic play to other forms of role-play that require students to enter other perspectives.

Mantle-of-the-Expert Roles

This technique differs from dramatic play in that students can work as themselves or in role, but they imagine they possess the knowledge, skills, and authority of experts. For example, for "The Fan Club," I could cast students as teachers, guidance counselors, psychologists, school board members, or other experts who have a stake in stopping bullying in the school, and who have expertise on the topic. I could frame such an enactment by saying, "As members of the school board, you must define bullying and put a policy into place that will help us address the problem of bullying in our school."

Though not always necessary, I usually find it useful to make "expert" views and information available to the students. The expert role they are playing should motivate them to read and find out some of what experts actually know and think about the issue. So, for example, for the topic of bullying, I might offer them the chance to interview our guidance counselor or to use various web sites to help them "get informed" about bullying before the big school board meeting.

Whereas dramatic play is imagining oneself in a new situation, and mantle of the expert is imagining oneself with new abilities and authority (though students may take on a different persona in these techniques), further along the continuum lies role-play, in which students take on the particular attitudes and perspectives of people who are different from them.

Role-Play Ideas for "The Fan Club"

During our reading of "The Fan Club," I ask my students to take on all of the major roles featured and implied by the story. They enact these roles at particular points in the story to deal with tensions, explore characters' situations, and play with different possibilities and responses. In this way, they become familiar with various positions and attitudes expressed, including those that may not naturally align with their own.

Frame It

Before reading, students count off as A's and B's. I ask all those who are an *A* to raise their hands, then everyone who is a *B*. This simple step is important, as students must remember who they are. If there are an odd number then I will take a role or will ask one A to switch to a B working together with another B (since Laura could talk with two friends).

I then tell the students their role and mission in the upcoming role-play so they will know what to pay attention to in the reading. For example, before we start reading "The Fan Club," I ask the A's to become Laura and the B's to be a friend who is enjoying school and who hasn't seen Laura for a while. The B's mission will be to match up with an A (I usually let students do the matching so they can work with someone they want to work with) and start a conversation with the purpose of finding out what is troubling Laura. They will report out about this to the rest of the group in the following forum.

Read Aloud

I read the first section. The students pay careful attention because they know they must use the section to do their Role-Play. At the section's end, I ask the B's to stand. I tell them that they are former friends of Laura, and their purpose is to find out how she likes high school.

State the Scene

Highlight your frame: "You are at the mall. You see Laura across the way sitting on a bench. You haven't seen her in a while, but you hear she's having problems. Go over, say hello, and see what you can find out. Laura, I don't know how you will respond to an old middle-school friend you haven't seen in a while, so you will have to figure out what you will say and how much you will reveal. B's, you have 10 seconds to find an A and start the conversation."

Because the A's are seated, it is easy to find those who are not yet working with a partner. Sometimes I ask the A's to stand when they are chosen, or to keep their hand raised until they are matched up. With a little practice, students become quick at finding partners. In subsequent role-plays, I ask students to choose a new partner with whom they have not yet worked. That way, they wind up working with a variety of partners, but always someone they choose to work with.

Play Teacher in Role

During the role-plays, I walk around and help students along or complicate things as necessary from inside the enactment. For example, if some are struggling to find their roles, I might enter in and say, "Laura, long time no see," addressing Laura and therefore making clear who she is. I might also say, "I heard you were having some problems…." Then I will turn to Laura's friend (B) and say, "Find out what is up; I'll be back in a moment." If a pair is coming to a pat conclusion, I might enter the enactment to complicate it. As a friend, I might say, "But Laura, I heard you complain about math class." Or, as a bully, I might say to Laura, "You don't fit in and you never will." And to her friend, "Ask her to tell you what the cool kids think of her!"

Revolving Role-Play: A Series of Role-Plays to Pursue Big Ideas

All of the techniques in this book assist and enhance student performance and learning. Therefore, each role a student is asked to play should meet a purpose (for example, the *micro-purpose* to find out how Laura is feeling, or the *macro-purpose* to explore the effects of harassment), provide a new perspective (for example, a person being harassed), or offer assistance in understanding something new or reading in a new way (for example, inferring characters' feelings). Depending on my students' needs and my teaching purposes, sometimes a single role-play is enough to set the scene and motivate students to enter into a perspective or bring their own life knowledge to bear on the text. But if my purpose is to guide them through an evocation and experience of a whole story—or to deal with ever more complicated ideas or processes like inferencing—I might continue role-plays throughout and after reading the story.

Anchor Standards for Reading, 1–3, 6

My favorite way of doing a series of role-plays is called Revolving Role-Play, in which students take on a different role from the story in each subsequent role-play (an idea I learned from Cecily O'Neill). If the story or text is long enough—for example, a class novel—I will take care that every student plays every major role once or twice to see the story from all perspectives. I also like to ask students to play the roles of minor characters or unmentioned characters (like Laura's parents), who would be affected although they may not even appear. In this way, we can look at marginalized characters or silenced voices and see how they would feel about or react to the situation.

Role-Play Different Characters

After students engage in the first role-play as students (close to home), I next ask them to engage as adults (farther from home). After reporting out and reflecting on the first Role Play, I announce that the A's will become one of Laura's parents and the B's will become Mr. Knowles, Laura's math teacher. I set-up that Laura's parents have found out about her problem in math class and made an appointment with Mr. Knowles. I add that I am the principal and may interrupt their conference to see what is going on.

The students must now pay attention to see what has happened in math class so they can play their roles. As we continue to read subsequent sections of the story, I might ask students to role-play one of the "cool kids" (Diane, Terri, or Steve) and have another student ask them why they tease other kids. Diane, Terri, and Steve are maligned quite a bit in the story and never have the chance to justify their actions or share their points of view. Students could also become Rachel or Laura interacting with the guidance counselor. The important thing is that there is a tension introduced between the two roles, perspectives to adopt toward the tension, and a clear goal to pursue.

He Said, She Said: A Transcript of a Forum Role-Play

After the first revolving role-play of "The Fan Club" between Laura and an old friend, I cast students as friends who have all recently spoken with Laura. I play the father of one of the friends. I orchestrate the drama with the "forum" of students in role.

ME (*out of role*): Okay, so you are all old friends of Laura who have just spoken to her. I am a friend's father, and you are at my house. I want to hear what you think is up with Laura. Our goal is to pool our knowledge about her problem and how to solve it. Now, even if you were Laura in the role-play, you know what you said so you can pretend you are Laura's friend and chip in. Right? And people might have been told different things—just like real life. [*Here I'm framing/purpose-setting from outside the enactment.*]

CLASS: murmurs of agreement

ME: Okay, ready to enter the enactment? Here goes.

ME: (*in role as father*): Hey, I heard a lot of you have seen Laura recently. You guys used to hang out with her a lot in middle school, but I haven't seen her around lately. What's up with her? [*framing/purpose- setting from inside the enactment. I also provide inferred information from the story: Laura has lost her friendship group.*]

JAKE: She's pretty unhappy. [*character inference and evaluation*]

ME: What makes you think so? [*push for textual evidence of interpretation*]

JAKE: Well, she was sitting all alone at the mall. And she said kids are teasing her. [*citing both explicit and implied evidence from the text*]

ME: Do the rest of you agree? (*Class nods.*) Did anybody find out anything else? Like about why kids are teasing her?

TOM: She's a loser. [*introduces new perspective/bringing life to literature*]

ME: What do you mean?

Report Out

In role-play, like almost all of my work with enactment, I want all of my students engaged and working *all of the time*. I like paired role-play because everyone gets to talk, explore characters, and make meaning of the story at the same time. Even so, I want the whole class to come together again to report out what they have learned in their individual role-plays. In this way, the kids can provide "peer assistance" to each others' readings; different readings and interpretations can be offered and tested against the text. And I, as the teacher, can get a sense of how it all went and get ideas to take up or address later in our enactment work.

ALICE: She wants to be part of the "cool" group, but they won't have her. And she doesn't hang out with us anymore, so she's all alone. But that's her fault. [*character inference*]

JOAN: No, it's not. I mean we just don't have classes together anymore. She's with other kids. It's hard when you start high school. Scary. [*uptake of other student's comment/provides another possible interpretation from using life experience*]

RY: It's the teachers, man, they have no control. It's not like middle school where people know you. And hallways are brutal. [*bringing life to literature/uptake/offers another perspective*]

ME: I think when someone is hurting, we need to help out. Why don't we invite Laura over? You could call her right now. [*shape drama, connect literature back to life, offer a challenge to the students*]

TAMMY: Dad, you are so uncool. You can't just, like, do that.

JOAN: That's for sure.

ME: Why not? That's what I would do with one of my friends.

TAMMY: She's a former friend. And it was her choice.

[*Students may be speaking for themselves here, from the protection of their role as Laura's former friends.*]

ME: What if she's changed her mind? It sounds like you guys are part of the problem. What if it were you having trouble? [*I push them to take Laura's perspective.*]

CAROLYN: You know, she told me something different. She said she really wants to fit in, but she doesn't know how. Like before you could fit in with lots of groups, but now you have to choose who you are going to fit in with. [*an alternative inference about what may be bothering Laura by bringing life to literature*]

ME: Do you think that's true? Does that really happen in high school? [*I ask students to explore this literature to life connection.*]….

For instance, I often take student ideas about how to address a problem from the enactment and incorporate these in later work on the story.

When students report out—which I usually have them do in role—I often play the devil's advocate, trying to reveal subtexts or other possible interpretations. If students are off the mark, I will push them from inside the enactment: "How do you know that?" If this doesn't work, we will move outside the enactment to discuss the importance of basing interpretations on textual evidence.

Report Out in a Follow-Up Group Role-Play/Forum

After the first role-play, I ask students to report out what they did and learned to the whole group. I have them imagine they are all friends of Laura. Even if they played Laura in the role-play, they know what was said and can report out on it as a friend. I tell them I will be the father of one of the friends and that we are all gathered around the kitchen table after their return from the mall. "I am going to ask you about Laura," I tell them, "and I want to find out what you learned by chatting with her." Giving the signal that the enactment is starting, I say, "Hey, I heard you saw Laura. She used to hang out with you all the time last year in eighth grade, and I haven't seen her at all this year. What's up with her?" (See the transcript of our dialogue, pages 78–79.)

Keep the Action Flowing

During enactments, my job—and yours—is to keep the action flowing, provide dynamic tension, and get more perspectives in play. If students provide conflicting information about what Laura said or did, I point out that we sometimes tell different people different things and we will have to figure out the "real story." If they all agree that she is being bullied, I might comment that this is part of life and Laura shouldn't make mountains out of molehills. If I sense that they disapprove of Laura, I may

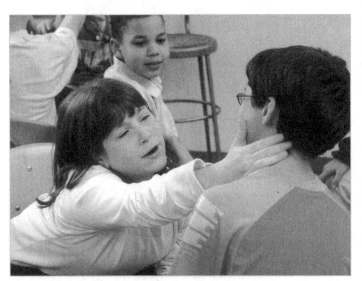

Stephanie, in the role of Laura's mom, asks Fiona, in the role of Laura, what is troubling her about school. Both must infer their reactions based on evidence from the story.

suggest they invite her to the next sleepover. All the while, I will try to get them to report out in role what they know and can imagine about Laura's feelings and what might be done to help her. In the next Role-Play I ask students to be Laura's parent or Mr. Knowles at a parent-teacher conference, exploring Laura's school work and experience.

Reflect and Consider Future Action

After this second scene, I might ask students what was hard or surprising about responding as a parent or teacher. These roles force them to see from perspectives they often resist.

I might also ask them to brainstorm the various reasons students do not engage in school, or to brainstorm a list of qualified people who are interested in helping students who are at-risk. To reflect in role, I usually cast all students in one of the roles that has been played— for example, as teachers at a teacher meeting. Again, even if students played the other role, Laura's parent, during the role-play they would still know what had happened and been said. I can run either meeting as the principal addressing the issue of bullying. Again, my role is to solicit student reviews of what happened during their individual role-plays, and to complicate their understandings in order to push them toward considering the issues more deeply.

Reporting out can be done quickly in this kind of group format or it can be done through student-composed Newspaper Reports, Letters, Diaries, Radio Show Announcements, or Public Service Announcements. *The essential thing is to structure the enactment so that students will report out and reflect on what has happened and why. All learning requires reflection to be consolidated and become part of the learner's schematic understanding.*

Framing: Keeping Role-Plays on the Rails!

As I said earlier, when an enactment does not go smoothly, it is almost always because I didn't frame it sufficiently. I usually find that a quick frame is all that's needed, such as taking a minute for a brief review of the roles, essential background information, the situation, a few hints about how to proceed, some prompts or question/statement stems, and a goal to achieve (e.g., something to make, create, or report out about). If roles or enactments are a bit more complex, I may have students prepare individually or in groups for a few minutes before the enactment. This allows them to go back into the text, review their reading, and prepare possible responses.

Role-Play Frames/Planning Sheets
Teacher's Planning Sheet

What are the roles?

Who is playing each role? (Confirm that students understand their role. If so grouped, ask all A's to raise their hands, then all B's.)

What problem or tension are they involved in?

What do they know about this tension and what are the differing perspectives on it?

What situation/context are they entering?

Who will they work with in the role-play, and what role is that student taking?

What will be their likely attitudes to the tension and the situation? How will they deal with this?

What do they need to achieve during the role-play and bring back from it?

How might they go about achieving it?

Who will start the role-play? How will it be started?

Role Player "Gut Check"

What is my role?

With whom am I role-playing?

What problem or tension are we involved in?

What do I know from the text/s we've read that will inform how I will respond during the role-play? What do I need to infer?

What do we need to achieve and be able to report out on? (What is the "deliverable"?)

Will I start the role-play? If so, how will I get it started?

How will I prompt or help my partner from inside the role-play if he or she has trouble getting started?

The Teacher's Role: Inside and Out

Enactments allow the teacher the unique possibilities of playing and teaching from new perspectives as well. The power of the teacher in role, of shaping enactments from within as a fellow role player, was pioneered by the famous drama educator Dorothy Heathcote (1978, 1982). From *inside* the enactment, teachers can

- assume any role that introduces tensions and new information.

- guide students into role and reinforce their task.

- enrich the material and purpose.

- complicate the action or extend the action.

- lend expertise and new ways of doing things. upgrade language—introducing new vocabulary, new concepts, and asking players to explain and justify.

- provide new opportunities for exploration.

- confront misconceptions.

- undermine and challenge simplistic pat answers, and in other ways extend student understanding of text and the world.

In this way, the teacher in role is a perfect position for providing Vygotskian-style teaching and assisting students through their readings and their ZPDs. The Vygotskian perspective demands that the teacher is always intensely present to the students and to teaching them by observing, lending expertise, setting up situations that will assist student competence and performance, upping the ante to provide more appropriate challenges, and introducing a new tension or information that will deepen understanding. To these ends, I can use various intervention techniques, such as voiceovers, to prompt, explain, or describe what students should do before a role-play or in the context of a role-play, or I can use narration to recount key textual details and prompt students to enact them. I can also summarize to focus attention: "Hmm, let's review what has happened. What can we do now?" I might choose to frame the reporting out of the enactment and the insights gained, or universalize our experience, connecting it to other texts and lived experiences: "I'm guessing this approximates how Native Americans must have felt when they were driven onto reservations." "The scientists working on controlling greenhouse gas emissions must have the same kinds of frustrations." (cf. Morgan and Saxton, 1987)

Must-Have Resource

Teaching Drama: A Mind of Many Wonders, Norah Morgan and Juliana Saxton (1987) London: Hutchinson. This is perhaps the most helpful book I have ever read about using enactment strategies in the classroom.

TEACHING DRAMA
A mind of many wonders
Norah Morgan
Juliana Saxton

The focus of the book is on using drama with primary grade students, but I found that it offered many unique insights which I could apply to my own use of enactment to teach reading. Morgan and Saxton explore all the "minute particulars" of the teacher's craft when using drama. I highly recommend it and have drawn significantly from this book in the writing of this chapter.

The teaching may be direct or indirect, but it must always be there. And again, the purpose of all reading, and of all learning, in fact, is to work toward changing and expanding students' understanding about human behavior, themselves, and the world they live in.

Variations on the Role-Play Theme

Anchor Standards for Speaking and Listening, 1–6

There are hundreds of useful variations on role-playing, depending on how you frame the work and what you hope to achieve through it. Here I will summarize a few techniques I've found useful for achieving particular ends.

General Processes of Reading

Literature Circle Drama Roles

Group reading structures, such as literature circles and reciprocal reading roles, are all designed to highlight the general processes of reading that every reader uses every time they read anything (Wilhelm, 2001/2012). In getting students to play the literature circle roles, I have found it helpful to cast them in roles and situations related to our reading.

For example, I might provide the frame of a News Show, telling students that they will be reporting on breaking news from a story, or about a scientific crisis or breakthrough from our unit of study. In order to broadcast our show, we will be interviewing a variety of people. Or I might cast them as detectives or news analysts. This can be done during or after the reading of a text. In any case, I tell the students that they will be playing various reading roles, which they will later turn into a final presentation of some sort. Here are some examples of how students might be cast to match general processes.

Summarizing: Telegram Writer/Cell Phone Message Writer/Tweeter. You are a reporter on the scene who can only communicate through your cell phone message service or tweets. You have to get all the important details down with as few words as possible and send them off.

Visualizing: Illustrator/Photographer. Because there is no video footage, you must create still photos of the key scenes or a mental model of the situation or issue (see Chapter 9 on tableaux).

Questioning: Reporter/Police. What questions do you have about the situation? What will you want to ask once informants become available?

Inferencing: Detective/Accountant. You must reconstruct the travels, life story, finances, and so forth of a major character. (Students could even be asked to recreate the checkbook or phone log of a character—a la Grue's "Trial by Cheque.")

Problem-Solving: Dear Abby Advice Columnist/Commentator. You have been asked to provide advice about how to proceed and you must consider all of the various perspectives.

Predicting and Elaborating: Fortune-Teller/Prophet/Futurist. Your job is to explain the "So what?" about what we have learned. What are the future implications? Predict what may happen next.

Monitoring and Analyzing: Expert Analyst. Explain the gist and importance of the textual information, such as behavior of the major characters. What does it mean? What might ordinary viewers find confusing, and how can you explain this to them?

Monitoring and Digging Deeper: Drama Diva. Create a drama that helps the class explore and understand more deeply a section of text you've just read. (This idea is from Jan Kwiatowsky who assigns this role in literature circle work, asking one student to come up with a drama activity to explore the text and its meaning. Once students are familiar with a variety of techniques, they can make such choices and justify their usefulness. The "drama diva" then directs other students to participate in the use of the strategy to dig deeper into the text's meaning.)

Considering the Author/Authorial Reading: Author or Author Spokesman. Create a Q&A for the author that will explore how the text was constructed to communicate certain meanings.

Stranger in Role

Many tasks that are perceived by students as empty academic exercises can be energized and given a new purpose through an enactment. For example, instead of asking students to summarize the last chapter of *Roll of Thunder, Hear My Cry,* the teacher could play Stranger in Role (in which the role-player "plays dumb") as an African American from the North, asking what is going on down here in the South. Now the summary has a purpose and must get at significance. *What does this stranger need to know? And why? What does he need to know if he is to stay safe and out of trouble?* If my students miss details about how the Northerner must change his behavior to deal with the prejudice here, I might say, in role, "Thought I would just drive on into Strawberry and get myself some lunch at that store." Such prompts get students to summarize the issues confronting the characters and move them to explore courses of social action. The importance of communicating the consequences of not knowing how to act are also clear from the story, and from historical incidents such as the Emmitt Till case.

Parallel Scenes (also known as Analogy Enactments)

When I feel that students' experience may be too distant from the text, I must provide experiences *before* reading that will build their background schema, allowing them to bring meaning to bear on the text. One way to do this is to ask students to engage in role-plays about situations in their own life that parallel or are analogous in some way to a scene in the story. When reading *The Incredible Journey*, for instance, I did not think my students would fully appreciate the feelings of the animals or the dangers they faced. I therefore led them through a series of parallel scenes—using each one before we read the corresponding scene in the text. I used guided imagery and role-play before beginning the story to have students imagine that they had been kidnapped, taken someplace they knew nothing about, and then left alone. What would they do? Most students voted to try to get home, though we were in the middle of the wilderness. They then brought to the text an understanding of the fear, loneliness, and desperation of the animals who have been left by their owners with a stranger. Parallel scenes were provided for each major scene of the story (see Wilhelm, 1997/2008 for the complete lesson plan of parallel scenes).

Character Walks

This is a variation on Revolving Role-Play. I seat a number of students in a circle facing outward and an equal number walks outside the circle. Those walking are assigned roles. As I announce a dilemma from the book and I ask the walkers to stop in front of a seated partner and report their feelings about a specific issue. ("You are Cassie, and your brothers are harassing you about becoming Lillian Jean's slave. Stop and tell the person in front of you what you are feeling and thinking.") Those seated take on such roles as friend or confidante and attempt to find something out or help the character. As such, students begin to enter into the perspectives and problems of a character. This can be done to review a text or to prepare students for issues they will read about.

Variations include having the seated students represent a timeline, with each chair representing an event—either an actual one from a story, or possible one. For this activity, I give the seated students a note card with an event, or allow them to write out an event of their own. When the walkers stop in front of a particular chair, they have to respond to the provided event or dilemma in a kind of "What would you do or feel now?" enactment. Alternately, seated students can be reporters interviewing the walking characters about the cited dilemma, and so forth.

Step by Step (also known as Freeze and Go)

If students cannot understand particular perspectives or they blame characters for being in certain situations, the Step by Step enactment can be useful. In this technique, the students imagine "step by step" how their life situation could change into that of the character they don't understand. During our "Space Trader" drama (Wilhelm and Edmiston, 1998), Brian Edmiston used this to great effect when students decided to trade convicted criminals to the space trader. He had them close their eyes and imagine helping a friend in desperate circumstances. When they had done this, he had them take a step. He then asked them to imagine that they told a lie or stole something to help their friend. Again, when they had imagined this, they took a step. In this way, he guided the students to a place where they could imagine being convicted of a crime, a position they condemned at the beginning of the enactment. Both physically and imaginatively, they ended up in totally different "places" through this kind of guided imagination. With this technique, students can imagine a sequence of events parallel to those experienced by characters or those in a historical situation. Many variations are obviously possible.

Character Think-Alouds

In a variation of the think-aloud technique (Wilhelm, 2001/2012), students take on the roles of characters thinking aloud and responding to their reading of a text. This works very well when a book character announces an affinity for a poem or text, for example Ponyboy from *The Outsiders* and his use of Robert Frost's "Nothing Gold Can Stay." But it works equally well when we know a character has strong feelings about a situation or issue and we can provide students in role with a newspaper article, poem, or other short text exploring that same issue.

After-Reading Activities

Who Am I?

After a reading, students can take turns portraying different characters. This could begin with mime— walking or moving like a character—and then move on to talking like the character, voicing his or her concerns. The rest of the class guesses which character is being role-played.

Character Surveys

Surveys and questionnaires are very effective as frontloading techniques (Wilhelm, Baker, and Dube, 2001; Smith and Wilhelm, 2002, 2010). A great adaptation for *after* reading is to invite students to become the author or a character responding to a survey. They must indicate their response and how they know from the text that the author or character would respond this way. In this way, students practice trying out possible themes and justifying them with evidence from the text. Given the importance of this skill and how poorly American students perform it (recent NAEPs show much fewer than 10 percent of graduating American high school seniors can do so), this is an important strategy to develop.

CCSS

Anchor Standards for Reading, 1–6, 8, 9

How would Shakespeare or Romeo, for instance, respond to survey items like those following? How would the corresponding characters from Sharon Draper's young adult novel *Romiette and Julio*, those from the movie *Save the Last Dance*, or the short story "The Chaser" respond?

1. Love means never having to say you're sorry.
Student in role as Romeo: I totally disagree with this statement. Love made me do a lot of things that make me really sorry. I'm dead, and so is Juliet. That was a total screw up. I killed myself and then she killed herself, so I'm pretty sorry about that. I am pretty sorry that I caused my friend Mercutio to die. I'm really sorry that I killed Tybalt, because that's why I got banished. The Prince himself announced at the end that "all are punished!" so he knows we all have lots to be sorry about!

2. Love at first sight is possible.
Student in role as Shakespeare: I would agree, and so would Romeo, I should think. Evidence: Romeo and Juliet see each other across a crowded room at the party and fall in love. I wrote that; obviously I think it is possible. Romeo experienced it. He knows it

can happen. But there's more to the story, like what happens when you are overpowered by the emotions of love. You should read my play to find out what I think about that! (For surveys about romantic love, see Wilhelm, 2007; Kahn, et al., 1984.)

Working in this way can also prepare students to do role-plays or interviews with authors and characters. Interviews could be conducted from the student's own perspective, as differences between the student's and the author's survey responses are explored, or in role as reporters, literary critics, and others.

Character/Author Interviews

Characters and authors can be interviewed in role or in a press conference. Students or reporters-in-role can ask what they think about issues from the book or ways in which the book might be revised. Characters and authors might even be asked to respond to events from other books, current events—like dealing with terrorism (The Prince and Friar Laurence from *Romeo and Juliet* have experience in this regard)—ecological issues, and so forth. They could also advise other characters or people from real life about how to behave, highlighting authorial generalizations and how the texts can teach us all to think about our lives. (For more information, see Q&A section, Wilhelm, 2001/2012.)

Minor Character Monologues

Minor characters are often very important yet receive little attention from readers. To draw attention to minor characters, students should brainstorm who these characters are and what is known about them. They can then write monologues in role as these characters, describing their role and their reactions to the story so that we can see not only their viewpoints (which will certainly differ from the major characters), but also their contributions to the story.

When my friend Michael Smith's Sunday School class was reading about the passion of Christ from the Gospel of Luke, students noticed the many minor characters, so he asked them to write monologues for characters that would reveal their roles and their reactions after the story. Students performed the monologues for the congregation, giving voice and insight from the minor characters. When Michael asked what they had learned, students responded that Jesus must think each of us is important since they felt the story revolved around so-called minor characters and how they were affected—characters such as Simon the Cyrene, the army officer, Joanna, the criminal, Joseph of Arimathea, Cleopas, and Thomas. The students' work was truly moving and allowed them to see parts of the story and meanings that were unavailable before. It also helped them to see themselves as part of the story.

Round-Robin Monologues

Another kind of spontaneous monologue technique, a Round Robin, can be used before, during, or after reading. First, students form a circle. Every one of them imagines they are the same character, faced with a particular situation that I provide. They should come up with one sentence that summarizes their feelings at this point, or what they want to do. Then, each student speaks his sentence aloud, going around in the circle. In this way, the group works to form a single monologue, which may consist of conflicting feelings, just as real life does. As an extension to this activity, students can build on, connect with, or disagree with what was said before. Obviously this requires more "thinking on your feet" and "uptaking" other students in-role comments. Uptake is the hallmark of true conversation and the dialogic exchange that leads to learning (Nystrand, 1997).

A variation of this technique works well in establishing background knowledge before reading. (I use this variation as a Getting Started technique.) For instance, before reading a book that examines fatherhood, like *To Kill a Mockingbird*, students could be asked to complete the phrase, "A father is…" and provide an example or definition. I participated in a workshop where Jonathan Neelands used this technique to great effect. Inevitably, the participants offered conflicting views, which Jonathan highlighted and which were then explored in the readings. After reading the text, students could consider the question, "Was Atticus a good father? How do we know? How does he compare to the ideas of fatherhood we initially articulated in our Round Robin Monologue? What does the author think? How do we know?" Clearly, this technique can be employed with any issue or idea to pool student knowledge and perspectives. This also gives the teacher a glimpse of student attitudes so she can develop additional enactment strategies to teach subsequent texts in order to address, enlarge, and explore these attitudes. Notice too how it develops the strategies of argument: stating claims, citing evidence, reasoning about evidence in warrants, and responding to reservations and other perspectives.

Drama Centers

Centers can be used to simulate a situation like a water shortage dilemma or to predict and explore the crises characters might experience. Students can visit Drama Centers around the classroom and pick up cards that present a new perspective or new information about the issue being read about. (Example for *Out of the Dust: You are a farmer whose soil is becoming salted from the water from the aquifer. You cannot grow your crops without water and will soon be bankrupt. Prepare a brief speech you'll present to the Water Council.* Or perhaps for *Romeo and Juliet: You are now banished from the person you love most. What will you do? Write a letter to her/him describing your plan of action.* Additional information and complications can be presented at each center, or a new enactment activity can be assigned. Students can rotate from center to center in groups.

Dress-Up Book Reports

I have had great luck with this technique throughout the years. Students choose a favorite character, real or fictional, that they've read about in their free reading, and dress up like that character and tell part of his or her story in role. Variations can include requiring the characters to comment on current events or thematic issues studied in the class. Characters from different texts can then meet to discuss issues or their responses to survey items in a kind of Meeting of the Minds.

Dress-up book report criteria:

- Choose a favorite character (or author) from a book you have recently read as a free reading choice during this latest unit.
- Dress up as you think the character would have dressed. You can also carry items or photographs that reveal the character. (Be able to explain how your costume fits the character and what you know about him/her.)
- Provide a 90-second summary of the book (or an important part of it) from the perspective of that character.
- Provide a 90-second commentary on the thematic issue we have been studying from the perspective of that character. Be sure to explain how your experiences as that character have shaped your views. (Try to talk using the language you think the character would use.)
- Role-play a short scene from the book or demonstrate a typical action of the character. If you are feeling creative, include your summary and commentary as part of your scene.
- Don't exceed five minutes.

Ways to Help Students Evaluate One Another

I always have students respond to each other's reports and I sometimes allow students to interview the character in role. I particularly like these three frames for getting students to respond to each other's work:

1. Praise, Question, Polish/Wonder

Praise: This is what I really liked about the presentation. (It is essential that the praise is specific.)

Question: Here are questions I had about the presentation.

Polish: Here are suggestions that could make the presentation even better in the future.

Another way of phrasing their "moves" is through these statements:

- What I really liked about the presentation was…
- Something I had questions about was…
- **Wonder:** I wonder what would happen if…/what would have happened if…

2. What? So What? Now What?

What? This is what I learned…

So What? This is the significance of what I learned…

Now What? This is the implication of what I learned, this is what I need to learn more about, and this is what we need to do as a result.

3. Contributions

My contribution to the enactment was...

The other groups members' contributions were to...

What I can improve/what I would like to try next time...

How I can help my group to work better next time:

These response schemes can work with all kinds of enactments, and other kinds of work as well. I've found that students of all ages have difficulty giving substantive and specific praise and advice, and these techniques assist them to do so.

Voices From the Field

These role-playing techniques and many variations of them can be extremely powerful in assisting students to engage with characters, authors, other perspectives, and the ideas each presents. They can also be very powerful for helping students to evoke and experience textual worlds, different perspectives, and to take on expert reading strategies like inferring, elaborating, reading for an author's generalization and justifying it, and many more.

I work with many teachers who have adapted these techniques in ways that are very exciting for them and their students. Once again, I'll conclude the chapter with an example of the kind of e-mail I receive regularly from teachers who are beginning to use drama strategies.

Jeff:

My rudimentary attempts at drama are certainly producing enthusiasm and very interesting classes! The best spin-offs result from the thinking the kids are doing about texts and the issues they present, and from their interest, too. Every class is asking for more!

This week in seventh grade we did enactments with [Jerry Spinelli's] *Maniac Magee*. I asked pairs of students to come up with a conversation that Amanda and Maniac might have if they were to see each other one more time. I told them *no scripts*, and they had three minutes to plan what would be on their minds and in their hearts to say to each other. We discussed how you don't usually plan out a conversation in real life, that it just happens, and that

continued on the next page

you take cues from what the other person says. Only one little girl wouldn't really get into character, so I took her place and asked her to become a reporter witnessing the conversation and to report out what she saw and heard. [Author's note: notice how Jane has asked this student to take an easier role, one closer to dramatic play than role-playing.]

That night at home, my daughter asked if we could do another enactment on Friday, and she suggested that we have Grayson's soul return to advise Maniac. (Yes, I have her for class and that's a whole new ball game!) She prefaced her comment with: "Do we have to do just a lit circle or can we do more with it by using some drama?" This is a child who has always loved reading but wants to push things and she sees the enactments as ways of doing that. Though she is sometimes uncomfortable with me being her teacher, she is immensely comfortable with me performing conversations in role, and I'm surmising that it is because I am Maniac, or Grayson, or Jerry Spinelli and not her mother! She has asked for no preparation next time. She thinks the class can do it—"just give us a partner and the situation and let us go!"

Now, in sixth grade, we are reading aloud *Hermit Dan*, and there are three kids who are going to explore a cave and the kids have brought lanterns with them. To frontload, I asked who had ever been in a cave. A couple of students had visited tourist caves, and one boy had explored a small cave near his house. I asked the students what they might find in one. Then I said we were going to enter a cave in our imagination using guided imagery and that they should move like they would in the dark and describe what they found.

This is a class with 12 kids who are really challenged by reading. I told them that what we imagined during our enactment are the kinds of things they should imagine when they read. As we read more about cave exploration, I think this activity helped them have stronger mental images and better connections, and that this will make reading more accessible and enjoyable.

So these are my experiences this week. I realize I'm a slow creature to change and need to hear and see things repeated several times to begin to internalize it. But now that I have made the leap into drama, I am so pleased with the results and the possibilities!

Thanks for listening to all of this!

—Jane

CHAPTER 6

SITTING IN THE HOTSEAT
Deepening Understanding
of Characters and Concepts

Hotseating, I've found, is the most student-friendly of all drama techniques. Students love it. They will use the technique on their own, in pairs and in small groups. They often call out, "Put him on the hotseat!' or as one student once called it, "the butt-blistering bench!" After lunch one day, I walked into my sixth-period class and noticed a bright red stool sitting in the front of the classroom. "What's that?" I asked. "We brought it in from the art room," Sam explained. "It's painted like a cinnamon Red-Hot, so we thought it would make a perfect hotseat!"

"Yeah," Nick enthused. "And a bunch of us decided at lunch that we needed to do some hotseating today!"

"Okay," I laughed, amused as I so often am by the exuberance of adolescents. "Just who do you want to hotseat?"

Even before the bell rang, Nick was in the hotseat playing the role of Eustace from our reading of *The Voyage of the*

Dawn Treader by C.S. Lewis. The class spontaneously peppered him with questions about his childhood, why he was such a "goof" (as Sam so eloquently put it), about his experience as a dragon, and about how he had changed and why. For part of the time, Belinda, without prompting, stood behind Nick and played his inner voice—adding comments that Eustace was thinking but not saying.

"Who wants to be Caspian?" Sam asked. Dan took Nick's place and was interviewed about the purpose of the voyage and his close shave on Deathwater Island. The kids were intrigued with why the promise of wealth had mesmerized the usually unflappable Caspian, and the means by which he shook this obsession.

My students had been studying a stock market simulation in social studies, and suddenly somebody yelled, "Let's put Mr. Wilhelm in the hotseat as Michael Milken!"

The entire class began chanting "Hotseat! Hotseat!" as I made my way to the stool. They continued pursuing their concerns about wealth and responsibility as they grilled me in my role as Milken, who had been in the news at that time for his junk bond dealings. Before long, the bell rang once again. I hadn't even taken attendance or implemented my lesson plan. But I was pleased. My students had been engaged with discussing key events in the book and how they related to the deeper real-world themes Lewis was expressing. They did it of their own accord, setting and pursuing their own agenda through the use of hotseating.

When I next collected and read students' journals, this comment of Sam's jumped out at me, perhaps because he had double-underlined it: "I can see why they call it the hotseat. You feel hot when you are in it! Instead of being bored in class, you feel alive. So alive you can feel your heart pumping pretty fast!"

Hotseating is a family of enactment techniques that intensifies role-playing by putting students "on the spot" so they can be addressed, advised, questioned, and so forth. This strategy invites students to hone their ability to analyze characters, infer, elaborate, and think on their feet. In the hotseat, the student assumes the role of a character or someone other than himself, tells about that person, and responds to questions and situations in that role. Students who are not hotseated can act to help and advise the character, connect his situation to wider concerns, and suggest social action, among other things.

Students can sit in the hotseat as a book character, an author, a real-life figure, a group or representative of a group (ecologists, violence prevention educators), as an idea (democracy), a force (electrical charges, inertia), a mathematical concept (density, area, commutability), and so forth.

Benefits of Hotseating

Hotseating

- brings text, characters, and authors, ideas, forces, or topics to life. Students can become, see, and relate to characters; they can hear their words, feel their presence, sense their emotions, and become part of the text.

- supports student exploration of subtexts—of a character's unspoken experiences in the past, present, and future. It also helps students understand the human dimension of various issues and dilemmas.

- helps students get to know characters deeply or understand differing perspectives on issues.

- aids inferential, elaborative, and analytical thinking as students fill in the gaps and consider how characters might respond to situations outside of the text.

- allows students to explore real issues and experiment with views from the safety of being in role.

- gets at main ideas/authorial generalizations/thematic meanings.

- provides a safe opportunity to play around with and change textual details or events—for example, asking "what if?" or trying out different interpretations and comparing them, linking interpretations to textual evidence, and so forth.

- offers opportunities to work on public speaking, interviewing, questioning, and other discussion skills.

Anchor Standards for Reading, 1–6, 8, 9

Speaking and Listening, 1–6

Language, 3–6

Preparation: Warming Up the Hotseat

The first few times I use any enactment activity, I make sure that each student knows what is expected and I develop a way to prepare in a group first. With hotseating, I make sure the group is ready and able to help the person in the hotseat by acting as his lifeline, or brain, which the hotseated student can turn to for advice on how to respond if and as needed.

It is important that students feel emotionally and intellectually "safe" enough to improvise and riff, so I emphasize that I value out-of-the-box thinking. Though we will occasionally stop the hotseating to reflect on whether certain responses fit what we have learned from our reading, it's always done in the spirit of reflecting, not correcting.

Let's take a look at how Nicky Gamblin introduced hotseating to her eighth graders.

Modeling the Hotseating Strategy

By Nicky Gamblin

Texts Used: Lois Lowry's *The Giver* and S.E. Hinton's *The Outsiders.*

Essential Question: *What does it take to belong?*

Subquestion: *What are the costs and benefits of belonging in different situations?*

1. Students fill out their planning guide in small groups. (See pages 98–99.)

2. I tell them that I really want them to understand the characters in these two novels. There are lots of characters, and they represent different social classes, ways of being, ways of belonging, attitudes, and perspectives, particularly on the issue of belonging. I tell the students that they can't understand a book fully unless they understand the characters, their conflicts, and their development, particularly in regard to central themes. I explain hotseating as a way of working through and using text—and of going beyond text—to understand characters and get to know them so we can use their experience to think with about central issues in the book and in our own lives.

3. Since we have just finished reading *The Giver,* I tell students I will sit in the hotseat as Jonas just before the end of the book.

4. I start with a prepared monologue, in which I talk about how apprehensive I am about turning twelve, about not knowing what I want to be but not wanting the Elders to pick my job for me. I also talk about my feelings for Gabe, my dislike for the routine, and my curiosity about Elsewhere. I make sure to comment on my sense of belonging and what I fear it might be depriving me of belonging from.

5. I ask the students to write on note cards the questions that they'd like to ask me. I want them to ask different kinds of Question-Answer Relationships, or QARs (Raphael, 1986): at least one "think and search" question, one "author and me" question, and one "on my own" question. (See Wilhelm, Baker and Dube, 2001, pp. 70 to 71, for an explanation.) That way, I—in role as Jonas—will be required to do some inferencing or elaborating. I want no "right there" questions, as this activity is not a test of my literal understanding of the text but is an exploration of the character's experience and what it might mean.

6. Students ask their questions, and I respond. If I have trouble, I ask a group of students to play my brain lifeline and advise me on what I might say. If I make a response I can't justify from the text, I "rewind" and am allowed to replay my answer. This provides a safety net for me and the students.

7. I tell the students that I have just modeled hotseating because we will now hotseat several characters from *The Outsiders,* the book we have just started.

8. We brainstorm "think and search" and "author and me" questions for each of the characters in *The Outsiders.*

Questions for Johnny: Why don't you run away from your parents? What would your parents think about you killing Bob?

For Cherry: Do you ever feel trapped by your social situation? What is it that you like about Ponyboy?

For Darry: What is it like to raise a family when you are so young? Why are you so hard on Ponyboy? What do you think Ponyboy thinks of you?

For Soda: What do you think of the way Darry treats Ponyboy? Why do you always act so funny? Can't you ever be serious?

9. We rehearse possible answers and justify these with the evidence from the text and from our own experience. *What makes us think these would be good answers?*

10. We write more questions and hotseat some of the characters.

11. For homework, I ask the students to write a reflection:

   • *If you were on the hotseat today, write about how it felt and what you learned about your character from doing this. Write also about insights you gained on the topic of "belonging".*

   • *If you were not on the hotseat today, write about new things you learned from asking questions and relating to the characters. Evaluate our use of this technique and suggest what we could do to improve on it. Write also about insights you gained on the topic of "belonging".*

One of Nicky Gamblin's eighth graders reflects on what it was like to be in the hotseat.

Name: Character: Johnny

A. What were you thinking and feeling when the blue Mustang pulled up?

   nervous, and scared. I remembered my servere beating I got from the socs.

B. What were you thinking and feeling when you knew that you were going to be in a fight?

   scared unaware what might lie ahead.   *Good stuff*

C. What were you thinking and feeling when Ponyboy's head was under the water?

   That I had to do something. Ponyboy is my best friend. I couldn't do that to him.

D. What were you thinking and feeling when Johnny was attacking Bob with the knife?

   interesting I was thinking only of Ponyboy and knew that what I did, although wrong, was a good choice.

E. What were you thinking and feeling when you saw that Bob was dead?

   relieved Ponyboy was okay, but scared and bewildered that I killed some body.

   really good thinking

Get Ready for the Hotseat
A Planning Guide

Title of Assigned Reading: _____

In a group of 3 or 4 students, choose a character from this text/unit that one of you will play in-role in the hotseat. (Your teacher may also assign you a specific character.) It is important that all members of the group agree on the following information about the character, so that any one of you could go to the hotseat and answer questions from the class, and so that you can help whoever is in the hotseat from your group. If the required information is not in the story, you will have to "infer" or make an educated guess about it.

Name of character:

Your age and physical appearance:

Your house, city/area, favorite place:

Your passions, "soap box topics," deepest desires (which may not be explicitly mentioned in the text):

Your main goal:

Your biggest obstacles and problems:

Your biggest influences:

Your greatest strengths:

Your greatest weaknesses:

What one or two words best describe you? Give examples of details or events from the text that demonstrate these traits:

List quotations from the text that reveal most clearly who you are and what you are about:

Optional: Prepare an opening monologue to introduce yourself, including your biggest passions and challenges, to the audience/forum for the hotseat interview:

The Actual Hotseating:

Members of your group not being hotseated will get to ask the first two questions. What will these questions be? And how will your character respond? How do you know that these responses are good ones?

1. Question:

Answer:

2. Question:

Answer:

What other questions might the other people in the audience ask? What will they want to know? How will your character respond and why will he or she respond that way? Rehearse a few with your group.

Using Inner Voices to Deepen Our Understanding of Character

Anchor Standards
for Reading,
1–3, 6

As with all enactment techniques, there are many variations to the hotseat. One of my favorites is called Inner Voice. In life, there are many things that we think but would never say. Why don't we just say what we are thinking? We might be intimidated by the situation, or the people we're with might get hurt or find our thinking inappropriate. It could be we have something to hide. Perhaps the consequences of telling the truth are too great, or we fear no one would understand us. Whatever the reason, characters are faced with these same issues. They might want to tell it like it is, but various forces prevent them from doing so.

The Inner Voice technique allows us to get at the essence of what the character might really be thinking about without any inhibitions or internal editing. It helps us to explore what the character might truly feel even though she may have said something else. It also helps us to judge the reliability of characters and narrators.

With this Inner Voice technique, the person in the hotseat responds as the character would publicly, withholding the full truth of a matter, or responding to get their way, impress people, or to meet their expectations. We hear a character's words, but the inner voice lets us know what really may be going on, as did the subtitles that articulated Woody Allen and Diane Keaton's conversation in the movie *Annie Hall*.

Each hotseated student-in-role has his "inner voice" (variations could be called "deep thoughts," "alter ego," or "conscience") stand behind him to reveal the thoughts that the character would not reveal. In other words, the hotseated student says what the character would say publicly—editing and controlling for the situation and withholding many thoughts and feelings, but the inner voice says what the character might really be thinking and feeling behind his persona or "mask."

This technique requires students to think beyond the literal. They must consider the influence of context, the meaning of words, tone of voice, and how they as readers must interpret the subtext of a story. This activity can help students think about reading their own behavior and situations in their own life, the messages that are sent, and the silences in the conversations. What is unsaid and why? What is really being thought? I have also found it useful in helping students to understand advertisements, political speeches, and responses to manipulative texts.

A related technique is called Alter Ego. The notion of an alter ego comes from Latin, literally: "the other I." The alter ego is considered to be a second self or alternate personality. Perhaps this is what a character wishes he could be, like James Thurber's Walter Mitty or Rose's Motorcycle Momma in the cartoon *Rose is Rose*. Perhaps it is a part of the personality rarely called on but who comes out in times of crisis or need. In psychology, the conscious self might be oblivious to the alter-ego who occasionally takes over and acts out on behalf of the self. (The term was coined in the early nineteenth century when "dissociative personality disorder" was first described by psychologists. A person with an alter ego was sometimes said to lead a double life.) Another meaning for alter ego can be found in literary analysis to describe characters in different works who are psychologically similar, or a fictional character whose behavior, speech or thoughts seems to directly and intentionally represent those of the author.

Hot, Hotter, Hottest With "The Fan Club"

Anchor Standards for Writing/Composing, 2–5, 7, 9

For "The Fan Club," there are several options for hotseat and inner voice prompts. The most obvious possibility is the conflict between Rachel and Laura because so much is unspoken between them.

We can start with a kind of "forum" drama in which the audience can give advice to the role players and help them along. To begin, we need a Rachel and her inner voice and a Laura and her inner voice. Here's an excerpt from a classroom transcript. The first two lines were assigned, then students improvised with some prompting and support from me and other members of the classroom forum.

1. Rachel begins the conversation with a quotation from the text: "Why didn't you come by last night like you said you would?" (This is what the real Laura hears and responds to.)

2. Laura speaks as she did in the text: "I was really busy."

3. Rachel's inner voice says what she really wanted to say: "I am really hurt because you keep ditching me!"

4. Forum suggestion: "You need to tell her you are hurt and why. Why do you think she's ditching you?"

5. Rachel's inner voice incorporates forum suggestion: "You haven't come over this whole school year, and my parents wonder what has happened between us. So do I! And you are dressing and acting different. You are forgetting me and who we really are! You are even acting like you don't love science!"

6. Laura's inner voice speaks to Rachel's actual comment (not Rachel's inner voice, which Laura cannot hear): "Are you kidding, Rachel? Like I want to hang out with you anymore. You just aren't cool enough! Get a clue! And it is uncool to show you love school or any subject!"

All the while, the forum can suggest ideas to get started, then make additions, deletions, and revisions. Once the students get the idea, the enactment can become more spontaneous. Typically, I have the characters hotseated and interviewed by students in role as guidance counselors or another role appropriate to the situation. Or characters could converse with each other. When first using this technique I tap or motion students to talk so that the students will know when to jump in (character speaks, then inner voice speaks).

Anchor Standards for Reading, 9

When I use this technique, I might have the character in the hotseat with the character's alter ego behind or beside that character. The alter ego must determine what "alternate" personality or side of the character's personality is being represented, and then comment on the core character's thinking and offer alternatives to it from the alternative perspective. This requires students not only to enter the character but to see how complex character is—how multiple and various and full of possibilities it can be instead of being monolithic.

You can also ask students to identify comparable character alter egos inside different works, for example, asking who might Jonas' alter ego be in *The Outsiders*. Or, students can be asked what character is most close to being the alter ego or mouthpiece of the author. These characters can be hotseated together and asked about their essential similarities (as well as differences), or they might engage in a correspondence drama exchange through letters and postcards. In this way, characters from different texts and the texts themselves can be put in conversation with each other. There are many ways to play with the idea of the alter ego.

Reflecting After the Hotseat

After the hotseating is completed, students reflect on the enactment by responding to questions such as the following: What would relationships and communication be like if we always knew what another person was thinking? What would change in your life if someone knew all of your thoughts? Or if you could only tell the truth (the premise behind the Jim Carrey movie *Liar, Liar* and the more recent Ricky Gervais film *The History of Lying*?

Other possible hotseat/alter ego enactments for this story would include Rachel and Laura being interviewed by local reporters about harassment in school. How would they be likely to respond? What do their styles seem to be? What would they really be thinking—what are their real concerns? Alternately, Mr. Knowles could be on the hotseat, being interviewed by the PTO about harassment and bullying in his classroom. What would he be likely to say in a public forum—and what would he really be thinking? What might the "cool kids" Diane or Steve say if they were called to task by a teacher, the principal, or their parents?

Variations on Hotseating

Interviewing Techniques

Interviews are great ways to solicit information from a character in a meaningful situation that students will recognize. Students hotseat in the context of a formal interview, a press conference, a trial, a debate, or even a game or game show (for example, hotseat characters as part of a *To Tell the Truth* or *Jeopardy* game). Groups or panels of students can be hotseated, and inner voices can be used.

Students can use their knowledge of press conferences, for example, to draft a press release and then be interviewed as the president, principal, or some other authority on the story or issue being studied.

Playing an Agent: Interacting With the Person in the Hotseat

In this next group of hotseat variations, the person in the hotseat gets to take a break while the rest of the class works. This set of techniques is great for reviewing information, inferring past situations, and considering how to help characters. In general, students act much like a Greek chorus, commenting on the action, interpreting it, wondering about it, and making predictions.

To begin, I have the class review a situation from our reading and then brainstorm about how to proceed before jumping in. For example, in *The Giver*, Jonas can benefit from help at several points in the story as he contemplates escape and actually leaves his community. He may also need help in the future in Elsewhere. How could we help him? What would he need to know?

Chad "whispers" to Jason, in role as Romeo, about what to do about Juliet's betrothal to Paris.

Voices from the Past

As a class, students consider what might have happened in the past that is affecting the character at this point. Then students come up to remind the character in the hotseat of his past and how it is affecting him. Every student can come up, or a representative can be sent from small student groups. In Ghosts, fears and doubts may come to visit the character. In Whispers, the students stand behind the hotseat and whisper anything that they think might be going through the character's mind at this point. In Prequels, students consider what makes a character the way she is. What is her past? What causes her to be this way? How could we help her? Students could psychoanalyze the person on the hotseat or ask her to remember past events that might be causing current responses. Or in a form of role-play, they could enact possible past events that would explain her current attitudes and reactions.

Good Angel/Bad Angel

This is one of my favorites, though I must warn you to use the Bad Angel carefully. Given the power of enactment techniques, I use it sparingly. I would never use it when hotseating the character of Rachel, for instance, because she is too vulnerable—and the issue she represents is too volatile and close to home.

One reason I like the Good Angel technique so much is because of Santayana's assertion that reading "should be an imaginative rehearsal for living." I agree. When we read, we should consider how we will use what we are learning and experiencing to make our own lives and those of others better. In my own research for *You Gotta BE the Book* (Wilhelm, 1997/2008), I found that one aspect of engaged reading was that readers want to act as "agents" for characters, abetting, advising, and helping them. Good Angel allows us to imaginatively rehearse our potential response to real-life situations and to act as helpmates for characters. It also helps us to understand the human dimensions and effects of the conflicts that run throughout stories and life and to connect these to our own lived experience.

In "The Fan Club," I use the Good Angel strategy when Rachel is being taunted during her speech. I call a meeting of guardian angels. Each group of three or four students is summoned because Rachel needs immediate help. What does she need to know or hear right now? Each group consults and then sends one angel to talk to Rachel. In all of these techniques, the hotseated character can either just listen or she can make comments or ask questions about the advice and converse with the angels.

When we read John Collier's short story "The Chaser," however, we use the Bad Angel as well. In this story, a young man named Alan buys a love potion that will make him "the sole obsession" of the girl he loves, but who does not feel the same way about him. There are several story clues to the disasters that await Alan, which he ignores. The Good Angels warn him in an attempt to dissuade him from making the purchase. The Bad Angels, on the other hand, urge him to go through with using the potion on his beloved. This always produces humorous situations. Afterward, I ask Alan, the student on the hotseat, who was most convincing. It is always the Bad Angels. This gives us a chance to "imaginatively rehearse for living" and review why the Bad Angels in our lives are so convincing. They are seductive and emotional, tap into our immediate desires, ignore long-term consequences, and play on our fears. Students can use this knowledge in their own reading and lives. Good Angel/Bad Angel works well with any moral dilemma or choice, especially if the character has some power to make the right choice and is not particularly susceptible to powers beyond her control.

Reflecting Afterward

After these activities, I always ask the person in the hotseat how it felt, and what advice was most and least helpful. The students generally enjoy being in the hotseat, and liken the good angels' advice to be "warm fuzzies," but sometimes they find conflicting advice very confusing. They prefer supportive statements like, "You know this stuff, just go ahead and do it," or "It will be okay; look, Laura is listening to you." They usually find the very directed advice like "Okay, this is what you do. First, change your wardrobe, then…" much less helpful unless they feel that their character is really at a loss or is in such a crisis that she cannot make decisions of her own. My students' preferences concur with the findings of discourse specialist Deborah Tannen and other researchers, especially regarding the response women seek when they are in trouble (they want support instead of being told what to do). Build in this reflection time—it will give you an opportunity to discuss how in real life, different people in different situations may need different kinds of help. They can reflect on how to ascertain what kind of help is needed, and how to get feedback. The enactment gives us a chance to reflect on our own experience and what kind of advice we should seek and give. It also helps us to consider how people in trouble may not be able to take our advice; if they are really in trouble, we must not tell them what to do, we must help them to do it.

This reflection on how the enactment relates to life is especially powerful when using the Bad Angel, because the Bad Angel's advice is generally more seductive, emotionally appealing, and immediate. The reflection allows us to freeze time and consider the options and why we may be so easily swayed to the wrong decision. It is easier to consider the consequences in a

drama than in real life. I have hopes that students may remember this "rehearsal for living" when they are faced with similar real choices!

Take a look at how Nicky Gamblin uses Good Angel:

Hotseat Techniques for *Lord of the Flies*

I chose the following scenes for Good Angel because the characters were in trouble, and because each scene highlights a theme in the book that I want to help the students think about.

The Theme: Teasing

The scene: Piggy is being teased again. He is the most intelligent boy in the group and important to their survival. But they don't see it. They reject him because he is smart and chubby and wears glasses. Everyone, that is, except Ralph. All students assume the role of Ralph and, one by one, whisper some words of advice in Piggy's ear that will help him deal with the teasing.

The reflection: After all students have had a turn, I ask them: What was the best advice? What was most helpful? Usable? What is the best way to deal with teasing?

The Theme: Power

The scene: Jack is considering dividing the boys so that he can become leader of the hunters. Half the class takes the role of Bad Angel, encouraging Jack to go through with his plan. The other half are Good Angels playing on Jack's logical concern for survival and his conscience. One Good Angel speaks, then one Bad Angel, and so forth.

The reflection: Why do people want power? What are they willing to give up for it? How can you best deal with a power-hungry person? What can happen to people who want and then get power? How can we protect against abuses of power?

The Theme: Terror

The scene: Ralph is being chased by the hunters who are chanting "kill the beast, cut his throat, spill his blood." He needs to do something or he will face certain death. You can whisper in his ear about past experiences that might help him, plans that he can use to escape, or just encourage him to keep going. Tell him whatever you think will help.

The reflection: What most helps people overcome terror? What most helps you keep going in the face of adversity? (Student responses can be used as the basis of a choral montage.)

Every Student in a Hotseat! Whole-Group Variations

Here are several twists that invite every student to be in the hotseat.

Tunnel of Advice/Conscience Alley

Have students form a circle. One student playing a hotseated character runs the gauntlet by walking around the circle of students who offer advice or speak as her conscience as she goes by. I usually have one student walk about halfway around the class circle, then start another student. In this way many or all of your students get the experience of being spoken to and advised in the hotseat.

Response Montage

Another way to involve every student in the hotseat is to ask students to respond to some questions in writing. For example, write in role what is your character's response to a particular event/comment/issue. Then ask the students to think of one line that captures the character's response, and write it down. Students can then recite their lines. The comments could be rearranged into a montage or choral poem. Likewise, students could offer the perspectives of different characters on an event into a montage. To reflect, students could determine which response was most interesting, then consider: How can we explain this response? How could we explore it further?

Two-Sided Character/Self Think-Aloud

On one side of a paper students can be asked to think aloud or write down a think aloud of their own responses to an event or to a passage as themselves. On the other side they can provide a think aloud from the perspective of a character or author. These can then be read aloud and compared. Or, on one side students could respond as a character would publicly, and then on the other side respond as he would privately, getting at the inner voice. Powerful lines could be underlined and used as the material for a montage.

Inside/Outside

Students form two circles. Those on the inside are in the hotseat and can confer about their response as if they were one person, or, of course, they could portray a group, like the Socs or Greasers from *The Outsiders*. Students in the outer circle play other roles, conversing, then posing questions and problems to those in the inner circle. Both inner and outer students speak one at a time, after conferring with others in their group about what their questions and responses will be. Often, I let them engage in individual conversations, all at the same time, then switching partners. Variations include the outer circle being a former or future self of the character with the current self seated in the middle, or the two groups play author and character, advisor and character, or reader and character.

Mantle of the Stranger

It's quite useful for me to take on the Mantle of the Stranger, meaning that I role-play a stranger who does not know the story we have read or the topic we have studied, but who has an intense need to know that information. I then put everyone in the class in the hotseat, asking them (in my character) what has happened or how things work. Once students see how this goes, they also enjoy taking on the stranger's role as they ask classmates to explain difficult concepts to them. To help students summarize the story after reading *Lord of the Flies*, I played the naval officer on the beach who asked for a full report of what had happened on the island. Not knowing anything about what had happened in my role, I could ask naïve questions and play the "dumb" reader. This required the students to identify key details, justify and explain their thinking, provide necessary background and context, and use many other expert communicative strategies.

Bending the Rules: Intensified Involvement

Some variations put a little spin on the hotseat in order to encourage students to think harder or from a new angle. Here are three ideas along these lines:

**Frozen Tableau—
Tapped Alive
(Conflict Intensifier)**

Intensifier: When a person is in the hotseat, the teacher can announce that something has changed in the character's situation. Now there is more tension, or the difficulties have just grown worse or more complicated. Then the interview or whispers can continue, but must reflect the changed situation. For example, after Cassie is pushed off the sidewalk by Mr. Simms in *Roll of Thunder, Hear My Cry*, students can be asked to whisper advice to her. Then, the situation can be intensified: What if Mr. Simms ordered her to kiss Lillian's shoes? What if Big Ma came to her aid and was grabbed by a mob? What if Mr. Jamison walked by but didn't see her? What if Uncle Hammer succeeded in physically beating Mr. Simms?

Hotseat the Author: Authors can be hotseated and interviewed. In the previous think-aloud book in this series, I outline several ways to talk back to authors, converse with or interview authors (the teacher or student playing the role of author), or use author monologues.

Personifications: When teaching math or science, I like to ask students to take on the role of a mathematical or scientific concept—like commutability, inertia, or symbiosis, or a force like an electrical charge. Students in the hotseat can be interviewed about their uses, relationships to other concepts, how they were discovered, and so forth.

After hotseating, remember to reflect and revise. Sometimes I form groups to review what went well and what answers they would change now that they have had time to think about it. Other times, reflection can occur as a whole class. One of the great things about enactment is that it's like a tape recorder— you can always "rewind" and redo things, you can erase, or you can fast forward into the future. Once students critique their work they can easily redo it. Too bad real life isn't like that!

Again, teachers who use the hotseat technique rave about the engagement it stimulates, and how it assists students not only in delving into characters and their motivations, but also in inquiring into the thematic statements authors make through characters about human nature, relations, and life.

Voices From the Field

Hi Jeff:

I was a participant at your workshop last week in Minnesota. I wanted to let you know what an impact you've had on my department. There were four of us from my school at the workshop. We returned to school the next day and found ourselves talking about your enactment strategies all day. During the week, each of us tried some techniques and felt great about the energy and success. So, I thought I'd share them with you.

G. went into class the very next day and had her students put Hamlet in the hotseat. She had good angels and bad angels giving him advice, and then various characters from the play entered in to tell Hamlet what would be best for him to do from their perspective. We finally got to hear what Ophelia really thinks!

R. was also working with Hamlet, and when her students finished the play, she had them form a different hotseat panel, taking on the roles of expert critics to get at different interpretations of why Hamlet acts the way he does. One critic explained everything in terms of the "ill-fated Hamlet," another the "evil Hamlet," another the "depressed Hamlet" and yet another the "confused Hamlet," and so on. They had to respond to questions from the audience, and we got to compare interpretations and decide which seemed most convincing and explanatory.

JM had her students visualizing and illustrating what they had read in Humanities from the perspectives of artists or just plain folks from various eras.

All in all, your workshop invigorated us at the end of a long term when we needed it the most. The enactment techniques were easy to use and helped even very good students delve deeper into the texts we are reading. And we are having fun exploring multiple interpretations of texts.

Other department members are jealously watching the rest of us with our heads together, planning what enactments to use to help our students' reading. They've requested that we spend some time on our upcoming in-service day to share what we learned. Thanks so much for sharing such an exciting set of teaching strategies.

—Mary

CHAPTER 7

MANTLE OF THE EXPERT
Learning to Read Deeply Enough to Develop Expertise

What makes reading powerful and transformative? Think about some of your own most powerful reading experiences. Did you find that a story made you feel something you never felt before, or to feel it more intensely? Did you see something from a new perspective? Were you shocked into seeing things in a totally new way, or that an article "got you into a different head" and gave you new expertise? Let's say you love reading mysteries, and discover as you read about an actual murder case in the newspaper that you have accrued quite a bit of knowledge about detective work. Or perhaps you read an astounding article in *The New Yorker* by a biologist who brings polluted watersheds back to health. The article is so powerful, you not only look at watersheds in a new way, but the biologist's way of thinking and her expertise affect how you think about related matters, such as conserving the tidal marshes near your home. This leads you to read other books on ecology. When there is a hearing to discuss preserving a natural watershed in your area that is now threatened by a shopping mall, you come to the meeting with knowledge, vocabulary, possible solutions, and informed questions derived from your reading. In this chapter, we will explore strategies that help students have reading experiences as powerful and educative as these.

Discipline Standards

The point of all reading, and of all learning activity, is to change our understandings and, as a result, our ways of thinking and being in the world. The goal of studying particular subjects is to understand a topic the way experts in that field understand it—to enter, as a novice, into that "Community of Practice" and to proceed down the "correspondence concept" continuum to ever greater expertise. In studying history, we want to learn how to read, think, and reflect like historians do; in science, we want to learn how to approach problems, consider data, and make decisions like scientists. In other words, we want to become "novice experts" who "take on" the language and strategies of the expert.

You might say that the enactment strategy highlighted in this chapter, Mantle of the Expert, trains the mental and attitudinal muscles necessary for gaining expertise. The strategy helps students read and think deeply enough that they learn more than the raw content—they learn the ways of thinking and knowing that experts use to understand, represent, and use that content. The phrase *mantle of the expert* means to wear the mantle (the cloak) of another, to step into another's shoes. Mantle of the Expert was pioneered by Dorothy Heathcote and is used by many other progressive drama educators. (See Heathcote and Bolton, 1995.)

Using the Strategy With Nonfiction: Studying the Depression

How does this strategy play out in the classroom? During a unit on the Depression, I asked my seventh graders to take on the mantles of various experts to explore this era from the perspectives of historians and documentary filmmakers. They worked in several different groups, with each group creating a video about a different aspect of the Depression. They ultimately pieced the parts together into a tremendous video documentary. Each student became a novice historian by learning how to conduct interviews, sift through data, read documents, study artifacts, and come up with complex analyses of what it must have been like to live during another time of history—and how we can apply this understanding today.

The students discovered that researchers don't just rely on existing knowledge. Researchers create new knowledge through action: conducting surveys, doing experiments, and so forth. My students used enactments to become hobos, farmers in the Dust Bowl, meteorologists, police officers, soup kitchen workers, and policymakers. These activities were phenomenological research into the experiences we were studying and provided a personal connection to that study.

To launch the unit, we watched two documentaries about the Depression, and used them to define "documentary" and the standards for making one. We also discussed ways of interviewing, types of interview questions, and ways of representing information, thereby taking on the mantle of expertise for documentary makers.

We then began our study in earnest. Groups were formed. Topics were selected. And students began reading. In their roles as historians and documentary makers, they had to decide what to read, who to interview, and how to fill in missing bits of information. When students identified gaps or displayed confusion, I aided them in using information they had found to create an enactment that would help fill that gap.

For example, Christine interviewed her grandparents about their experiences living through the Depression. Based on her grandparents' stories, she and her group decided to focus their documentary video on the various ways people entertained themselves during these lean times. Still, they did not understand why people just couldn't "get a job" or "work harder to get money." The Mantle of the Expert enactments helped them realize the consequences of competing for jobs with people who were willing to work for less, who would work for food, or who did not have a family to care for. They further realized that many of those people had to live in an encampment called a "Hooverville," which would eventually be torn down by health officials. "But we have no place else to go!" Christine complained in her role. And in that moment, she had filled the gap and entered into the experience of the time. "But isn't there something that could have been done?" she asked. I gave her group a copy of Jerry Stanley's *Children of the Dust Bowl* and they were able to learn more about the challenges of the time and how some courageous folks were able to meet those challenges.

These enactments became the basis for many scenes in their video. Afterwards, this is what Christine and another group member had to say:

"When we started I didn't understand how all the people were so poor. I just thought they were lazy or something and that they should have tried harder to get a job, or should have moved where the jobs were. So then we tried it out in the drama and I couldn't get a job. Then I got one and somebody accepted less pay, and then only meals, but I had a family so I couldn't do that. And I moved, but I couldn't find work there either and in the end I lived in a cardboard box and I was really frustrated and angry. Then the people [health inspectors] came and kicked us out.... It really made me understand.... I just didn't get it when I [heard or read] about it."

—Christine

"School is about facts—mostly boring facts—drama is about making facts exciting because you add the feelings.... Drama takes facts and asks how they might have been different or how the facts might affect you or someone else and how all that would feel. That's why I like drama."

—Mike

The power of Mantle-of-the-Expert work is clear. Without it, the students would not have reached the professional understanding nor felt the personal experience for which historians and video documentary makers strive. (See Wilhelm and Edmiston, 1998, for more on this Depression unit.)

Roles Students Adopted

In the macro-frame of this unit, students took on the mantle of:

- documentary filmmakers
- historians

Why? Because we were creating a historical video to show others and, therefore, needed to understand the standards and conventions of people in those professions. This set a higher standard for our work and made clear what and how we could learn from historians and documentary filmmakers. It gave the project real purpose because we understood our need to be apprenticed into these expert communities. In the micro-frames for this unit, students took on the mantles of:

- rum runners
- economists
- hobos
- policymakers
- Hooverville residents
- meteorologists
- Dust Bowl farmers
- police officers
- breadline workers

Again, *why?* We needed to explore perspectives and conditions that were distant from ours in terms of time, space, and experience. We interviewed actual "informants" when they were available. When they weren't, we used enactment to provide an in-role substitute for them. The enactments allowed students to connect personally to the experience, to feel the conditions under which people of this era lived, and to play with ways of representing this experience to others—something that historians and documentary makers must be able to do. As such, the micro-frame enactments supported the ways we performed as novice experts in the fields of history and documentary filmmaking.

Benefits of Mantle of the Expert

Anchor Standards
for Writing, 1–10,
esp. 6, 7, 8, 9

Mantle of the Expert

- provides a purpose for learning and the tools for gaining, applying, using, and sharing knowledge.
- infuses facts with feelings.
- helps students experience curricular "facts" and their uses.
- requires students to take a stance and action.
- positions students as purposeful, involved, and cooperative community members.
- helps students ask "What if?" and experiment with the possible.
- develops the ability to monitor one's own thoughts, feelings, and meaning-making processes, which leads to metacognition and self-monitoring strategies.
- turns students into inquirers and provides research methods and tools, ways of re-seeing the world
  - as ethnographers—enactments enable students to observe and experience distant cultures, situations, and historical eras.
  - as phenomenological researchers—enactments allow students to become "insiders" to the experiences of others.
  - as action researchers—enactments encourage students to take action, reflect, and evaluate the effectiveness of the action and how it changed the situation. (cf. Wilhelm and Edmiston, 1998; Edmiston and Wilhelm, 1998)
- provides a situation that closely resembles how experts develop and deploy specific kinds of knowledge, for example: language, strategies, approaches, and applications (making the classroom a laboratory/workshop).
- develops expert ways of knowing.

Mantle of the Expert enhances reading of fiction as well as nonfiction. You can use it for quick enactments during or after reading (as I did in "The Fan Club" by casting students as guidance counselors who were interviewing Rachel on the hotseat). But it's most useful as an extended strategy, one that threads through before, during, and after one or many readings, as was the case in our study and inquiry of the Depression.

The Teacher's Role: Coaching Students From the Sidelines

You may choose to become an expert working along with students or someone who serves the experts, like a dispatcher or aide who provides information, complicates matters, or reminds students of their roles in various ways. As the teacher, you should lend "expert" language, information, perspectives, and strategies that would otherwise be inaccessible to students. For example, during the Depression study, I played the role of a police dispatcher who introduced the concepts of prohibition, organized crime, fraud, and embezzlement. I introduced language like "whistle blower" and "take a bath in the canal," and challenged the police force to look for the causes instead of just the symptoms of crime. In other words, I situated the learning, modeled language and concept use, and guided students to work in their zones of proximal development, helping them gain new and more expert understandings. I framed the enactments, shaping the roles and interactions, but in a secondary and supportive role, and providing the language and strategies that students used and developed.

Unlike Heathcote, who favors the imagination instead of actually making things in the midst of this activity, I almost always have my students create a "knowledge artifact" that makes their learning visible and demonstrates their application of processes used by the experts they are emulating. Nonetheless, anyone who uses Mantle of the Expert is standing on the shoulders of Heathcote's genius, and I refer interested readers to descriptions of her work. (O'Neill, et al., 1988; Wagner, 1976; Heathcote and Bolton, 1995)

Using the Strategy With Fiction: "The Fan Club"

For "The Fan Club" story, I chose a short Mantle-of-the-Expert strategy after the third section of the story. I introduced the strategy by asking students who might be an expert on the subject of kids having trouble at school, of not fitting in or engaging. They listed guidance counselors, social workers, psychologists, teachers, and parents. I then asked them who might be the most appropriate expert to bring in for Laura, and they agreed that it would be the guidance counselor. (Sometimes I let students choose the expert role; other times I will choose from their list or make a suggestion based on possibilities I see for exploring issues and ideas.)

For the enactment, students "became" guidance counselors who help Laura. Generally, if there are things that students need to know to play a role, then I provide them with that information at this time, perhaps by sharing information or by inviting in an expert to be interviewed by the students. Given that these students were familiar with the role of guidance counselor and were conducting a *short* enactment (they were not trying to develop more expert counseling strategies, but simply to understand a character and her feelings), we brainstormed some ground rules for counseling. The students suggested things like making the student comfortable with easy questions first and asking oblique questions to get at the real issue. From there, we proceeded with the enactment, first by holding a meeting of guidance counselors about bullying in our school, and then by putting Laura on the hotseat and interviewing her in role as if we were her guidance counselors.

Extension Ideas

Doodling

Another strategy I use with stories is called Doodling. I have students take a role, such as Laura, and doodle or make notes in her notebook that we think she might have made during math class. Or students could compose a diary or journal entry after the class. Later, as guidance counselors, we look at the pictures or notes and try to decipher what they tell us about Laura's state of mind. We might even choose to pair up as guidance counselor and student to talk about the doodlings.

Mentor Group

Another strategy I like is called Mentor Group or Problem Protocol. The character brings her problem to a group of other students who are cast in expert roles. She describes her problem, and the group asks questions. Then, the group explores her problem, her choices, the consequences and possibilities, and provides advice, while the character listens quietly and takes notes. At the end, the character says "thank you" and describes what she has learned. For "The Fan Club," I ask students to play Laura, Rachel, a parent, or Mr. Knowles. The character then chooses which experts she wants help from and addresses a group comprised of those experts.

After reading the story, I asked the students what issues it raised and which, if any, remained unresolved for them. Since they were all troubled by what had happened to Rachel, I asked them which experts might be able to help her. They brainstormed ideas like the school board, the police liaison, the principal, or a lawyer. In this case, I seized upon the idea of a lawyer because I could see how it connected to the theme of civil rights that we were studying. Besides, we had recently read about Thurgood Marshall and other civil rights lawyers. I asked the students to become civil rights lawyers and, in teams, use the story as a legal transcript to decide whether Rachel's civil rights had been violated. The students knew something about civil rights legislation from our current unit, and I added some information about laws governing schools. Their job was to decide whether civil rights laws had been broken and to propose a course of action to help Rachel.

Clearness Committee

This idea comes from Parker Palmer (2007). Palmer uses this approach, which comes from Quaker tradition, as a way to help people achieve clarity about a specific problem they are experiencing, but I have found that it works very well in-role as well. First, a person (or character) writes out a problem statement that must include three elements: 1) a clear statement of the nature of the problem, 2) the background of the problem, including prior relevant experiences, and 3) the foreground of the problem, what is seen on the horizon when the problem is held in view—what the character foresees if the problem is not addressed. This step is powerful in itself. A second step is for the person (or character) to choose three or four other people (or characters) who she thinks might help her to understand and navigate the problem. These people (or characters) sit in a circle and give undivided attention to the focus person.

The clearness committee itself is only allowed to ask questions. They are not to provide solutions or suggestions. The purpose is to understand the problem, not to try to fix the person having the problem. At the end of the activity, the focus person can request "mirroring." Mirroring is not providing advice, it is simply mirroring back what has been heard and observed ("When asked about A, you said B" or "When you spoke about X, you sounded tired, but when you mentioned Y, you seemed energized and your eyes brightened.") I have found this technique to be very powerful in my mentoring of teachers, and as a drama technique with students. I think it is a great rehearsal for living—the writing about problems, the winnowing of feelings from facts, the requesting for help, the deep listening and attention we give to others, and the withholding of advice in service of helping another. All of this can transfer to living a more responsive and responsible community life and the cultivation of something that might be called wisdom. (Wilhelm and Novak, 2010).

Planning Mantle of the Expert

Below, I highlight ways of planning Mantle-of-the-Expert work based on "The Fan Club" project and two other extended projects by colleagues. The first is a project by Janett Jackson, with whom I worked during my sabbatical in Australia. Janett teaches in Aboriginal communities, and she and her students created an anti-smoking video documentary that was distributed within their own community and beyond. While working on the project, students became experts about the risks of smoking through their roles as health officials and researchers, and gained more expertise about theater and video documentary from their work staging and filming short scenes.

I'll also feature the work of Seth Mitchell, who used enactments within a more traditional ninth-grade curriculum featuring two required texts, *The Iliad* and *The Odyssey*. He chose to do an extended Mantle-of-the-Expert drama by casting students as historians and as designers responsible for creating a theme park organized around these two epic poems.

To demonstrate our planning and implementation processes, the following section shows the steps. Specifically, I show the thinking behind my short strategy and Janett's and Seth's more extended use of Mantle of the Expert.

Notice that in order to play the expert in any of these cases, *students must have read the central texts*. In turn, the enactment helps them understand this text more deeply, the issues it raises, and the community of practice that produced it. You might also require students to read and learn about what various experts know and how they work.

12 Steps for Planning Mantle-of-the-Expert Work

STEP 1: Teacher sets (or students and teacher negotiate) the curricular topic or text, and frames it by articulating an essential question and thematic issue to explore.

Jeff: My class was studying civil rights. I chose "The Fan Club" as a story that could be a useful part of this study. For the short enactment using Mantle of the Expert, the issues to explore were school bullying and harassment. Our essential question was: How can we protect and promote civil rights?

Janett: The curriculum required that we do a project on health risks to the community. The Aboriginal students with whom I was working identified smoking as a risk. Our essential question was: What do we need to know about smoking to promote Aboriginal teen health?

Seth: The English curriculum required the reading and study of *The Iliad* and *The Odyssey*, so I chose the theme of the human journey. The essential question was: How can we best meet the challenges that all humans face?

STEP 2: Teacher, perhaps with students, brainstorms experts who could deal with the issue, and what they know and do.

Jeff: Who knows about bullying and harassment? Guidance counselors, psychologists, social workers, and lawyers.

Janett: Who knows about the effects of smoking on a community? Doctors, health officials, physiologists, medical researchers, ethnographers, and anthropologists.

Seth: Who knows about *The Iliad* and *The Odyssey* and its importance in our culture? Literature specialists, archaeologists, historians, experts on Greek antiquity, and psychologists.

STEP 3: Teacher asks: Who could use the knowledge offered by the experts—and for what purposes?

Jeff: Kids being bullied, kids doing the bullying, parents, teachers, policy makers, social workers, and police officers.

Janett: People from our own and other Aboriginal communities, people in the wider community—basically everyone, since smoking is a pervasive health risk!

Seth: Folks who want to reconstruct/understand the history and culture of a people or a period to know what they were about, how they lived, and so forth—people like Von Schliemann, the guy who found ancient Troy; people who want to understand current events and problems, and what we might do about them, from a new perspective, for example, Fleischman, who wrote *Dateline: Troy*—a great young-adult read; others who want to understand the human condition, our cultural heritage, where we have come from and where we might be going; and some just to be entertained.

STEP 4: Teacher asks: In what form would the expert knowledge be created, shared, and applied?

Jeff: Through a meeting, counseling session with student, presentation to teachers or parents, self-help column in teen magazine, and so forth.

Janett: With a video documentary.

Seth: Through a movie, play, or story; psychoanalysis; or a game show or theme park.

STEP 5: Teacher introduces the situation: the purpose, the roles, the audience/clients, and the task to be performed.

Jeff: I used "The Fan Club" as the backdrop of the drama, and gave students a focus for the drama by pointing out that Laura had a problem that guidance counselors could help to address.

Janett: I asked students to write about their future personal and professional goals and then summarize these to the class. I gave them each a "chance card" with a symbol that represented how smoking had affected his or her life. Students had to interpret the symbol and explain how it would affect their personal and professional goals and futures. In other words, students were asked to imagine, or become more expert, on the impact smoking would have on them. Some students traded cards if they had a personal reason for doing so.

Seth: I set up the roles and tasks for students through a "client letter," asking them to become historians, literary experts, child psychologists, and others responsible for using their expertise to design a theme park. I explained that, though the class would design only a proposal, we would construct a few exhibits that would be used by classmates.

STEP 6: Teacher explains what students are to imagine and what they are to produce.

Students should produce something if it motivates and requires them to use skills that are important to the community of practice. Jeff's students produced an interaction with Laura. They could have created a guide for guidance counselors about bullying: what to look for, how to help those who are bullied, things to say and do, things to not say and do. Janett's students created a documentary for use throughout Australia. Seth's students imagined themselves as theme-park designers who created plans and models within that role.

STEP 7: Teacher and/or students choose specific tasks.

Jeff: I had students imagine they were guidance counselors needing to find out Laura's problem, then propose a solution for her that would also address the issue of harassment and bullying at school.

Janett: Students became novice health experts and (video) filmmakers participating in the production of a video documentary that would teach others about the effects of smoking.

Seth: My students created a proposal for a theme park based on *The Iliad* and *The Odyssey* to be built in time for the Athens Olympics. They decided that the park's theme should celebrate the heritage of Greek antiquity and engage visitors in ideas and events from these two epics that could be applied to their own lives and "human journey."

STEP 8: Teachers and students decompose the task and plot out a time line.

Less time usually means more when it comes to enactments because the pressure to create, or come to a tentative conclusion, stimulates thinking. The enactment can always be extended or set off in another direction as needed. When in doubt, put the pressure on! Constructing a timeline requires students to "decompose" the elements of a task, sequence how to complete the task, divide up responsibilities, make plans, and so on.

Jeff: I gave students five minutes to come up with a list of reasons bullying occurs and possible ways to eliminate it. I then gave them five minutes with Laura in the hotseat to identify her problem(s) and how to help her. We then discussed whether Laura's situation fit our original ideas about bullying and how to address it. Finally, we revised our thinking about helping those who are bullied and put it in the format of a guide.

Janett: The students knew that we had two weeks to plan the video and one day to film it with a crew. The date was set, so we had to be ready. There was a "drop-dead" deadline.

Seth: I introduced the Mantle-of-the-Expert project before the class began reading, that way students could read the texts as if they were theme park designers or advisors. Once the reading was completed, students took seven class days to plan out the theme park, create the models, and make presentations to other classes. I required them to emphasize how the theme park design mirrored the essential elements of the hero's human journey, the challenges faced, and how to overcome them.

STEP 9: Students plan how to manage the task.

Either in or out of role, students have to plan out what needs to be done, who will do it, and by when it must be completed to meet the final due date.

Jeff: Time management is not a big problem in a short Mantle-of-the-Expert scene. Nonetheless, some kids would say things like: "We have only five minutes to prepare this report for the principal. So we have to get our list of reasons in the first three minutes and then list solutions in the last two."

Janett: I provided the overall time line and engaged students in activities that gave them ideas for developing their scenes. It was up to them to decompose the task and figure out what they needed to do. Then everyone negotiated how the scenes might go together in the final video as there was more time for the editing process.

Seth: The students formed their own groups and had to figure out how to get the job done. I was the project manager and, thus, approved, challenged, and asked for amplification, as needed, to make sure every group had thought things through and was appropriately challenged.

STEP 10: Students assume a role—or multiple roles.

In a short scene, students will probably only play one role, which may be assigned or chosen. In a longer enactment, multiple roles may be involved, both an overarching role and service roles. The overarching (macro-frame) role has to do with the design of the knowledge artifact or the completion of the project. In service (micro-frame) roles, students learn what is necessary to perform the overarching role—for example, a cultural leader exploring how smoking affects children and the culture of the tribe—so this knowledge and their perspective can put it in their presentation, such as a video. They then return to the overarching role—for example, that of video producer.

Jeff: My students acted as guidance counselors. During the story, they also played the roles of parents, teachers, and students, which indirectly helped them understand the people they were serving. From the brainstormed possibilities, they chose the role of guidance counselor for this Mantle-of-the-Expert scene.

The Great Theme Park Challenge

A prestigious architectural firm who specializes in multimillion-dollar theme parks has come to this class and asked for help. The Disney Company has contacted them and would like them to submit a plan for a new theme park based on the travels of Odysseus. Since you are such an intelligent and creative group of individuals, the firm is nearly begging for your assistance. Your task is to design the park as you read *The Odyssey*; at the end of the book you will have a detailed layout of a family fun-park that chronicles the journey of this great hero.

In order to successfully create a working model, the class will need to work together to make sure that all tasks are being fulfilled. The following jobs will need to be taken by members of the class:

Rides and Attractions: All amusement parks need to have rides, and yours is no different. You are in charge of designing rides that are not only entertaining, but also closely fit the story line. Each ride should have characters that accompany the theme, and should be logically placed. The result should be sketches of six rides, and brief descriptions of each that include the relevance of the ride to the story.

Games: This task will require that six games be created that parallel the book. These games should reflect important points in the story, and show a great deal of creativity. Each game should be drawn out, with brief descriptions that show connectedness to the epic.

Food Court/Menu: Food is one of the best-selling items at theme parks. Your task is to create four food booths for the park, with a complete menu for each site. Disney wants to see the menu exactly as the park visitors will see it.

Museum/Visitor's Center: It will be important for families to gain a better understanding of the time period in which *The Odyssey* takes place.

Seth Mitchell's assignment cover sheet for his "Great Theme Park Challenge" project.

Janett: The students were health researchers and video documentary producers. But while creating the video, they also played the parts of cultural leaders, victims affected by smoking, friends or family members of the victims, interviewers, data analysts, video technicians, and others.

Seth: The students' overarching role was theme-park designer, but their service roles included being literature specialists, historians, engineers, financial planners, family experts, child psychologists, and children.

STEP 11: Teacher assumes a role.

The teacher assumes various roles that can assist students by providing them with challenges, questions, directives, and information. Her job is to extend old tasks and devise new ones, so that students continue to develop deeper understanding and skillful use of expert strategies and tools. This can be done from a role outside, alongside, or inside the enactment.

Jeff: I assumed the role of colleague, a guidance counselor who had organized the meeting. I reviewed the reason for the meeting and opened it up to questions for Laura. Then I pretty much stayed out of the way, except to emphasize an insight, complicate things that seemed too pat, or to encourage discussion.

Janett: I was alternatively the head video producer and fellow actor, critic, archivist, and research assistant to those students in role as researchers.

Seth: The role of the client who had commissioned the proposal was mine. Of course, I always wanted to know how things were going and offered suggestions. Sometimes I took on service roles—as a finance director who put new constraints on designs, or as a kid visiting the workshop who offered feedback.

Heathcote asserts that teachers can often help students the most by being in a subservient role in which they need assistance or direction from the student. The role of colleague also works well.

STEP 12: Groups, in role, engage in a series of tasks.

For extended Mantle-of-the-Expert enactments, classes are usually broken into different groups with different tasks. Any time students are engaged in the complex activity of making and designing things, a series of tasks must be completed. Teachers assist in this process by involving students in enactments that help them accomplish parts of the task, or they can use the momentum of the overarching task to help shape the work.

Jeff: In this short use of the strategy, the kids had two tasks: on the story level, to find out what is bugging Laura and try to help her, and on the more general level, brainstorm causes and solutions to bullying, based on their own experience and on Laura's case.

Janett: I involved students in a series of tasks, like the start-up strategy, to assign them a circumscribed area of expertise and then employed various role-plays and tableaux to get them to see the human consequences of smoking. When they'd had sufficient experiences and knew enough to consider the issue thoroughly, I gave the students more freedom to experiment and script scenes of their own. I became their technical assistant, teaching them blue screen, lighting, or aging techniques that served their purposes.

Seth: We did some different enactments during our reading, like hotseating Odysseus and holding debates between Athena, Telemachus, Penelope, and the suitors. But once we were done with the reading, creating a theme-park proposal became the enactment, and I intervened as necessary to challenge students in their overarching roles as experts or in the service roles.

Anchor Standards
for Writing, 7–9

Anchor Standards
for Reading, 6–8

Sample Roles for Mantle-of-the-Expert Enactments

Documentary Maker. Students make a documentary about an issue or series of issues. Jamie Heans and his student teachers, Jennah Doughty and Jessica Hyde, for example, had students watch *Looking for Richard*, a documentary about Shakespeare's *Richard III*, and the writing and staging of the play, before they read *Romeo and Juliet*. They asked students to create a documentary called *Looking for Romeo and Juliet* that would explore historical precedents and issues that came up for them in the play. Students ended up researching Verona, the history of the story, the history of family feuds through the ages, the conventions of dueling, different conceptions of justice, ideas about love and romance, and many other issues all delivered in a frenetic style with music that was inspired by *Looking for Richard*. Last year, Jamie focused student inquiry on language use and subtextual meaning in the play. Students then created a video in the role of Shakespearean scholars, called *Looking for Deeper Meaning in Romeo*.

Website Designer/PowerPoint Designer. Students produce a website, or other electronic artifact, for use during a presentation that documents what they have learned, offers a public service announcement (PSA), or other such information.

MTV Video Producer/Advertisement or PSA Producer. Students enjoy making MTV-like videos that are based on poems, convey a social message, or communicate the perspective of a character or author. They particularly enjoy performing parodies of popular music videos and songs.

Movie Producers. Recasting or reproducing scenes from stories to make them more modern or close to their own lives, much as director Baz Luhrmann did with *William Shakespeare's Romeo and Juliet*, is a popular and rewarding enactment. Any kind of movie-scene remake can be interesting to students and get them to see parallels. Some of my students once made a great update of a dance using *Pride and Prejudice* characters in a modern club/rave scene.

Radio-Show Host/Producer or Record-Company Producer. Students produce NPR-like documentaries on various topics. I sometimes use the National Writing Project CDs, which contain student writing and poetry about living in Maine, to inspire students to produce and

Mantles:
A Springboard
to Social Action

Many mantles can lead to social-action or service learning projects. When engaged in such work, I have the students go through the process of asking: *What? So what? Now what?* By planning and engaging in social-action projects, students actually become novice experts instead of just playing them, and the purposes of school become aligned with the purposes of real life.

Social-Action Thought Guide

What? What issue have we explored? What have we learned about it?

So what? What is the significance of what we have learned? Why is it important and to whom is it important?

Now what? What should we do? What should authorities do? How could we begin to work for or enact changes? What have experts decided and suggested be done? What will we do?

burn their own CDs with their own writing and music. (Order "Rural Voices Radio Shows" at www.writingproject.org.)

Museum Designer. Students design an exhibit, kiosk, or whole museum. (See Wilhelm and Edmiston, 1998, Chapters 1 and 3.) Teacher Julie Housum created an interactive Egyptian museum with her sixth-grade students (Housum, 1998). Upon entering, visitors to their museum walked down a time line of the Nile back into the past. Exhibits were arranged historically and involved Egyptian fashion and makeup, embalming and mummification, and Egyptian religion and gods. At the end of the tour, the Sphinx would foretell a visitor's future, if he or she wanted. The students played Egyptians from different eras and were well versed in their area of expertise. They could discuss their work, worldviews, and understanding of their exhibit topic at length.

Living Wax Museum Designer/Living Figures. Sixth-grade teachers Brian Ambrosius and Nancy Cook use this technique for a medieval fair their students hold. Students research particular historical figures (for example, Richard the Lion-Hearted, Saladin) or roles (serfs, minstrels) and create a living wax museum. Students pose as wax statues, and visitors step on buttons on the floor to get them to enact a typical action, recite their name and place in society, or to interview them.

Co-authors/Supplementary Material Editors. I ask a group of students who have read a book, perhaps in a literature circle, to create supplementary materials to aid future readers of the text. They might add sidebars to the text, suggest resources and websites for further information, create an About the Author page, make illustrations to go with the text, put together a study guide or jackdaw kit, or a "connections to today" section. They could also add ancillary information pages on particular topics that arise in the text, or create an award application for the book (a project that would entail learning about various book awards and writing an application). This information can be created electronically or posted on the Internet.

Blue-Ribbon Panel. After reading the young adult short story "Eva and the Mayor" (Okimoto, 1997), fifth-grade teacher Sharon Murray had students become a blue-ribbon panel trying to eliminate home-work problems and copying. She began by having Eva and Keneisha, two characters involved in a copying scandal, appear before this panel of teachers and child psychologists, using hotseat and alter-ego techniques. The panel then went on to deal with real cases and to make real recommendations. Such expert panels can address any kind of issue faced by a host of characters or by the kids in your school.

Public Relations Experts. Fifth-grade teacher Georgia Rhodes uses a technique she calls "critical review challenge." She begins by explaining that publishers have supplied important reviews on a particular book, then distributes the reviews, as well as excerpts from the book itself, for students to read. She goes on to inform them, "Even though the reviews were great, the book is just not selling. Your job is to create a PR campaign to jumpstart sales. You must include a new book jacket design, a poster illustrating an important scene or theme from the story, and a TV commercial. You might also choose to create playing cards, a game, or another kind of promotion. Your information must be factual and accurate, and your work must incorporate a quotation from a critical review. The company representatives want to see your work next Wednesday at 2 P.M. You will present you work and your justification of it at that time."

A possible variation would have different teams compete for a PR award, presenting all of their work at a convention where judges choose the best campaign.

Social Activists. Students take on the roles of environmentalists, protest organizers, or anyone with a soapbox topic to pursue and the desire to achieve some kind of social change. My students have engaged in many social action projects based on their reading and study.

Peer Counselor. Nicky Gamblin used a combination of Expert Panel and Peer Counselor to explore issues around drug abuse and depression while her ninth graders read *Go Ask Alice*. (See her guide, right.) The students then learned about peer counseling and role-played ways to approach Alice about her problem.

Advice Columnist. A variation is to write *Dear Abby* letters of advice to Alice. Students write advice to characters who experience conflicts or they can address real-life issues. This can also be done in talk-show format with characters meeting each other to hash out differences.

Topic
Issue
Points
Details

Go Ask Alice

Alice's Friendship

What problem can I help Alice with based on what I know about the situation?

What is the problem I want to deal with?	How is the problem affecting Alice's life positively and negatively?	How did Alice's environment fail to help her in her time of need?	What options would have helped Alice the most? In what ways would they have helped her?

The peer counseling guide that Nicky Gamblin's students used after reading *Go Ask Alice*.

Critics. Students write reviews of films, books, and projects. They can even review school policies, school facilities, cafeteria food, and so forth.

Historians. On several occasions, I've had students create and participate in a living history museum or consult with a local historical society, Civil War round table, and other groups about creating one.

Forensic Scientists/Archaeologists. Students look at, interpret, and evaluate evidence from a crime, environmental disaster, and other life-or-death situations. (See *The Wildlife Detectives*, Jackson, 2000.)

Scribe/Archivist/Record Keeper/Data Analyst/Research Assistant. In these roles, students help collect data, find background information, and record findings.

Political Advisor/Analyst. Acting as political advisors to historical figures, students hold a political summit or reenact a historical event such as the Yalta Conference.

Reporters/Writers/Authors. In a role such as reporter, op-ed writer, or commentator, students write about an issue being studied by summarizing events, weighing in on a controversy, or providing a personal opinion.

Lawyers. Students represent a client from a story or historical event and pursue a class-action suit on their behalf.

Psychologists. Students analyze characters, explaining situations and actions or trying to help resolve problems. Eleventh-grade teacher Patti Baldwin uses this technique with *The Scarlet Letter*. She has Hester Prynne visit a group of students cast as modern-day therapists trying to identify her issues, and Dimmesdale appears on a talk show to be interviewed as a deadbeat dad. You can see all the possible permutations!

Voices From the Field

Jeff:

The big thing I've learned is that "instructions" are not the same thing as "instruction." I used to think of instruction as telling students information. Now I am rethinking instruction as finding ways for me, as the teacher, to collaborate with students on real tasks where they learn through the process of actually doing or making something. Thought you'd be pleased to hear this. Maybe you passed the Mantle of Expertise on to me, and now I have a way of passing many such mantles to my students. Thanks.

—Thom

CHAPTER 8

EXTENDING OUR REACH
Using Technology With Drama/Action Strategies

I've long argued that teachers need to get hip to current technologies and integrate them into ongoing classroom projects (Wilhelm and Friedemann, 1998). On their own, technologies are somewhat limited. Technologies are meant to extend human capacities in order to do important and substantive work. Technologies always hold the promise of helping us to take on the "mantle of the expert" as we extend our capacities towards expertise and give us expert venues for discussing and sharing our learning. When we integrate technology into our classroom activities such as drama, we tap into what MIT psychologist Sherry Turkle calls the "natural holding power" of technology and of "game-like structures" like drama—this gives us an edge in leveraging technology to do compelling work.

In addition, being literate in the 21st Century, by anyone's definition, means being able to use the culture's most powerful tools to create, to communicate and receive meanings, to solve problems, and to represent what has been learned in usable ways. The new Common Core State Standards require the integration of technology across the curriculum in ways that will promote deep engagement and understanding.

We can extend any substantive activity in new ways through technology, and thus engage and extend our students' capacities. At the same time, everyone might learn how to use a specific technology, understand its limitations, and determine with a critical eye how and when to best use the technology. This kind of critical literacy and critical use of technology absolutely needs to be cultivated in schools. All technologies have tremendous benefits and also potentially significant costs. Sometimes technologies extend our capacities and sometimes they distract or truncate them. Nonetheless, I am a stalwart proponent of critically aware integration of technology across the curriculum.

One strategy I've used to help me integrate new technologies is to invite students to suggest how to use technologies in our class, or to find a knowledgeable teaching colleague to help me. This past year I worked with Rachel Bear at Boise High School who helped immeasurably as we infused technology into all of our work, including drama/action strategies. Equally helpful has been my colleague Dianne Ruxton at Boise's Capital High, who serves as my National Writing Project site technology liaison. Find friends like these, be willing to learn from your students, and you'll extend your teaching with technology in exciting and useful ways.

Integrating Technology: A Promise and a Warning

Classics scholar Jay David Bolter (1991) has argued that being literate has always meant the capacity to use a culture's most powerful tools for making and communicating meanings. In our studies on boys and literacy (Smith and Wilhelm, 2002; 2006), we found that our informants were cynical about teachers who did not use technology. "They teach us with paper and pencils for a world of calculators and computers," one boy sneered. The boys in our studies wanted literacy in school to match and prepare them for the literacies they encountered and saw used in their lives beyond school. There is no question that our culture's most powerful current tools for making and communicating meanings are now electronic, digital, and multimodal. If we are not using these tools, we are not preparing students for literacy in the future, or even for the current moment. This promise is one we must work to fully actualize for our students, and drama activities are an excellent starting point.

However, there is also a caveat: Technology is not a substitute for substance, either conceptually or procedurally. As one expert put it: "We should not just review our curricula, but our everyday lessons for relevance, for some connection between students' education, experiences and future" and realize that "a superior tool giving us superior access still does not constitute deep thinking or understanding" because "computers cannot substitute for substance" (Kathriner, 2007).

21st Century Literacy

CCSS

Anchor Standards
for Reading, 1–9
Anchor Standards
for Writing, 1–9

There's been a lot of talk recently about 21st-century literacies and what constitutes them. I like this definition: Students use critical thinking skills to plan and conduct their own critical inquiries, manage projects, solve problems, make informed decisions, and take informed actions using appropriate digital tools and resources.

Students:

- identify and define authentic problems and significant questions for investigation.

- plan, decompose, and manage activities to develop a situation or complete a project.

- collect, organize, and analyze data to perceive patterns, explain patterns, extrapolate and interpolate, identify solutions, and/or make informed decisions.

- use multiple processes and diverse perspectives to explore alternative solutions.

- represent understandings and take informed actions—using technologies throughout as appropriate to do so.

In-Role Correspondence Dramas

We used a variation of Good Angel/Bad Angel with students posting comments on a Facebook page created for fictional characters from students' readings, or through a blog or wiki format, at the point of decision/ethical dilemmas. For example, when students were reading *Frankenstein*:

Purpose: Explore the various motivations and perspectives of an ethical dilemma facing a character and the possible consequences of various actions. In this case, we will consider whether Dr. Frankenstein should chase down and eliminate the creature he has created; later we will alternate roles as good or bad angels and discuss whether he should create a mate for his creature.

Process: Use a discussion board or character Facebook page. Those assigned to be good angels brainstorm and post your advice about what to do and why—you are allowed to say anything that you think will convince Dr. Frankenstein to do what you believe is the right action. Bad angels, you respond to the good angels and make your own argument to convince Dr. Frankenstein to do something that you think cannot be ethically justified.

Deliverable: Read through all the comments from the good and the bad angels. Write a one pager in role as Dr. Frankenstein: What arguments most convinced you? What are you now going to do and why?

In-role Blogging

Individual wikipages are great for a blog-in-role. We often use the discussion feature on each page to comment ourselves as teacher on blogs, but we can also comment in role as another character, just as one would with a real blog. We also sometimes use the discussion feature on each page to do various kinds of correspondence drama. You can embed a chat window on the wikispace to do a synchronous "chat-in-role."

These kinds of chats can occur with teacher or students playing the role of the author or a popular culture figure interested in the inquiry. In the case of *Frankenstein*, our inquiry question was about the costs and benefits of technology, and we played Mary Shelley, Steve Jobs, Bill Gates, Galileo, Alan Turing (who helped break the Enigma code during World War II by inventing the Bronze Goddess—the first computer), and many other figures who have strong opinions on the subject.

RAFT (Role—Audience—Format—Topic) writing and responses using GoogleDocs, which embeds comments or revision suggestions from other characters about what has been written.

RAFT Example for *Frankenstein*:

Purpose: To explore how popular culture figures, authors, or characters from other material we have read during this unit or this school year might feel about the costs and benefits of technology.

Process: Brainstorm well-known figures from our unit, school year, or the world who would feel strongly about the issue of technology and its costs and benefits (Steve Jobs, Okonkwo, Winston Smith, Dalai Lama, scientists from our frontloading PowerPoint).

Identify the **role** you want to take. Who will serve as your **audience**? What **format** do you want to use: informal letter, Public Service Announcement, op-ed piece, argument, extended definition of technology, script for introduction or ad for a documentary, and so on.

Topic: What are the costs and benefits of technology, in general or in particular, e.g., cell phones in schools, Facebook, and interaction with friends?

When complete, you will comment in your role on the compositions shared by two other students in-role as characters by using the GoogleDocs comment feature.

Video Technologies

In my experience, students love to make videos. The past two years, working with Rachel in her AP English class as well as working with younger and struggling students in other classes, I've seen many kids gravitate to making videos. This has become easier and quicker to do over time with the advent of tiny video cameras (in most cell phones) and video editing software like iMovie.

My friend and NWP fellow Jamie Heans assigns students reading *Romeo and Juliet* to form video production teams. Each team has a couple of important scenes and is assigned a literary convention from each. Their job is to create a video glossary entry, a summary of their scene, and a video production trailer for the play. Students read their scene and identify the literary convention they were assigned as they consider how the use of this convention contributed to the meaning of the scene. They create a video that summarizes the scene, defines the convention assigned to them for that scene, and then demonstrates and explains how that convention helped to create the experience and meaning of that scene. These videos are put together on a CD or DVD which is given to each student. The result? Each student has a video glossary of all the major literary terms required by the curriculum, a summary of all the major scenes in the play in order, as well as a model trailer for a proposed film version of the play, and often a series of bloopers!

**Anchor Standards
for Reading, 3–6**

Jamie's students often create these videos fairly quickly. Though they do a lot of planning, the actual recording and editing often occurs over a lunch or study hall period. The videos are funny, creative, and point-on correct. They often include asides and commentary and comparisons with issues in the students' own lives.

Videos as Frontloading

In Rachel's class we used videos in several different ways. For our "What work does funny do?" unit on satire and parody, our frontloading was to have students post YouTube videos that they thought were funny onto our class wiki. Students then ranked the videos for their funniness. We then classified the videos into "types" of funny: slapstick, misdirection, satire, pastiche, parody, etc. We identified the different kinds of work each kind of "funny" or humor could do. To throw in a drama component, we asked students to identify what was funny or worked for them in-role as different characters from our past units.

Teacher Tip

Google Launches YouTube for Schools

Google is aiming to provide educators and students access to educational content through a network called YouTube for Schools. The site is designed to link participating schools to educational videos from more than 600 partners such as the Smithsonian Institution and TED. Users also can access some 300 playlists created by teachers and organized by subject and grade level. Ubergizmo.com

We also had students form video teams where they took on the "mantle of the expert" as designers of various kinds making documentaries and "how-to" videos, ranging from demonstrations that were more conceptual to those that were more procedural (e.g., a conceptual documentary about slavery based on *Heart of Darkness*, with students interviewed in various roles from the novella; a satiric how-to/process video about how to destroy another culture based on *Things Fall Apart*). The final project for the class involved the option of creating a video that explored, in role, a theme that had run across the year. My daughter Jasmine and her friend Laura created a wonderful video entitled *Still Waiting for Godot* that traced various forms of existentialist philosophy across various works. They played the roles of Estragon and Vladimir visiting Meursault from *The Stranger*, Gregor the cockroach from *The Metamorphosis*, and other characters to get advice about where to find Godot as well as insights on other pressing existential topics.

With some of the younger groups I've worked with, we created a variety of different Into the Past/Into the Future Choral Montages that we videotaped and shared. We created montages in which characters reported their current feelings and thoughts about a situation, then stepped into the past or into the future to report on changes, predictions, or what they used to think and why this had changed. We did a variety of before and after montages in role to explore character change and to explain this change—which always led us to rich discussions of thematic meanings.

Using Audio Tools With Role-Playing

Talk Radio Show/Podcast

Another fail-safe technique is the talk radio show. I've used it in many different ways, with and without technology, and it is always magic. Follow these simple steps: present a true dilemma, brainstorm roles, allow students a brief period to rehearse their in-role contributions, and you and your students are off to the races.

Example from *Frankenstein:*

Purpose: To tie *Frankenstein* to our overall inquiry, exploring how the book comments on the inquiry about the costs and benefits of technology and how this commentary relates to the world. Bringing different perspectives offered in our readings and in popular culture together in conversation to see points of contact, similarity and difference, to justify different points of view and see the reasoning behind them, and to come to our own justified and reasoned point of view on the issue: What are the costs and benefits of technology?

Process: Brainstorm characters who would have strong feelings and arguments about this topic, and cultural points of view about the topic. What would our characters say in answer to our inquiry question? What comments might they make to Dr. Frankenstein at this point in the story (e.g., when he considers killing his creation or running away/when he knows the creature is killing/when the creature asks him for a mate)? Rehearse and practice.

Option: You could do a hotseat version with Dr. Frankenstein as a guest, or with Dr. Frankenstein and some other characters as a panel who will answer questions.

Deliverable: In-role contribution to your small-group radio show and then our large-group radio show. Also respond, in your role, to the comment of one other character. We will record and archive the shows as podcasts. Share your podcast with someone who is not in this class and get their reaction: What points of view most convinced them and why? What do they think about the topic that was discussed? Do they know any real or fictional characters who would have strong feelings and thoughts about the issue of the costs and benefits of technology? If this person had entered the conversation, what would they have said?

My students enjoy audiotaping voiceovers or musical scores to go with their presentations of slide shows, making this presentation into a multimedia extravaganza. Sometimes they also use lighting, dance movements, and other multimodal features and videotape their presentations.

CHAPTER 9

TABLEAUX
Visualizing Meaning Through Image and Gesture

Tableaux are yet another set of drama techniques that are easily adopted and adapted by students. A group of fifth graders is reading and talking about *Sukey and the Mermaid*, by Daniel San Souci, in a literature circle. After their final discussion, they present to the class a series of tableaux, or living statues, culminating with one of Sukey's fiancé Dembo rising from his coffin and pointing at Mr. Jones. Kirsty, playing the role of commentator, says, "This is the last major scene of the story, and it's kind of the conclusion because now Sukey and Dembo can get married, and Mr. Jones gets his just desserts!" The students in the statue now melt from their frozen postures and create a new statue, with two students holding a swath of blue cloth that they flutter to simulate the ocean waves. Another student rises from behind the cloth and puts her hand to her forehead, looking out into the distance. Three students to the right hug each other as a fourth lies at their feet. Kirsty explains to the class: "This statue represents the meaning of the story.

The family is safe because they stuck together, which we show with the hug. Mr. Jones dies because he wouldn't follow the rules of the community. And the mermaid is watching everything to help things work out. We think the [Gullah] islanders tell this folktale because they believe you have to stick together to fight for what is right, and that there are powers like the mermaid that will help you fight for what is good!" The rest of the class claps wildly as the students in front of the classroom take their bows.

Afterwards, Kirsty has this to say: "You know how they say a picture paints a thousand words? Well our slide show (or series of tableaux) did that same thing. With pictures, it told the whole story, and what it meant, in about three minutes flat. We were that good!"

Tableaux: A Definition

The family of enactment strategies we will explore in this chapter is called Tableaux. It makes use of visual and kinesthetic intelligences, which are often not used in schools (Gardner, 1983). The word "tableau" (singular) derives from the French word for visual presentation. In enactment, this can be done in a variety of ways, using the body or bodies in combination. It generally takes the form of a frozen scene or pose that captures a physical, psychological, or emotional relationship. This technique can be adapted to include some movement, speaking, and other features, variations described in more detail below. These types of variations are known as a "tableux vivant." Or several scenes or poses can be strung together to form "tableaux" (plural), which can work together as a kind of slide show, as in the example above. Tableaux help students visualize and explore both the text and the subtext of a narrative, including settings, scenes, situations, characters, relationships, and meanings. They can represent vocabulary, create mental models of complex concepts and procedures, or visually translate a host of themes and ideas.

Benefits of Tableaux

Tableaux help students visualize, perceive, and consider

- characters.
- relationships between people, forces, or ideas.
- scenes, settings, situations, contexts, and situated meanings.
- key details and features of a text or textual experience, and how these relate to make patterns of meaning.

Tableaux also help students

- represent understandings in a unique way.
- attend to thoughts and feelings of characters and an author.
- explore and portray an author's thematic generalizations.
- identify and understand text structure.

Anchor Standards
for Reading, 1–10

Anchor Standards
for Writing, 1–4

Anchor Standards for
Speaking and Listening,
1–6, esp. 4–5

Tableaux require students to

- be active.
- speak with each other.
- experiment with various depictions and ways of representing what is thought and known.
- consider textual meaning deeply.
- communicate their own interpretations.

Tableaux develop

- kinesthetic intelligence.
- an ability to work our understandings and responses into the physical fabrics of our being, our "body memory".

Tableaux also give students the opportunity to

- share literary experiences.
- create a concrete experience to see, share, and reflect upon.
- voice their own opinions.
- be active and interactive; to make and do things.
- work together and to share with others.

Creating a Tableau: Guidelines for Students

To create a tableau, familiarize students with these steps:

1. **Choose the story, text, or part of a text that you wish to depict visually and share with each other or an audience.** (A tableau works with any kind of text, data set, or information.) In Kirsty's class, studying how to give voice to the voiceless, her literature circle chose to read some shorter texts, like *Sukey and the Mermaid*, a folktale from the Gullah islands; another group chose to read Whelan's (2000) *Homeless Bird*, a story about Koly, who is subjected to an arranged marriage in her home of India. Both groups decided to share their reading with the rest of the class through the use of tableaux.

2. **Identify central concepts (informational texts) or events (narrative texts) that are crucial to understanding the whole text.** Kirsty's group used tableaux to share the main events of

their story—and through these the cultural significance of the story itself and its use of a mermaid. Those reading *Homeless Bird* used tableaux to share the key events from the beginning of their book and to demonstrate the cultural traditions, such as marriage customs, that affected Koly and how she was silenced.

3 **Review the important ideas, events, and/or details that an audience will need to know regarding each concept or scene.** Kirsty's group identified these key events: Mr. Jones's ill treatment of Sukey, her meeting with the mermaid, Mr. Jones's attempt to catch the mermaid, Sukey's life with the mermaid, Sukey's return, the murder of Dembo, and Mr. Jones's being brought to justice through Sukey's using of her newfound voice. The group working with *Homeless Bird* paid scrupulous attention to teasing out cultural information like the effects of overpopulation and hunger on girls, the importance of a dowry, and the age at which a girl is marriageable.

4 **Work with your group to consider how to present these scenes visually in a way that will communicate the important details and implied meanings to the audience.** Kirsty's group discussed the possible messages of the folktale and why it has been retold for so many years. When they decided it was about facing problems and working together to meet them, the students experimented with ways of showing people sticking together (like the group hug) and ways of conveying that someone was outside the community because of his actions.

5 **When you are done with your tableaux, be sure the audience has help in "seeing" and understanding the whole story or the importance of the concepts explored.** The *Homeless Bird* group wished to show how and why boys and girls were treated differently, particularly why Koly was denied an education. They decided to do mirror tableaux, with boys on the one side and girls on the other. They ran through a series of scenes that were mirrored, for example, boys in school writing, girls at home embroidering. To make sure that the other students understood difficult concepts like caste and how it affected marriage arrangements, the figures in the tableaux would come alive and explain how their scene reflected these concepts.

Tableaux can also be created through drawings, collages, and other fine art media. (See Wilhelm, 2004/2012, for explanations of visualization strategies like visual tableaux.) I used the brainstorming sheet and guidelines on pages 138 and 139 with fourth and fifth graders who were inquiring into culture to help them create tableaux about a folk tale or fairytale.

Building Background

To assist students in considering the power of a single gesture to communicate a theme, have them make various gestures and challenge other students to tell their theme or meaning. Gestures such as placing one's hand over one's heart during the Pledge of Allegiance, a military salute, a flag flown at half mast, a wave hello, a raised clenched fist, the peace sign, a thumbs up, a high five, and grasping your head let students see how to communicate significant meanings. The same can be done with various body postures and facial expressions. All this will help students see the variety of gestures available to them when constructing tableaux.

Tableaux of Folk Tale or Fairytale Brainstorming Sheet

Name:

The culture my group is studying:

The title of the folk tale or fairytale we have chosen:

I think the story reveals that this culture cares about and values:

Meaning of the tale to the culture/the reason they tell this story:

The 4 to 6 major scenes to be presented in the tableaux will be:

1.

2.

3.

4.

5.

6.

The meaning (main idea) of the story will be shared by:

Elements of folk tales (the number three, use of riddles, use of youngest sibling, for example) will be depicted in the tableaux by:

Our tableaux will show some of the following cultural information as indicated:

1. traditional clothing or costumes, by _____

2. architecture, by _____

3. setting/geography, by _____

4. typical activities, by _____

5. rules for behavior, by _____

6. values, by _____

7. other cultural artifacts or information, by _____

8. education/raising the young, by _____

Guidelines for Creating Enacted Tableaux/Slide Shows

The pressure is on! You have 20 minutes to create and rehearse your tableaux, then present them by the end of the class period!

1 **Pick out four to six scenes that you feel summarize the story or display aspects of the central concept.** (This number may vary depending on the text or assignment.) Decide on the characters (or forces or ideas), setting, and other details that need to be visually communicated.

2 **Write or describe short telegraphic summaries of what each tableau should communicate about the event, detail, or conceptual aspect that is being displayed.** Determine how the characters (or forces or ideas) will move and what they will do visually to depict the important details, emotions, aspects, and the significance of what you are presenting.

3 **Create, act out, and freeze the scene or mental model into a tableau, as if you were suddenly made into statues, at the high point or most illuminating juncture of your scene/depiction.**

4 **"Melt" the tableau and reform it into another one that captures the next event or key detail.**

5 **Rehearse and perform.** Your complete presentation of several tableaux and commentary should be approximately three minutes. (This length may vary depending on task, text, or assignment.)

Using Tableaux With "The Fan Club"

During the story drama that I use to support reading "The Fan Club," I have used different kinds of tableaux.

Prequel

The purpose of a prequel is to get to the pretext of the story, the events that happened before the story begins. To get started, I ask groups of students to consider Laura's past. What from her past causes her to be the way she is? I then ask students to form a snapshot of a scene that probably happened to Laura in her past that may be causing the particular attitudes and sensitivities that she displays. In the case of "The Fan Club," the students could depict a scene from school that is actually described, but I most often ask them to infer a possible scene from Laura's life that would have explanatory power about her current character. This in turn can lead to diary writing or hotseating, through which a student in role as Laura can be asked what she remembers about a particular incident and how she thinks this has affected her.

One Thing

Another kind of tableau is called "One Thing" because students think about one thing in the past that might have changed this character's life, and then enact or display it. These techniques help students to see how powerful events and relationships can shape our character, and how decisions we make can change our situation, our attitudes, and our very being. I also like how it foregrounds "agency," the recognition that we have the power to change our lives and others' by choosing to make decisions or engage with each other in particular ways and to respond to events more positively, seeking the possible value that might come from them. Many of my students do not feel a sense of agency, and I want to explore with them some ways they actually do possess agency and ways they might exercise this power.

Commemoration

Commemoration is effective in exploring an author's thematic generalization and helping students to articulate the ideas and beliefs they should take away from a story. I use this technique often because

I know that few of my students are expert at identifying an author's point and justifying it with evidence from a text. Indeed, the national assessments over the past twenty years show that fewer than 10 percent of graduating high school seniors are adept at this skill. Yet this ability is profoundly important: It allows a reader to "converse" with authors, to learn from their reading, and to use their reading for thinking and acting. Reading cannot transform us if we cannot understand what the implied author is communicating to us (see Wilhelm and Novak, 2011 for a full exploration of this idea).

After reading "The Fan Club," I ask groups to create a statue commemorating the meaning of the story events. I sometimes tell them these statues have been commissioned by the student council or school board and there will be a competition to decide which statue should be built and placed in front of the school. This lends reality and purpose to the tableaux. If I think the students need more help expressing the story's central thematic generalization, I might provide a bit more framing. For example, I might tell them that the statues are being commissioned by representatives from a history museum doing a display on how civil rights are violated in our communities, by a concerned citizens' group organizing a Bullying Awareness Week, or by school officials as part of a campaign to eradicate peer harassment.

If I do not feel it is necessary to provide this information, students independently come up with the story topic, or general subject, themselves.

Another way to assist them is by telling them to remember our TDP Strategy:

(T) Every text has a major *topic* (a general subject that it explores—in fact, most texts have several topics but as long as students can justify one that they think is general and major they are using the strategy).

(D) The identified topic is explored through the use of *details* or *events*.

(P) The syllogism, or scheme, or pattern and trajectory of details or events and their consequences lead up to or accrue to a *point* made about the topic of the piece that can be generalized and applied to life or the human condition. (For a complete heuristic of reading for main ideas, see the think aloud book in this series, Wilhelm 2001/2012).

Tableaux Evaluation/Reflection Sheet

Name: Douglas

Group members presenting tableaux: Fiona, Jaggy, Denali, Scott
Silky + the Mermaid

1. What were the major ideas or events depicted in the tableaux? That Silky had lots of problems but she got through because she asked the mermaid for help.

2. How was one of the ideas or events creatively depicted? They had Silky being pulled apart by reality on one side and escape on the other

a. How did this enhance your understanding and/or enjoyment? What did you realize or learn that was not obvious from your reading? I realized Silky wanted to escape her problems, but then saw she had to face them! I didn't realize the mermaid helped her do both things.

3. What personal connections did you make to the information or emotions presented? I realize I feel the same way sometimes. I know I have to face my problems but I want to run away.

4. What central idea, concept or theme are you taking away from the experience of watching the tableaux? The story's main idea is to face your problems head on + you can overcome them.

5. How might you use the information or ideas presented? In your further reading, in your life, etc.? It's a good story to think with— I wonder who my mermaid is? Like a fairy godmother?

6. What might have made the tableaux even better? Add movement- Silky being pulled one way then the other.

A student's filled-out Tableaux Evaluation/ Reflection Sheet.

I tell my students that through their tableaux, the *point about life* needs to be clear to the audience. In other words, whatever they learned as readers through the accumulation of detail and, most of all, by the ultimate consequences and conclusion, must be conveyed through image and gesture. This needs to be a lesson learned from the pattern of details in the story or text, that can be applied to their lives outside of the story.

Sequel

Another tableaux technique that I use with "The Fan Club" is sequel or "scene after the story." I ask students to imagine a future scene between Laura and Rachel, or Laura and the rest of the "cool kids" in the fan club. To complicate it, I ask them to make two (or more) tableaux of various possibilities—for example, the best possible scenario and worst possible scenario for Laura or Rachel, or the most and least morally satisfying scenes. Afterward, we might vote as a class on what seems most likely and discuss why. We talk about which ending we like best or find most satisfying and why. We talk about the different lessons or thematic generalizations that would be conveyed by these two different story extensions. This best/worst scenario technique also works nicely at a climax or a point in the story when a character must make a major decision. Tableaux can be created to explore the possible consequences that could occur

Choosing the Enactment Strategies to Use

cannot emphasize this enough: Use enactment techniques to help students through their ZPD (zones of proximal development), to see and do *new* things as readers and thinkers. If all, or even most, of your students already know or can do something, then don't use an enactment technique (or any other instructional strategy) that merely encourages kids to do what they already can do. Choose a technique that helps them develop a strategy or understand a concept that is not yet available to them, or has not yet been mastered.

I use different techniques depending on my assessment of which strategies students already use and which they don't. Enactments can always be a formative assessment: they are great for revealing to me what students are understanding and, by implication, what they are not understanding yet. In this way, using one enactment can help me plan the next one based on what I find out my students can't yet do, but could do with my help. Enactment makes the things the students understand and how they are thinking visible to the teacher, so assessment is continuous and support can be delivered seamlessly at the point of need.

And again, for each general enactment strategy, there are hundreds of variations. Choose one, combine or adapt some, or even invent one of your own to help your students learn something new. To quote Austin Powers of cinema satire fame, "Play with it, baby. Work it!" Work it so that it fits the needs of your students.

based on various decisions. This allows students to examine ideas like probability or moral satisfaction, the effect of consequences and endings on the thematic generalization learned from a text, and promotes social imagination and decency.

A Sample Tableau Plan for *The Outsiders*

(Adapted from the work of Nicky Gamblin)

Goals:

- To understand, see, and feel the events from Chapter 4.
- To make inferences about character relationships, thoughts, and feelings.
- To understand the causes and consequences of the chapter's events.
- To make connections from the text to personal reality and the community/world.

CCSS

Anchor Standards
for Reading, 1–7
Writing, 7, 9
Speaking and
Listening, 1–4
Language, 3, 5

1. Build background knowledge.

Word association activity: PANIC (3 minutes)

We will stand in a circle and speak in turn to the following prompt:

> What does the word "panic" mean to you? What thoughts, images, or ideas does it bring to mind? Keep responses short to a word or phrase.

When done, we will write a poem or montage about panic based on the responses. A recorder can write down responses on chart paper, or students can be asked to remember their lines.

In your journal: Think of a situation that caused or could cause panic in your life. Write about the feeling and how it made you react.

Speaking in turn: Based on your journal writing, we will stand in a circle again and speak in turn to the following prompt: How does panic make people feel? (I will start with "Like a deer in the headlights.") We will make a poem or choral montage with what people say.

2. Have students read Chapter 4, the fountain scene, in literature circle groups.

3. Assign homework.

In your journal: Everyone in the group will write a diary entry, dividing up the roles of Ponyboy, Johnny, Bob, or Randy. or will write a group police interview transcript involving these characters. You will work in a group, and each member should choose a different role. You will have to make inferences about your character's thoughts, feelings, goals, and reactions—get inside the mind of your character. Answer the following five questions, which will set the scenes for your Tableaux:

- What were you thinking and feeling when the blue Mustang pulled up?
- What were you thinking and feeling when you knew there was going to be a fight?
- What were you thinking and feeling when Ponyboy's head was being held under the water?
- What were you thinking and feeling when Johnny attacked Bob with the knife?
- What were you thinking and feeling when you saw that Bob was dead?

4. Plan and perform tableaux.

- Work with another group to create a "slide show" of the chapter. The slide show will depict each of the five most important scenes. You might choose to act and freeze, then act your way into another frozen picture, or you can simply depict one frozen scene after another. Groups will be paired: One group will do scenes 1, 3, and 5, the other group will do scenes 2 and 4 and provide a final commentary explaining the lesson or generalization we can take away about the topic of "panic" from this pattern of events.
- Make sure your audience can "see" what is happening in each scene.
- During each scene, we will use the "unfreeze/freeze" technique. Each character will unfreeze and say what he is thinking and feeling, then freeze again.

5. Consider another option.

Create a tableau for a "what could have happened" scene to show how someone could have made a different decision and thus changed everything.

6. Reflect.

- After we have seen every group's tableaux, we will discuss how people in general and characters in particular react when they are panicked, and compare this to how they could have and should have reacted. We will then discuss why we do not react more rationally, reasonably, or appropriately, and how we might train ourselves to respond positively in negative situations.
- We will also evaluate our use of tableau techniques. What worked well? How did groups work differently? What did we know from the text and what did we have to infer? Why might an author only tell us so much about a character or situation and leave us to figure out the rest? What interpretations fit best with the information given in the book? What do we wish we had tried? What might we do next time?

7. Follow-up.

Each group creates a Conceptual Tableau or Concept Machine (this is a kind of tableau where each person does an individual tableau followed by the next person and so on—so that the audience gets a machine-like series of pictures of a story or sets of connections) that explores or expresses the concept of "panic." If you choose, two groups can work together to depict this psychological state through the concept machine.

Variations of the Tableaux Techniques

In *The Outsiders* example, we saw many tableau variations being used: slide show, unfreeze/freeze or melting tableaux, what could have happened, machines, and conceptual tableaux. Here, I'll explain some of those techniques, and others, in more detail.

Gestos. Defined by Bertholt Brecht as "an action on stage that shows the true relationship between characters," this is a mini-tableau that can be performed by one or two people. The idea is to get the student or students to summarize the relationship between characters (or ideas, objects, or forces) quickly, with a simple gesture and expression.

Snapshot. When students are reading, ask them to stop and imagine a snapshot of the action. The result can be hand drawn, created on the computer, or performed as a dramatic tableau.

Slide Show. Here, students put together several tableaux to tell the coherent story of how several events (or ideas, objects, or forces) relate to each other or lead to one another. The slides can be animated and then frozen, start frozen and be tapped awake, or they can simply remain frozen. A variation on the slide show (or any other tableaux) is to add the Mantle of the Expert to get an informed commentary—for example, having a student play the role of a professor explaining a phenomenon to his classes, or a detective or expert witness describing a crime scene.

Machine/Concept Machine. This technique is similar to slide show in that it progresses element by element, and the presentation builds step by step. I first used this technique at the Chicago Teachers Center. Jackie Murphy, the leader of the session, asked the students participating how a particular character was feeling. When they said he was "stressed out," Jackie asked them to form a machine showing his psychological state. The first student stood in the middle of the class and acted like she was pulling her hair out in a repetitive motion. One by one, students had to add a layer to the machine. The second student paced back and forth behind the first student. The third student put her hand above her eyes and peered about robotically as if looking for a solution. Three more students joined the machine. Then Jackie asked what would happen if something happened to add more stress. The machine quickened its pace. Finally, she had the students consider what could happen that would relieve the situation. Answers were given and students were asked how the character would feel then. They made another machine for "relieved"—the centerpiece of which was a student lounging on a beach.

I've also seen this technique done in a kind of forum where the audience advises the student joining the machine what he might do. Another variation is to have one or a few students represent a main idea of a text and then have others add ideas and elements that support that idea. Still another variation is to require that the first event or image causes or leads to the next one in a way that is obvious or can be explained.

Conceptual or Vocabulary Tableaux. The main-idea machine can become a kind of conceptual web that visually depicts the relationships of ideas. In a recent science unit, my students were building bridges. A group of four boys pushed on two sides of a bridge made of cardboard boxes to represent the physical force of "compression," then pushed down on the boxes to represent "tension." The group created a bridge with the two boys on the sides pushing in and the two on the top pushing down to show how these forces work together to keep a bridge from falling down.

Frozen Tableau: Tapped Alive

Tapping Alive/Hotseating. The teacher, student, or a group member can tap participants in a frozen tableau to come to life so they can make a comment or be interviewed as if they were in a hotseat. They can explain their actions, feelings, or details of how the story got to this point. For *Homeless Bird*, the group created a tableau representing Koly's wedding picture. Koly was tapped alive to tell what she felt on that day and what she felt years later looking back on that day. I've also used tapping alive with science by having kids in role as elements or electrical charges explain the role of individual elements or of negative charges in different physical conditions.

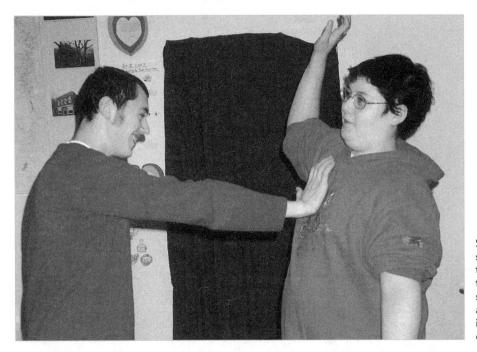

Students stage a two-person tableaux summarizing a character's internal dilemma.

Talking Statue/Talking Portrait. Students can become statues or portraits that come to life and give their views. Again, for *Homeless Bird*, Koly and the others in the wedding party took turns reciting monologues about their feelings.

Re-enactment Drama: Entering a Story World

Dorian Gray. Using the Oscar Wilde story of *The Picture of Dorian Gray* as inspiration, students can use snapshot or portrait tableaux to show the inner psychological condition of the character or characters.

Family Portraits. Noted drama educator Cecily O'Neill uses this activity as a "getting started" technique by having students create a family portrait of characters before reading or experiencing what happens to them, based on the book's cover, title, and introduction, and the students' background knowledge, expectations, and reading to that point. For example, for a story about pioneers in America, students could pose as characters on a wagon train preparing to head West. They might depict the "family" relationships, which don't have to be blood relationships, but relationships among characters or even ideas. From within the frame of the family portrait, individual characters can be asked by the class what they are looking forward to, what they fear, what they will miss the most, or what they may regret. The technique can also be used to form a kind of slide show or family album, tracing changes in the characters and their relationships as the story continues by adding new snapshots, candids, or portraits. And, of course, there can be a final family portrait from which characters look back on their experiences and comment upon them or are interviewed about them. I often take photos of the dramatic tableux to create a scrapbook of the story, something you'll see on the DVD in the re-enactment drama.

Remember, too, that characters don't have to be the basis for or subject of the Tableaux. Forces (such as electrical charges, gravity, greed, or jealousy), concepts (such as addition, diffusion, or friendship), inanimate objects (such as important or symbolic objects from a story), or ideas (such as democracy) work as well. In this case, the purpose would be to put related ideas into families and to depict their relationships, or how relationships, for example of chemical elements, change under certain conditions. Students can wear name tags of chemical elements or other visual devices to help identify who is representing what.

Baby Book/Timeline/Personal History. Taking their cues from a family photo album, students can create a series of events from a character's life, or tell about a character's history, through a series of images or events presented through tableaux.

Daily Life. When team-teaching history, my colleague Paul Friedemann and I often tried to get students to imagine the daily life of women, minorities, or common people whose stories were not told. In the context of a unit, after the students had enough information about their subjects' daily life, we asked them to imagine they were people from that era and then create "stills" or "moments," showing what it was like getting up in the morning, at mealtime, at work, and in their homes. There was generally no speaking as students worked together to show the daily life of a particular group.

Curtains/Hidden Scenes. In a class taught by Seth Mitchell, I observed groups of students creating tableaux of poems. One group doing "Richard Cory" formed a human curtain and then opened it slowly to reveal the surprise ending. This technique works well when the author presents a sudden change—when the reader expects one thing and receives another. The human curtain delays the revelation, giving it more effect.

What If /Missing Scenes/Multiple Endings. In *The Outsiders* tableaux, Nicky Gamblin had her students enact a "what could have happened" scene. Similarly, students can also enact missing scenes or possible "behind the scenes" tableaux of details the author could have included. One variation I quite like is Multiple Endings, which I usually do before the end of a story, or at the end of a story when we don't know what will happen to the characters as a result of their actions, as with "The Fan Club."

Students create tableaux to explore different possibilities. For example, they could create tableaux for

- the most desirable outcome for character 1; least desirable outcome.

- the most desirable outcome for character 2; least desirable outcome.

- a compromise ending.

- an alternative/completely different ending.

Students then have experiences to think with as they discuss questions such as:

- Which ending is most likely? Why do we think so?

- Which is most dramatic? Why?

- What is most desirable from your point of view? Why?

- What point is made by each ending? What ideological position would the author be taking in each case?

In this way, authorial choice is foregrounded—the students can see that texts are constructed to make certain points and could be constructed differently to make different points.

Kamishibai. In this itinerant storytelling tradition from Japan, the Kamishibai man announces his arrival by clapping together two wooden blocks and preparing a stage. As he tells his story, he uses drawings to illustrate. In my classroom, the storyteller claps the blocks and retells his story, while his "assistants" create physical tableaux to illustrate meaning. Sometimes they create a slide show or video version of the story. Though my students and I usually rehearse before a presentation, we also work spontaneously if the students are sharp and on top of things!

I quite often use this strategy when groups of students are reading different stories or texts around the same topic. Kamishibai becomes a way to share the stories and their meaning with each other in a highly ritualized manner. The group helping the storyteller can also provide sound effects, music, and other devices to aid the storytelling. Interestingly, the Kamishibai man was also a candy seller, so we often have treats when we do these performances.

Voices From the Field

Jeff:

My fifth grade science class is still "exploring space." You have heard so much about this already, I am sure you feel like you are part of the unit! We are studying the life cycle of stars and ages of stars (depending on color, etc.). I put the kids into groups and instructed each group to take on the role of a star. Each had to dramatize a personal lifeline of the star from birth to death.

I then asked the same groups to act out the various stages from the beginning to the end. Though there are six stages, I added a substage to each. The students, therefore, needed to depict through their tableaux 12 different points in the life of a star, including many scientific concepts about each. Not only did they have to describe the facts through their depictions, but also show what a star might "feel" like in that stage.

Each student in the performing group came to the front of the class. All the lights were out and the shades shut to set the mood of being in space. A spotlight illuminated the group's speaker, who usually had made and was wearing a costume of the star's stage (optional but most of the kids did it!). The other kids were frozen in a tableau, and the speaker explained their depiction. When they were done, the group illustrating the next stage came up.

It was fabulous! The students' ability and willingness to put themselves into the roles were extraordinary. The kids got into it in a big way. I should have known it would work because kids like to be active and involved. Their ability to show and recite the facts was superb. Sure, some were better than others, but they all worked so hard and referred to their reading—even the reluctant kids—so who am I to ask for more than that?

We had fun, and the desired knowledge was learned and shared. Everyone was involved. Another desired outcome was the kids' ability to work together, so much better here than during other times. They made up their own ground rules for working together and abided by them. Tableaux is certainly a strategy I would use again!

— Paul

CHAPTER 10

REENACTMENTS AND INTERVENTIONS

Playing to Deepen Understanding of How Texts Work

> **"** *The best way to understand how a text works. . . is to change it: to play around with it, to intervene in it in some way (large or small), and then try to account for the exact effect of what you have done. In practice—not just in theory—we have the option of making changes at all levels, from the merest nuance of punctuation or intonation to total recasting in terms of genre, time, place, participants and medium.* **"**
>
> —Rob Pope, *Textual Intervention*

For many years now, I've done a unit on civil rights and social justice with middle-school students. When I ask students to brainstorm how their civil rights are violated by school, they quickly brainstorm long lists and fill the board with their complaints. But at the same time that they are so sensitive to slights to their own rights, they are defensive about their own respect for others. As the pre-reading activities continue, my students indicate how savvy they are to positions of tolerance. They are quick to point out how kids of different races get along in our school, how mixed their friendship groups are in terms of gender and ethnicity. But, at the same time, I hear them heaping disparagement on their classmates, often dismissing them on the basis of body image, level of "coolness," sexuality, or perspective.

I'm convinced that Dorothy Heathcote is right when she asserts that we cannot best transform our students' understanding and ethical selves through a direct approach. The students know the game; they have their guards up. The indirect approach goes in through the back door and is typically more powerful.

In light of Heathcote's insight, I include texts by and about people who are different from us, particularly in my civil rights unit. And I use reenactment techniques and intervention techniques to help students grasp what these people are saying in the texts through which they speak. Intervention techniques are especially rich, allowing my students and me to "play" with the text in ways that force us to confront our understandings in a powerful and sometimes shocking fashion.

For instance, a few years ago, Brian Edmiston came to my classroom to participate in the opening of our civil rights unit. We used a story drama based on "The Space Trader," a story by Derek Bell in which a traveler from the universe comes to the United States in a time of crisis. He agrees to clean up our environment, save our economy, and put political turmoil to rest—in exchange for all the least-valued members of society. The story clearly and compellingly shows how racism and prejudice are rife in our culture.

To begin, we had my students imagine they were U.S. Senators trimming the budget. They brainstormed all the services supported with government funds and decided which one was least worthy. In all of my five classes, the students chose either the prison budget or the welfare budget (which was a bit ironic, since I was teaching in a "prison town"). As Tony exclaimed in role as a Senator, "The [people who benefit] are worthless anyway!"

During the ensuing drama work, the students were put in roles as the prisoners or welfare recipients, imagining how they came to be in prison or on welfare, writing a farewell letter to a loved one before departure with the Space Trader, and imagining the best and worst possible scenarios of what might happen to them.

The students then became Senators again to reopen discussion of the Space Trader's offer. Brian and I reminded them of their previous position on the issue and their judgmental statements about the prisoners or those on welfare as human beings. In this way, we obliquely but powerfully pointed out some of the many prejudices they harbor, and the potential effects of these—prejudices and effects they had previously denied they were capable of expressing. Because the prejudice had been expressed *in role,* we could discuss the nature and effect of prejudice in a safe way that did not personally indict the students.

At the end of the "Space Trader" enactment, Jenny had this to say: "At first, I thought that the aliens could take [the welfare people] because we didn't need them. Then, after I thought about it, I kind of changed my mind. You can't put a price on a person's life. It was very prejudiced for me to do that. Maybe it was a mistake and they regret it, and then it would be too late for them. Maybe they couldn't help not getting a job. We were all too selfish and too quick to decide." (Wilhelm & Edmiston, 1998)

When teaching the civil rights and social justice unit, I like to return to these kinds of drama experiences using texts such as *Roll of Thunder, Hear My Cry*, a story of the Logan family's struggles as African Americans in the Depression-era South; *Reaching Dustin*, about coming to understand and care about an antisocial boy; or *The Eighteenth Emergency*, which chronicles how Mouse discovers something human in the toughest boy in the school. Books such as these help us consider the points of view of characters and authors who are different from us, and invite us to consider our own prejudices and ways to address our habitual ways of seeing and being in the world.

Smashing the Frozen Seas Within: The Power of Authorial Reading

Though we teach many things—informational content, skills and strategies, and much more—working for transformations in understanding is perhaps an educator's most important work. Reading is a powerful way of expanding and transforming our understanding, but only if we have the willingness and the tools to see other points of view, reconceptualize our understandings, and change our thinking and behavior. Enactments can make that happen.

The reader's first responsibility is to understand the text as it is written, to responsibly fill in the "forms" offered to us by the text, as Iser (1978) puts it. Reenactment strategies help readers responsibly ascertain and "placehold" the meaning of a text (to represent a difficult concept so it can be studied, tested out, and reflected upon) in the way that the author's construction and coding of the text asks us to read it. Once we have worked to comprehend a text the way its construction asks us to comprehend it, we have other things to do: play with the text, see what other meanings may be hidden or suppressed, and decide whether to embrace, adapt, or resist the authorial vision we think is being offered. And then, of course, we need to decide how to enact and live out our decision about the authorial vision in the social worlds we inhabit.

This vision of reading comes from the powerful theoretical orientation of "authorial reading" offered by Rabinowitz and Smith (1998) in their seminal book *Authorizing Readers*. These authors argue that the New Critical orientation, the dominant one in schools, asks the text-centered question: *What does this text mean?* Subjective Reader Response theorists generally ask a different kind of question centered on personal response: *What does this text mean to me?* Neither question considers the purposeful coding of the text by the author who constructed the text, nor the importance of reading the text in the way that its construction would indicate that we should. Rabinowitz and Smith argue that we must first respect authors before we decide if we want to embrace or resist their visions. Otherwise we cannot learn from texts and the intelligences that create them; otherwise we would not even know what it is we are embracing or resisting. Authorial reading requires a wide-awake understanding of how texts work, how we are asked to read them, how we articulate the meanings texts communicate, deciding whether we want to embrace, transform, or resist these visions, and how to enact this decision.

The authorial reading question posed by these theorists is: *What does this text mean to the audience for which it was written* (an audience that understands the concepts and codings presented and how to responsibly comprehend these) *and how do we feel about that?* Reading in this way emphasizes that literature is a human construction and serves meaningful human purposes. This construction is meant to communicate in agreed upon ways called "conventions" for making meaning. These are powerful points that are often lost in the way literature and reading are typically taught in school.

The authorial reading question is more powerful than the previous two because it subsumes and goes beyond them. It requires that we attend respectfully and carefully to texts, *and* that we apply our subjective personal responses—not to whatever meaning we choose to create, but to the closest possible approximation of the meaning originally constructed by the intelligence behind the text. New Critical theory lines up with *teacher and text/information-centered views* of education; subjective Reader Response with *student-centered views*; and the theory of authorial reading and transactional reader response with Vygotskian *meaning/learning-centered views* (see Wilhelm, Baker, and Dube, 2001 for a full discussion of these theoretical positions). The most powerful educational theories and current cognitive research support the learning-centered view as the most explanatory and helpful to teachers and learners alike.

The two different families of enactment techniques explored in this chapter parallel the two phases of authorial reading. The first family of reenactment (or pre-enactment) strategies is excellent for supporting students in figuring out and representing the literal and implied meanings of a text's construction. These are fairly straightforward techniques, and I will provide only a quick overview. The second family belongs to strategies for "playing" with meanings by intervening, reframing, recasting, changing, and probing texts. These intervention strategies are used in order to determine what the texts are and are not saying, what is voiced and what and who is silenced, how a different construction would change the text and its meaning, and what the texts might mean to us if we choose to adapt or resist the author's coding and vision. In this way, intervention strategies aid the reader in fulfilling the second phase, and the obligation of the authorial reader, to play with the text to figure out *how do I feel?* about the vision expressed (or suppressed) by the text and *what do I want to do about this as a result?*

Benefits of Reenactments

Anchor Standards
for Reading,
1–6, 10
Language, 1–6
Writing, 3, 10

Research shows that reenactment strategies require the skills that are necessary for reading comprehension and engagement. Reenactments (like most other forms of enactment) sharpen students' ability to

- identify, remember, and represent key details and events, and the patterns between them;

- analyze and answer questions, particularly higher-order ones;

- pose and solve problems;

- understand and integrate the relationships between various pieces of information (in other words, infer and explain deep meaning);

- recognize and develop understanding of syntactic and textual sequences and structures;

- comprehend word meanings and tone; and

- remember, recall, respond to, and transform the thematic meaning of what has been read. (See, for example, Ross and Roe, 1977; Siks, 1983; Wilhelm, 1997/2008.)

The enactment strategies you'll learn about will assist students with these processes by helping them recognize, imagine, and reconstitute textual meaning, and then reflect and work on it, transforming it and trying it out, along with alternative meanings.

Basic Reenactment Strategies

Reenactment Drama:
Entering a Story World

Basic reenactment asks students to represent the events and the meaning of a text in dramatic form. Students can focus on literally stated meaning, implied meaning, and/or the directly stated or implied central focus of the piece as a whole. Even though reenactment implies that students would engage in it after reading, you can actually use it any time—during reading, after reading, or even before reading—to predict and bring knowledge from other texts or life experiences to bear.

Many of the techniques in this book work for the same purposes of establishing and "placeholding" a text's literal or implied meaning. Tableaux, for example, can establish key ideas as well as express a thematic generalization, and role-play can get at the subtext and complex implied relationships expressed about a character's experience. So, the strategies here can be abetted by the drama techniques featured throughout the book.

Telling Tales. Ask pairs of students to recount the story as a storyteller would. One student tells the story and the other listens. The listener prods and asks questions, playing Stranger in Role, trying to piece together the details. This technique works with informational texts as well, by having the teller recount an important historical event, mathematical concept, or scientific discovery, as the listener plays the role of historian, mathematician, scientist, or reporter, trying to understand and apply the importance of this understanding to specific situations or to the inquiry currently being pursued. Telling Tales can also be done with the whole class working together to create a summary, with the teacher playing Stranger in Role. In this case, I usually have a couple of students record important details on the chalkboard or anchor charts.

When using Telling Tales, I prefer a large group for complex texts and pair work for texts I think students can work through and summarize with the assistance of a peer. For example, I was recently working with sixth graders reading Byars' *The Eighteenth Emergency.* The students worked in pairs, with the teller playing the role of a witness to the climactic fight between Mouse and Hammerman. The listener wrote a summary of the fight and made a prediction about how the incident might change Mouse and his friends' attitudes and lives. Two weeks later, we used the same technique as a whole class: I asked students to report to me, a stranger from another planet, about the history of civil rights in America. They were to recount the most important situations and events and their consequences, both immediate and eventual, in a story-like form and to extract ideas that would help me—and themselves—think about how to preserve civil rights in the future. This summarization activity was one of our culminating activities for the unit.

Guided Imagery. I ask students to close their eyes and listen as I read aloud a passage. While I read, they visualize, elaborate on, and reenact the text world in their minds, using prompts such as, "What are you seeing now?" and "Where are you now?" or more specifically, "I see the inside of a cave and feel the dripping cool wetness on the wall; what else do *you* see and feel?" Sometimes I play mood music to accompany the reading. Other times, I prompt a reconstruction by citing key details and asking students to add to these as we relive the text. Students call out their thinking. Later, students sometimes write or draw to guided-imagery prompts.

Mime. Students can also be asked to act out a scene silently as it is being read, reconstructing the visual details or illustrations. After a reading, students might also discuss how to block and stage the key details of a scene: What details need to be included? How could they be conveyed? Are there details that aren't necessary? What details could be changed, and what effect would this have?

Scene Writing. In groups, students write a script for the scene to be performed, perhaps by another group, class, or for reading buddies. They must attend to key details and features of script writing so that this group will know how to act out the scene. This is a great technique for teaching students about the conventions of dramatic scripts, such as incorporating stage and set directions and indicating speakers.

Our Town. At times, mimes or scenes are improved by adding a narrator, commentator, or stage manager who can explain the deeper meaning of what is going on. This narration can also provide background or transitions that connect scenes to each other so that all information does not need to be acted out, as Thornton Wilder did in *Our Town.*

A Day in the Life of a Chemical Reaction: Mental Modeling in Action

Dear Jeff:

I have found over the years that scientific principles readily lend themselves to drama. Recently, after unsuccessful attempts to teach chemical reactions to sixth graders, I mixed your ideas about Analogy Enactments and Mental Modeling into the classroom formula, and the level of understanding increased tenfold.

Types of chemical reactions:
Composition A + B = AB
Iron + oxygen = iron oxide

Replacement A + BC = AC + B
Magnesium + Hydrogen Chloride
= MgCl + H

Switching AB + CD = AD + CB
Lead nitrate + sodium iodide =
lead iodide + sodium nitrate

Decomposition AB = A + B
Sugar = Carbon + water

"Yeah, right, Ms. Mourkas!" the kids responded, eyes glazed. I knew I needed to make this concrete… something on their level that they could understand. My solution: a party or a dance. Each student was assigned to be a different element or compound. There is a party or dance going on, attended by everyone in the room. Couples or individuals are announced as they enter and act out the reaction.

Composition: Iron and Oxygen come to the party stag. At the party they get to know and like each other and leave the party together as Iron Oxide. We talk about what attracts people together and what attracts chemicals together.

Replacement: Magnesium comes to the party alone. Hydrogen and Chloride come as a couple. However, at the party, Chloride discovers Magnesium, and dumps Hydrogen, since Hydrogen is a bit unstable anyway. We talk about what keeps people together and what might make them "dump" someone and get someone new. Then we analogize this to chemicals.

This scenario continued through the other two reactions. I then had students research common reactions and add them to our list. It worked really well!

Thanks, from me and my students.

—Anne

Analogy Strategy. If students are having difficulty comprehending and reenacting a scene, it is likely that the information is too distant from their experience. Asking students to make an analogy, comparing their personal experience to the new and unfamiliar one, can be helpful. I have students enact a personal experience that parallels, in some way, a scene from the reading or a detail from a text. While reading *The Incredible Journey*, many of my students did not understand the scene in which Luath asks the other animals to join him on his journey. So I asked them to mime out how they would convince friends to join them to clean the yard or do some other challenging or undesirable activity. When studying colonization, we acted out scenes from family life where parents directed the kids' activity. In each case, I introduced parallels from the story, or the world of history, and asked students in what ways that analogy was similar or different from the personal experience we had enacted.

Mental Modeling. This technique works well with complex concepts or ideas. I use it quite often in science. When studying electrical charges, my team assigned some students to be positive or negative charges, and other students to be natural laws governing their behavior. I then introduced phenomena that would affect the charges and they had to respond correctly. If they did not, then the natural laws would step in to advise them. (And I guess I was playing God, because if things didn't go right, I would blurt out, "You can't do that!" and stop the enactment to correct misconceptions.)

Later on, students constructed mental models of electrical circuits in a kind of moving tableaux. These mental models made clear what the students did and did not understand. For example, one group created the model of a party. The partygoers were charges who were aligned in a conga line dance, demonstrating the understanding that charges stay in the same order as they flow through the circuit. The refrigerator was the battery, required to move the charges along. As one boy said, "no fridge, no fiesta!" The parents were the resistors, using energy from the charges to shed light on the dark corners of the party. And other kids were clamoring to get in—showing that they did not understand that circuits were closed systems. I introduced new lab activities to further our study. From there, students revised their model to show that the doors to the party were closed and no more charges would be allowed in.

Dance/Movement Reenactments. Some of the most exciting reenactments I have seen involve dance and body movement. In my work at the Chicago Teachers Center and its Summer Academy, we match up students with content experts and artists. The content experts help the students engage with questions such as "Why did the dinosaurs become extinct?" or "How does the experience of war affect people?" The artists then work with the students to help them represent their understandings.

Last summer, the dinosaur inquiry group at CTC worked with a dancer and drummer to portray different theories explaining the dinosaurs' demise. Though the middle-school students were reluctant at first, they eventually became engaged and animated. In one dance, performed for the other Summer Academy students and their parents, students used an entire basketball court to demonstrate a variety of dinosaur life and five different theories about their demise, prancing about like raptors, flying like pterodactyls in highly stylized ways, and combining together to become Tyrannosaurus Rex. At the end of the performance, the drummers began drumming insistently and the dinosaurs gathered together. One boy, depicting a giant meteor, ran as if slung across the court, then ran back and jumped into the group of dinosaurs with a mighty leap as the drumming reached its crescendo. As he landed, the dinosaurs all fell prone in a giant circle. Afterward, the students explained the theories, the various places such a meteorite might have hit the Earth, and what effects that might have caused.

In another class, which was studying war, the students used current event stories and a reading of *My Brother Sam Is Dead*. The teacher began by asking the students to determine the overriding theme of the study. After negotiation, the students settled on "war brings

Newscast Activity

One of my students' favorite reenactment activities is the Newscast. I generally use this at the end of units or longer texts to summarize and consider the most important details.

Video Newscast: Directions for Students

You and your group members have the job of producing a ten-minute news show about *The Incredible Journey*. You must come up with a network name, select stories that will be of interest to viewers from our school, write the stories, create reenactments, prepare props and backdrops, rehearse your show, and be prepared to go LIVE and ON THE AIR by Wednesday! (With the weekend, this gives you four days to prepare.)

Purpose: to review the most important ideas and events in the book for viewers.

- Your show *must* be between 9 and 12 minutes.
- Each group member must be the primary author of at least one script and act in two.
- Each group member must help out with organizing, props, and videotaping.
- During the newscast, each story/script must be identified by type: "Hello, this is Jon with a special feature on animal heroes…" "And now over to Andrea with a view of how weather affected the journey."
- You may tape your show after school or on the weekend with your own video recorder or one you borrow from me. Or you may tape during class on Monday with editing time Tuesday. All shows will be aired on Wednesday.
- You don't have a lot of time, so you will have to pack information into the show in the form of visuals and the spoken word.

Required stories:

Top news story: the most important event/idea in the book

Other stories: a review of the other key events/ideas in the book

confusion and pain to people who are not on the battlefield, but history doesn't pay attention to that." Groups of students became individual characters from the book, with a central group as Sam. A group playing the boys' mother did a stylized dance of grief, putting their hands on their hearts, and spinning out of control. As they fell, the Sam group turned to their father, and this group responded with anger. The fathers backed away and the Sams turned to their friends, who displayed fear before sitting down. Then the Sams turned to their brother, the narrator of the story, and this group showed disappointment and sadness, wiped away a tear, and reached out to Sam who held out a hand but fell to the ground.

Feature story: a story about a related topic of interest suggested by the book—animal heroism, navigation, how to prepare your pet when you travel, animal rights, geography of Western Ontario, and so forth

Review: a review of the book, the movie version of the book, a performance in the book (Bodger's victory dance after slashing the other dogs), or one of our dramatic renditions of scenes from the book

Advice: personal or consumer advice directed toward characters or readers of the book, such as animal lovers or pet owners

Commercial or Public Service Announcement Related to Themes from the Book

Commercial/PSA: regarding products or items featured in the book, or that would have been useful to characters in the book

Optional stories:

- **Interview:** with character, author, or reader
- **Sports news story:** for example, the story as an endurance event or report on Bodger's fights
- **Weather:** how weather affected the story, or metaphorically how the mood or tone of the story shifted at certain points
- **MTV music spot:** song must be related concretely or thematically to the book
- **Cartoon:** must be related to events or themes from the book
- **Opinions and commentaries**
- Any other idea that will review and examine important ideas from the book

Teacher note: A Newscast can be expanded into a full-fledged documentary or news show that explores the topic of study. Students almost always want to take the videos home, show their parents, view them at parties, and trade them with other groups. So be prepared!

I'll never forget seventh grader Joe who having participated in the dance, told me, "We wanted to recreate the story, literally, but we wanted to do more than that. We wanted to add stuff, put in our own interpretation, be symbolic, make it meaningful to anybody thinking about war." He knew the importance of understanding a text on its own terms, but then intervening and adding one's own productive interpretations.

A third group, studying the Depression, created a dance showing how the displacement, poverty, and hunger of many people contrasted with the lives of people who were relatively unaffected. A central group danced a waltz and mimed drinking champagne, while all around them other students depicted people picking through trash, being rolled out of their shacks, and being turned away from every doorway they tried to enter. Afterward the students in role as displaced people wrote letters to President Hoover about their plight.

A Day in the Life/Magic Schoolbus. I have most often used this technique to help students imagine what it would be like to have lived in different historical periods. Students imagine and reenact a typical day or the day of an event—what it would be like waking up, what the first chores would be, how people would gather and prepare food, what typical problems would be faced, and how would they be handled. Another version of this is a "day in the life of…" an object, a scientific principle, or a math concept. How would this object or principle be used? The use of the A Day in the Life technique requires detailed understanding from prior study and reading.

Taking *The Magic Schoolbus* books as a model, I have the students imagine they can shrink and travel through the bloodstream or through a plant to learn about the system they are studying. They can enact or report out on their adventures and findings. Or, like *The Incredible Voyage,* they may be given a mission to cure a disease, or complete an operation.

Headlining/Lead Writing. When reading a text together, I ask a small group to do a daily summary by coming up with a title for the material, writing a lead for a report about it, and sometimes even creating a quick headline news drama. Groups revolve each day so everyone gets to provide his or her summary enactment during the course of the unit. Some groups add graphics, music, and implications—but the challenge is to tell all the news in one minute.

Pre-enactments. Anything that can be reenacted can also be pre-enacted. Students are introduced to a situation that will occur in the text and asked to predict or enact what will ensue. This can be done for story events, historical situations, or scientific phenomena.

Basic Intervention and Transformation Strategies

Recastings/Reframings. It is useful to work on *what* an author communicates (the authorial theme/vision/generalization) and *how* this has been communicated (the textual coding and construction) in tandem, since the *how* so intimately affects the *what*. After reading "The Fan Club," for example, I ask my students to consider why the author made the choices she did and what she was trying to communicate through those choices. They can do this by considering other authorial choices that she could have made instead:

New circumstances: What if Rachel were considered cool? What if she were really good at something that was privileged by the culture of her community, or knew about something more valued by the school culture, like sports?

New context: What if the teachers had been more responsive and paying more attention? What if the story occurred in a school where none of the kids came from privileged backgrounds?

New age or time period: What if the students were back in middle school, or at the college level? What if the story occurred in the 1960s?

New narrator or genre: What if this story were rewritten from Laura's point of view? a teacher's? Bill's? Rachel's? What if it had been written as a poem? as a confession? as a ballad?

New conclusion: What if Laura had stood up for Rachel?

Students could enact the new possibility through role-play or tableaux, or write out the recast version. In any case, they discuss how the meaning of the story and its implications may have changed.

"What If?" Scenarios. When studying civil rights and social justice with fourth graders, we read about Harriet Tubman. We enacted a slave escape led by Harriet. Along the way, we engaged in several "What If?" Scenarios. What if we could not take the usual route along the Underground Railroad? What if a man from the escape party turns around and says he will return to the plantation? What if Harriet threatens to shoot the man? What if one mother's child cannot keep up and the mother cannot keep up when she carries him? In role, students had to brainstorm and act out solutions, or the costs and benefits of different courses of action.

Interrupted Action/Slow Motion/Speeded-Up Motion. A climactic event or action can be interrupted and frozen and the characters interviewed or advised. The action can also be sped up, or even slowed down so decisions can be more considered. Like a tape recorder, the enactment can be rewound, edited, and a different way of dealing with things can be tried. We can also fast-forward from an event in to the future, or experience an event and then rewind to what must have gone before. All this helps students to infer past and future action and to see patterns and connections between events and details.

Alternative Endings. Enact different endings and discuss their meanings. Explore themes such as "best and worst scenarios for different characters" and "least satisfying/most satisfying for the reader" or another character from this book or another text, of a popular culture or historical figure.

Intensifier. A situation can be intensified, a character trait can be magnified, new consequences or conditions can be introduced, requirements made more stringent—the ante can be raised in any form—and the students can explore how the rest of the story might be different. For example, to intensify the situation in *Where the Red Fern Grows*, we imagined that Billy's family was even poorer, that Old Dan is hurt badly enough by the big raccoon that he can no longer hunt, and that Billy's father is less understanding. Then, we explored how these situations could change the book and its meaning.

Temptations/Tensions. A new element, temptation, or tension, is introduced. Students explore what might have happened.

Two-Sided Story/Re-Viewpointing Stories. This technique connects kids directly to a text by requiring them to recast or reset the story in some way. It's good for exploring and understanding symbolism, double meanings, alter-egos, and allegory, and it's fun.

I type a fable or a summary of a story, leaving space between each line for students to retell their own version. I usually take a story or legend from the distant past or a different culture from ours and ask students to recast and rewrite the story as if it had occurred in our school. Or we sometimes take a current event issue from the newspaper or from the school and rewrite it as a myth, fable, or legend. Students then compare the characters, events, actions, and meanings in the two versions of the same story. The story can also be recast from another character's perspective (from inside the story or outside the story), or could be reset in a different situation or culture. Anything works here, and kids often have a rollicking good time with it.

Students do the same thing by role-playing parallel scenes, enacting a scene as written in the text, and then reenacting it in different contexts or parameters, with different eventualities and consequences.

The Leap at Rhodes   by Aesop

The Big Fat Basketball Blather   by Jason

A certain man who visited foreign lands could talk of little

When Tom (not his real name) moved in from Milwaukee

when he returned home except the wonderful

all he could talk about was what a great hoops

adventures he had met with and the great deeds he

stay he had been at his old school.

done abroad.

One of the feats he told about was a leap he had made

He told about how he could stuff it, jam it

in a city called Rhodes. That leap was so great, he said,

and slam it in his old school's gym, his style

that no other man could leap anywhere near the

was so amazing that he was called "Slammer" for

distance. A great many persons in Rhodes had seen

a nickname. All his friends had seen him

him do it and would prove that what he told was true.

and could prove it!

"No need of witnesses," said one of his hearers. "Just

"No worries, man!" said Dr. J (the real one),

suppose this city is Rhodes. Now show us how far you

"Just imagine this is your old gym. Now

can jump.

show us your stuff, Mozart!"

Moral:

Don't do the brag if you are a lag!

Jason's two-sided story based on Aesop's fable "The Leap at Rhodes."

Game Show. I used Game Show with a class that was reading George Orwell's *Animal Farm*. At the end of our reading, I asked the class to create a game show that would highlight the key details and meanings of the book and explore possible interventions. The class had one 90-minute block to create, rehearse, and perform their show. They decided to do a show called *Animal Farm Family Feud*, parodying the show *Family Feud*. Group members began making masks of pig noses and other animal noses with paper cups and construction paper as they planned out the show. (I have often found that time pressure can stimulate creativity and productivity!) The students decided that Snowball, a pig, would be the host and judge (which was appropriate since he is the spokesperson for the pigs in the book), and that the competition would pit the pigs against the rest of the animals. Snowball, with the help of other students, devised questions about the book that got at important details and the authorial generalization about the topic of power and civil rights. The animals provided answers that were sometimes disingenuous, sometimes insightful about the way things had evolved in the book. They were always judged wrong by Snowball, even when they were clearly right. The pigs were then given a chance to answer and were always judged right and awarded points and prizes to great applause from the pig faction.

Near the show's end, the animals answered two questions and were buzzed, and the pigs gave the same answers and were given points. When the animals complained, Snowball told them, parodying a line from the book, that "All animals are right, but some animals like pigs are more right than others." In the end, the pigs won 1000 to 0, and Snowball summarized the meaning of the book. Most of the students then collapsed laughing, as the end of their show coincided with the bell.

The Rest of the Story. I got this idea from the old Paul Harvey radio show that my father loved so much. I ask students to create a summary of the story and then to tell "the rest of the story"—the subtext or follow-up that wasn't explicitly told. What happens later? Whose story wasn't told that we will now get to hear? What surprising twist or information did we not get that will be revealed to us now? And how does this change our understanding of the story?

Tunnel of Time. This is an enactment in which characters go back or forward in time to see how the past or future might impact the story. Another version is to have students go back in time to interact with historical characters or live a day in the life of people of a past era. Or like the *Back to the Future* movies, how would changing the past of a story change its future?

Third Rock from the Sun. Like Professor Xargle from Jeanne Willis' stories, students act as if they are beings from another planet on a mission to gather information or help people in a different time period, culture, or world. I have also used a technique I call **Rip Van Winkle** or **Sleepers Awake** where students imagine they've been asleep for many years and wake up to a very different world. How would a new situation appear to them if they did not understand the history behind it? And how would these new understandings affect them? Students can write as "stranger in role" as a naïve, unknowing observer, as when Professor Xargle writes about how "earth hounds own humans and walks them each day."

Three Women. This idea is inspired by Edward Albee's play where three phases of the main character—as a young woman, a middle-aged woman, and an older woman—come together, blaming each other and explaining to each other why things went as they did. Variations could include a meeting of the past, present, and future of the main character or of situations to explore why things have turned out as they have and what could have been different.

Scrooge Looking Down. With this technique, we examine what in a character's (or situation's) past could explain the current status. We look closely at the present, and examine possible futures should things continue as they are or if some change is enacted. Other versions are Looking Forward/Looking Backward, where a character considers past possibilities and dreams of possible future lives.

Extended Interventions

Debates and Trials are two types of extended enactments that work to intervene and elaborate on texts and textual information.

Debates. My students love to engage in debates, and any book or unit will offer many possibilities for debate. Students have debated with gusto topics such as the best possible moral for a fable or story, the importance and fairness of immigration policies (as revealed in Karen Hesse's *Letters from Rifka*), current events news stories, the most just and fair conclusion for a story like *The Outsiders*, and many other issues.

Debates can be pursued in role as characters, or students can play themselves. There are advantages to in-role debating, especially when an issue is sensitive or when students all tend to adopt a similar point of view; doing debates in role requires that they take on a perspective that is not their own and means that a rich diversity of viewpoints will be considered and explored.

An informal kind of debate could be conducted in the form of a CNN town meeting. My students in Maine were familiar with the proceedings of town meetings and take to it readily. For those not so familiar, the CNN model can be used.

Trials. Another technique my students really enjoy is a trial. My students have put Macbeth onto the stand, and the defense was able to get him off by demonstrating that he was an unwitting accomplice to his wife's manipulations. We have engaged in a trial of Alfred Nobel, the inventor of dynamite, and his legacy, as well as that of Robert Oppenheimer, the head of the Manhattan Project, which created the first nuclear bomb. We have put current food and drug laws on trial. After reading *Roll of Thunder, Hear My Cry* and before reading *Let the Circle Be Unbroken*, the class engaged in a trial of TJ for his role in the robbery of the Wallace Store; we did this in role, so we could experience the unfair restrictions placed on African-Americans during trials of that period. Any literary characters, historical figures, or even scientific advance can be put on trial. This helps students interrogate positions or circumstances that are accepted unquestioningly.

Possible roles include prosecution and defense attorneys, defendants, plaintiffs, witnesses for both prosecution and defense, and perhaps a jury. Students can also play multiple roles, and

I often ask everyone to play a role, then become themselves at the end when they form the jury. As with most enactments, I help to organize the brainstorming and put a strict time limit on preparations. The trial itself, like the debates, is meant to last for no more than a blocked class period. Sometimes trials can be scripted and staged, but most often we engage in the trial as it would play out in real life.

Students may need to learn about the court systems, both criminal and civil, the conventions of trials, or even laws—but this is usually not necessary unless it is a goal of instruction to learn about such things.

I have also engaged students with less elaborate legal proceedings such as an **Inquest** or a **Hearing** into why the dinosaurs went extinct as part of our "Who will survive?" unit.

The close reading and discussion of the text that students pursue in such instances is astounding. One student participating in the dinosaur inquest e-mailed one of the world's top authorities, Paul Cereno of the University of Chicago, for his expert opinions. When he received a reply, the student used this "expert testimony" at the inquest. I was astonished that Paul Cereno would respond to a seventh grader doing a school project, but my student was nonplussed. I guess that's the democracy of the Internet! Likewise, during our Macbeth trial, another student called the drama scholar Sam McCready at the University of Maryland-Baltimore County for his opinion, whose statement was recorded and played for the classroom court.

Lesson Plan for a Debate of Lois Lowry's *The Giver*

By Nicky Gamblin

Debate Topic: Euthanasia/Death Penalty

Question: Should the community adopt a law that would institutionalize a systematic approach to "release"? ("Release," according to the story, is a system of euthanizing humans. It could be due to medical incapacity before or at birth, or during life, to control population or punish those who do not conform.)

Situation: You are members of the community described in *The Giver*. There has been controversy surrounding the laws around "release" and the Elders have agreed to a debate of the issue and to reconsider the law.

Each of you will be appointed to a task force of Elders assigned to consider all the pros or all the cons of a "release law," to address medical problems, overpopulation, the relief of human suffering, and to deal with those who refuse to adhere to the laws of the community. You will not necessarily be assigned to the task force researching the position with which you agree. Nonetheless it is your duty to the community to explore and defend the position you are assigned.

Brainstorming Sheet

Anchor Standards for
Writing, 3–5, 7–9

Opening Statement/Claim *for* or *against* "release":

Evidence supporting your claim (this can be from *The Giver* or from other sources). *What makes you think so?*

1.	
2.	
3.	
4.	

Warrants explaining how each piece of evidence connects to and supports your claim. *How do you know this evidence supports your position? What rules or principles does your reasoning exhibit?*

1.	
2.	
3.	
4.	

Cross-examiners:

Reservations about the opposing group's position, evidence, and warrants:

1.	
2.	
3.	
4.	

Responses to opposing team's reservations or attacks on warrants (provide backing):

Closing Statement:

Voices From the Field

Dear Mr. Wilhelm:

I've never much liked English class. So I guess I wanted to write you a thank-you note for helping me to enjoy tenth grade English. It was an enjoyable and cool experience for me.

My favorite parts were the dramas that we did. I really liked the newspaper simulation and putting Macbeth on trial, and I loved talking to Professor McCready about Macbeth and using his expert testimony. I still think Lady Macbeth got stiffed though, because she was clearly getting it from Post-Menstrual Syndrome (yeah, we learned about it in health). There was a new moon and blood everywhere. And Professor McCready said women all used to be on the same cycle with the moon. (Weird, huh? I wonder what other weird things the world is full of?)

But anyway, I was thanking you, especially for the drama stuff. I liked that you didn't tell us what to think and that the dramas helped us think and express our own thoughts. I don't want to be taught what to think but *how to think,* and I liked how you tried to do that in really active, fun ways that made the things we read really come alive.

English can be really boring (believe me, I'm an expert on that!), and you made it exciting. I know it was hard work sometimes, but I wanted you to know it was worth it.

I liked, too, how you said a couple of times that you will be my tenth-grade English teacher forever, and that's why you were so serious about it.

Well, I wanted you to know that I see myself as your tenth-grade English student forever and that is why I am going to be serious about reading and thinking about things—as a kind of compliment to you and to myself. Cool, huh?

Sincerely,

Steven, your tenth-grade student forever

WRITING IN ROLE

Radio Shows, Voice Collage, Memory Circles, and Other Correspondence Activities

W e were in the final phase of our civil rights and social justice unit, where the kids form small groups and engage in their own critical inquiries that extend our classroom topical inquiry into civil rights. Sean was in a group of five boys who chose to research the protest movement during the Vietnam War. From my early discussions with them, it was clear that the whole group thought the Vietnam War was "totally bad" and the protesters were "civil rights fighters." Though I was sympathetic to their point of view, I wanted them to see beyond facile understandings and consider all points of view on the subject.

To do this, we engaged in a variety of enactments involving writing. After reading about the rise of Communism and the Cuban Missile Crisis, the boys played the part of President Kennedy and his cabinet, writing memos about the "Vietnam problem" and what could be done about it. While reading excerpts from Ron Kovic's *Born on the Fourth of July*, we engaged in enactments as protesters and military personnel at a recruiting center. Afterward, I asked the boys to write diary entries about the events from both perspectives –as a protester and as a military recruiter. We read Tim O'Brien's *If I Die in a Combat Zone* and some of his short stories, and the boys role-played a family whose elder son volunteered for service and whose younger son was considering dodging the draft. They wrote letters to each other. The boys then became a Vietnamese family with similar divided loyalties. And finally, the boys took newspaper accounts of the war and rewrote them for the *Stars and Stripes* and *Rolling Stone*.

Anchor Standards
for Reading,
1–7, 10
Language, 1–6
Writing, 1–10

Afterward, Sean told me, "I liked writing the letters and acting as the soldiers and the Vietnamese people, the protesters, the President, and the families and all that because it made me see things from new directions…and that made me understand it all in a really stronger way." His group partner Tony said: "Now I think the Vietnam War was bad even more strongly—because now I think that instead of believe it—and I think it with some doubt because I know there are other ways of thinking about it."

These writing activities are part of the family of correspondence enactments, which are any kind of composing that is undertaken in role. Correspondence enactments are powerful because they provide the student writer with a persona, a purpose, meaningful information, a situation, and an audience—all of which help him or her compose. Plus, writing in role requires careful reading; students know they need information from the text to advance their point of view. It also develops students' awareness of how texts are constructed, since they are to write formal letters, newspaper articles, memos, and so forth.

Benefits of Correspondence Enactments

From inside a correspondence activity, students can

- become characters or figures from history or science
- become interested in learning more about these figures and the complex situations that shaped them
- take on and contend with differing points of view
- experiment with various forms and styles of writing

- adopt a writing voice different from their own (which enhances their facility with writing and the development of their own voice)
- learn the conventions of reading and writing different genres, variations and kinds of texts

- confront and compare issues in historical and current contexts
- consider underlying causes and consequences
- make inferences and elaborate on their reading;
- address situations and plan social action
- reflect on textual experience from the inside, and much more

Reading and writing inside enactments humanizes literacy. It makes literacy personal and immediate. It provides an immediate context of use. The DIY and JIT (Do it Yourself and Just in Time) culture of kids is put to use. The texts we read and the facts they contain become "more personal, real, and have it more pop" to quote my student Erv. What follows is a template I give students to guide their in-role writing.

Feel free to adapt the template to meet your needs. You might have students write as real historical people. During a study of the Manhattan Project, for example, I've had students take on the roles of Bohr, Heisenberg, and Oppenheimer. Whether the individual is real or fictional, students correspond from the perspective of major characters in fiction or players in history or the news.

Another tip: Use *The Jolly Postman*, a children's book by Janet and Allan Ahlberg, to teach students about the form and conventions of different kinds of correspondence, or bring in examples from the daily mail.

Forms of Correspondence: Some Ideas to Try

Many kinds of correspondence can be composed in role to deepen understanding and engagement with text. All of them will allow readers to see things from new angles, deepen comprehension, notice sub-texts, and identify and fill in silences. In the technology chapter, I highlighted various uses of Facebook, blogs, wikis, GoogleDocs and other platforms for doing dramatic correspondence. Here are a few other possibilities, which I've arranged into three categories: social network, social action, and pop culture.

Social Network

Telephone Call/Telephone Tree. Telephone Call works best when characters have markedly different experiences. Students imagine making a telephone call to characters to advise them or get advice from them, or imagine calls between characters about a problem in the story. Scripts of the conversation could be written and performed, or this could be done spontaneously as an in-role drama.

In a Telephone Tree, one character calls two others. Those called could be cast by the original caller as she starts the conversation, for example "Ponyboy, I am so glad I got a hold of you!" Or you might prefer to assign students' their roles prior to the enactment. The characters make subsequent phone calls to other characters. Every character has to summarize all key details that have been shared with them and add their own perspective or interpretations as the character they are playing. This telephoning technique can be run with the entire class listening in on the conversation between the callers, though I usually get several calls going at the same time in small circles so that more kids are involved. Of course, the same idea can be played out on Facebook or through texting or instant messaging. Examples of Telephone Tree enactments with specific texts, are on pages 173–174.

Basic Correspondence: Guidelines for Students

In this enactment activity, you will be asked to become one of the characters from the text you are reading or a character who would have an interest or perspective on the issue with which you are concerned. You will then compose a form of correspondence based on or suggested by your experiences as this character. You may write

- from a character in (or suggested by) the text to a character in another text, situation, or era, or to a historical figure or popular culture figure.
- from a character in the text to an imaginary character, or vice versa.
- from a major to a minor character, or vice versa.
- from real people to characters, or vice versa.
- from you to a character, or vice versa.
- from a character to the author, or vice versa.
- from you to the author, or vice versa.
- anything else you can think of . . . the possibilities are endless!

Steps to Take

Decide:

1. from and to whom the correspondence will be.

2. the purpose of the correspondence. This purpose must relate to the text or the unit topic.

3. what form the correspondence will take, given your purpose

a. formal letter	d. thank-you letter	g. advertisement	i. memorandum
b. business letter	e. bill	h. public service announcement	j. business contract
c. informal letter	f. postcard		k. invitation

4. whether your correspondence will be handwritten or typed. Why?

5. the kind of stationery and envelope. How will they reflect the character of the letter and writer?

6. the address for each correspondent and why the address is appropriate.

Now write the correspondence.

Other Possibilities

Exchange! Now we will all exchange the correspondence. The classmate who receives your missive will write back to you in the role of the addressee. Perhaps later you and your pen pal will meet face to face (in role) and talk about the issues raised in the correspondence.

Poster Presentation! Write several letters in a correspondence between characters and mount them on poster board. If writing postcards, create illustrations. Provide photographs and other enclosures or visuals that may be appropriate to include with the correspondence.

Postcard Assignment for *The Incredible Journey*

Here's a sample Correspondence activity I use frequently in my classes.

Imagine that you are one of the three animals from *The Incredible Journey*; either the starving but courageous Luath, the humorous but lagging Bodger, or Tao, the tireless Siamese cat. You have just departed on the final leg of your journey across the Strellon Game Reserve. Not only is this the final leg, but it is also the most challenging. In your weakened condition, you may not make it. Take this opportunity to write a postcard to your master. (Remember that Tao's master is Elizabeth, Bodger belongs to Peter, and Luath is the faithful retriever of Dr. Hunter, the children's father.) You will receive a large note card or sheet of paper to use as a postcard. On it:

1. Write about your thoughts and feelings at this point in time as one of the animals. What needs to be said if this is your last chance to say what is in your heart?

2. Recount your favorite adventure so far in the journey and what it meant to you/what you learned from it.

3. On the reverse side of the postcard, create a picture of your favorite adventure. Remember, this may be your last chance to communicate with your friend and master. Tomorrow we will play the roles of the pets' owners and we will reply to the postcards delivered to us.

To: Susan,

Peepicheep is such a great mouse. I cant wait till we get to Aslans Country. We saw beautiful seapeople. It was the most amazing thing ever. Caspian is so sweet. I'v also seen Asian a couple of times. He's just as great as I remembered him.

Love
Lucy
P.S I cant wait to get home

To: Susan
From: Lucy

Dear Uncle,

It's me Lucky. Strange things have been happening here on Mercury. First Scott Mindes ("He showed us the 'ghosts' of Mercury) suddenly snapped & tried do me in with a laser pistol! Then when we went to doctors office with him Dr. Gardoma acted very suspiceos. Then the Senator's Spy Urteil showed up at Gardoma's office. After that encounter Dr. Peverale showed us to our room where I found out one of our suits was slashed inside & outside to kill us easely out on the sun side! How are things there? Write back soon.

Your Nephew,
David Starr

P.S.: Watch out for Sabotovers!

"The Fan Club." Teacher Donna Dachs used the Telephone Tree technique to help students explore the possible reactions of parents and teachers to the incident at the end of "The Fan Club." She herself made the first calls as the mother of Steve. What had happened at school today? Why had Steve come home giggling uncontrollably? He wouldn't tell her what had happened, and she was concerned about the atmosphere of the high school and what the kids were learning there. What did other parents think?

Donna's first step was to break the class into two circles, and then assign each student in the circles a role. Each circle was composed of several assigned and different roles in the same order in each group, so that she, as Steve's mom, would initiate with a call to the students in each group who were playing Terri's mom, and then the student in each circle playing Terri's mom would call Carol's mom, seated to her left in the group, and so forth.

The first few roles in each circle were parents of the in-crowd (Terri, Steve, or Bill), then of Laura, then of Rachel. The last few students acted as the teachers, principal, guidance counselors, and social workers.

While Donna made the first two calls (to Terri's parents in two different groups), the whole class watched and listened, then those two students called the next person (Carol's mom) in their separate circles. As these two talked, the students tried to piece together the whole story about the community reaction, judge the credibility of responses, and so forth. It often helps focus students if they have to somehow synthesize what other students have said either later in the activity or at its conclusion. In this case, students could have assessed various people's views for a report to the superintendent or for a *60 Minutes* exposé.

Roll of Thunder, Hear My Cry. I used Telephone Tree a couple of times when teaching *Roll of Thunder, Hear My Cry.* I used it first after Cassie is pushed off the sidewalk by Mr. Simms, and again when the cotton field fire is noticed, near the end of the book. Any crucial event around which there may be different perspectives or strong reactions, or where different people may have different information, is a good springboard for this activity. Readers of *Roll of Thunder* will know that the major characters all had different perspectives on these events and reactions to them, and will also know that Papa, Mr. Morrison, and Uncle Hammer personify very different ways of dealing with prejudice. The order of callers I used was designed to get people with different perspectives calling each other and exchanging their views on what happened and what to do about it.

When exploring the scene of Cassie on the sidewalk, I formed four or five circles of students (depending on the size of my class; I like about six students per circle). I acted as a reporter for *The Strawberry Gazette* who was writing a story about the incident.

I started by calling the first student in each circle, who was cast as Big Ma. I wanted to know what had happened (so I solicited a summary from this perspective) and her response to what had happened. (Given the sensitive nature of the incident and the potentially lethal consequences, I could've done inner voice or alter-ego responses here, meaning that we'd tease out the differences between what Big Ma said through the filters she had developed to protect herself in a racist society, and what she was actually thinking. Students would, thereby, get the "official" story and the "unofficial" silenced story.) I sometimes start Telephone Tree by talking to each student who plays the character in turn, for example, talking to each Big Ma (from the different groups) while all students in each circle watch. This allows us to compare responses and get off to a good start. It also challenges later Big Ma players to find some new scrap of information, a new insight into the incident, or to draw on information from earlier in the book or Big Ma's life. Sometimes the third or fourth Big Ma feels all the good stuff has already been used. To address this issue, I sometimes start the activity by doing a Party Line, in which I talk to all four Big Mas at the same time, and they in turn pool the information they have collectively expressed to make their next individual phone call within their separate circles.

I arranged for the phone calls to proceed in this order: from Big Ma to Stacy, from Stacy to Cassie, from Cassie to Hammer, from Hammer to Mr. Morrison, from Mr. Morrison to Papa, from Papa to Mr. Jamison or Harlan Granger, and from this white community leader to Mr. Simms, then from Mr. Simms to the white shopkeeper or another white friend. Obviously, smaller circles could work, with students taking on different roles each time they made a call. You could even do this activity in pairs, with roles switching with each call. Another option is to have each callee become a reporter before or after making the next call along the tree.

Sometimes I'll allow students to call whatever other character they choose, casting the next student as they do so. Characters can call someone for advice, someone from a different story, or someone not present in the text being read. They might even call an expert, casting a fellow student in the Mantle of the Expert.

Social Action

Public Service Announcements. Students are asked to identify an issue, topic, or danger explored in the text. From there, they create a PSA directed at characters to advise and help them by providing information that they need. The announcement can also be directed at classmates and members of their community. Often, I have students script and film their PSAs, which usually follow some strict requirements regarding factual content, the inclusion of real help-line numbers, real agencies that can help people, and actual website addresses for further information.

As readers of my other books know, I am passionate about inquiry, issues-oriented instruction, and social action projects. Any text or curricular topic can be organized around "essential" or "existential questions" that pertain to "contact zones"—issues that can be easily connected to our students' lives. This kind of instruction lends reality, importance, and purpose to reading, making it part of the students' "here and now," and motivates students, particularly when they know they will engage in a social-action project. This should come as no surprise considering that people have always written and read literature to address issues that matter deeply across time and situation. The reason we study any subject is to use it to think and act, so why not make that purpose immediately obvious in school?

Public Service Announcements are a quick and easy social action project. My school has a cable channel that often broadcasts student PSAs. Students also publish PSAs in poster form around the school, or in the school newspaper. Often I've had students engage in significant social action projects through PSAs with palpable effects. Our "Hostile Hallways" project, for instance, led to peer mediation programs and the creation of brochures about harassment. There was a "Clean Up Our School" community project that led to recycling, reuse, and conservation practices in the school and community, with proceeds going to buy a tract of rainforest. We also participated in a "Read Poetry" project, where students posted short "poems for the hallway" around the school. These poems dealt with social action issues we were studying, and the poems were changed with each new unit.

Informational Brochures/Campaigns/Eco-Guides. Students can create brochures or eco-guides that inform or advise people about an issue, or how they could personally address a problem. My students have created guides about diet and nutrition. (I've had students move from shock to social action, reforming personal habits after reading *Sugar Blues, Fast Food Nation, In Defense of Real Food, The Ecology of Commerce*, and/or various medical reports like the Mayo's Sleep Clinic website.) They've written powerful pieces about how much sugar Americans eat, the effect of cola drinks on bone density, the amount of additives in food and their influence on early maturation, and a host of other issues. Student groups have focused on pollution, global warming, water use and the depletion of aquifers, energy use and conservation, erosion, the use of fertilizers and alternative farming practices—the list could go on and on. And what they all have in common is this: writing for real purposes, writing to effect change, correspondence undertaken with the mantle of novice expertise.

Protest Manifestos/Political Planks and Platforms. I often encourage students to choose a topic that comes up in our reading or study unit and form a political action group. I ask them to create a political plank or a protest manifesto. (The Internet has many examples of declarations and manifestoes. Many political agencies and parties now post their platforms.)

Students sometime choose to align themselves with an established political party. I have had several student groups contact and use the local Green party as a resource for environmental projects. Other groups have used Greenpeace, Amnesty International, the ACLU, the local Democratic or Republican Party, local churches, or the Moral Majority. My purpose is neither to proselytize nor to have students adopt my personal point of view, but to make students aware of many issues that are currently affecting their lives and will continue to do so. When we debate, I want them to understand why the issue is being debated, what is at stake, who is winning and why that is, and what groups are involved and why. I also want students to think about short-term versus long-term effects of decisions and actions. Of course, to make these discussions and activities worthwhile, we need to foreground how students could make a difference by addressing these issues.

To act as if we do not live in a world of contact zones and crises, to refrain from highlighting the many ways in which people make the world a better (or regrettably, a worse) place would be, in my opinion, to renege upon my responsibilities as a teacher. Research findings suggest that most students do not feel any personal agency, or see the possibility for it, or ever actually exercise choice in school, and that is something I find threatening to their happiness and to democracy (see Smith and Wilhelm, 2002). I also do not expect that the conclusions reached in my class will be end points; I hope they will be starting points for lives full of social consciousness, social inquiry, and social action.

In my classes, if students in different groups come up with conflicting platforms and perspectives, we welcome this diversity because it offers us a chance to converse and see other points of view. I do not push for conclusive answers, rather I work to help students stake "categorically tentative" positions that they are willing to change with new information or situations.

Popular Culture

Songs/Anthems/Music Videos. Students usually embrace any opportunity to bring popular culture into our classroom, particularly if it connects to music. In most cases, however, students use music as identity markers, but don't often think about the meaning of the music, lyrics, or related texts.

To build on their interest and examine songs both textually and musicologically, I ask students to choose a song that could be an anthem for them and to explain how the song summarizes some important attitude toward life or seminal life experience. When studying poetry, I often ask students to make a music video of a favorite poem. (I have seen stunning poetry videos about the content and meaning of poetry from the canon, such as Shakespeare's Sonnet CXXX, "My Mistress Eyes Are Nothing Like the Sun," Frost's "A Road Not Taken," Robinson's "Richard Cory," and also for contemporary poetry like Ginsberg's "Howl" or the poems of Gary Snyder.)

A variation is to have students become a character, author, or authority and choose a song that expresses their worldview or attitude toward the events in a story. I sometimes provide a list of songs and ask students to match characters or authors to the song that best expresses their worldview. I am probably showing my age, but I've found this technique works better with the songs of the sixties, seventies, and early eighties, but it works with contemporary music, too, and with older swing, jazz, or blues tunes. I have students provide song lists too. Students have to teach me and each other about their music, and their tastes seem to be more divergent than in the past. Still, this allows them another opportunity to bring what they know into the class, to stake their identity, and to teach the teacher and others.

Horoscopes/Fortune-Telling. Students can play astrologers and write horoscopes for particular book characters to express predictions about their futures, or they can clip out published ones from the local paper or magazines that seem apt for particular characters. Horoscopes can also be used to predict bigger events like the future of an ecosystem or the earth under certain circumstances, or a charge in an electrical circuit, among other things. As a variation, students can assume the role of a fortune-teller or prophet and recite predictions.

Movie Casting. I ask students to imagine they are directors or a production team for a movie version of a poem or book that they have read, or for a documentary about an issue we have studied. They choose actors that would be good for each role and justify these choices. For the documentary option, students identify experts or authorities that they could interview.

They can also be asked to propose ideas about the filming, using other films they have seen for ideas about techniques and approaches. They might even choose a director, or a musician, or particular songs for their soundtrack. I've even had students cast classmates for a movie version of a text, asking them to provide a positive justification for each choice.

As If. I got this idea from a game my daughters often play. "If I were the author/God/an authority/had special powers, I would…" This simple exercise can be done as a fill-in-the-blank to create a Choral Montage or Voice Collage. "If I were the author, I would…" "If I were God, I would help the Logans by…" "If I were an ant, I could…."

Subverted or Mirrored Correspondence. With any of the techniques, it is possible to have students compose a response and then rewrite it after new information has been introduced. For example, have students write diary entries before and after an important event or crisis, or at the beginning or end of a book. Students can rewrite a diary entry from another character's point of view, or critique or dispute it as that other character. The initial writing is on one side of the paper and the mirror writing goes on the other side.

Jazzy and Stephanie exchange letters as characters in *The Giver.*

Other Correspondence Ideas

- Letters of complaint

- **Author-reader exchange:** Write and, perhaps, send a letter to an author.

- Invitations or cards

- Character belief statement

- **Dear Abby letter** (and/or Abby's reply)

- Yearbook page

- Job Fair advertisement

- **Character résumé:** Create one at the beginning and again at the end of a text.

- **Campaign speech:** Imagine that a character or an author decides to run for office. What would his or her agenda and platform be?

- **Quotations book:** Collect quotes from a favorite character and illustrate these in a book of quotations. Or, assuming the role of a character, collect quotations from the Internet, *Bartlett's Familiar Quotations*, and other books that would appeal to that character.

- Job application

- Photo album

- Medical report

- Psychological profile

- Map/floor plan

- **Play-by-play:** Write up the events and actions of particular sequences or predict them as a sports event play-by-play. This can be quite fun when applied to historical or scientific processes such as oxidation or reduction, or to predicted events like the end of the Earth or our solar system.

- Interview with character on the scene

- **Person/reader on the street interview:** Question an unmentioned/unnamed observer or classmates who respond as readers

- **Ghost chapter of missing scene:** Put together a chapter or write a scene that seems to be missing, or that you think would be good in this story. This is great for texts with inference gaps, especially diaries and epistolary novels. It's akin to what many students do in on-time fanfics.

- **Character dream/dream journal:** Describe dreams in the text or those you imagine characters might have.

- **Character fantasy:** Express what the character or an affected person fantasizes as the best and worst possible future scenarios.

- **Character monologue:** Insert an explanation from a character into the book, explaining or justifying why he did something.

- **Shipwreck story:** Imagine you are a character shipwrecked on an island or another planet. How would you retell what you know or have experienced to the inhabitants there?

- **Myth/legend:** Explain and encapsulate, in mythic terms, what you have learned through this text or this unit study. Write your own myth or compare the situation or circumstances from a story to a myth or legend you know.

- **Magazine profile of characters**

- **Bill of sale:** Prepare a bill of sale for an important object or artifact. It can be satirical, such as the bill of sale for clean rivers like the sacred Penobscot sold unwillingly by Native Americans to the paper companies.

- **Newspaper:** Produce one that is set in the time and situation of the story, or one published now.

- **Job announcement:** Create one for a character or for the kind of person who could help solve issues that have come up.

- **Personal ads placed by characters**

- **Hidden conversations/secret tapes:** I used this hidden tape or video recorder technique with *Roll of Thunder, Hear My Cry* as readers figure out what was said or what happened in the car between Uncle Hammer and Mr. Morrison. This works well using texts with inference gaps—parts of the story left to our imagination.

- **Photographs:** Make or find photos that might have had significance for or been appreciated by a character, or that depict events, situations, and feelings from the story.

- **Related activities:**
  - Come up with captions for photos or descriptions of the photos in role.
  - Create a scrapbook belonging to a character or group of characters and respond to each other's scrapbooks in role as characters looking back several years after the story.
  - Make a collage of the photos; you can do collages from the perspective of different characters, then compare and discuss them.

Techniques Well-Suited for Story's End

At the climax of a text, the end of a text, or the end of a unit of study, these techniques will help students explore character experiences and elaborate future directions:

- Final phone call or phone call from the future
- Last will and testament
- Bequeaths, legacies, or last wishes
- Last meeting, or meeting between characters in the future
- Conversation between characters—a year, five years, ten years after the story

Voices From the Field

Dear Jeff:

Letter writing. Epistolary enactments. Correspondence.

I have taken these ideas and run with them, or to be more accurate, my students have run with them. Highly appropriate as I have looked up the etymology of correspondence and found it goes back to the Latin root of courir—to run, to deliver, to give currency to.

I began by having students write e-mails to each other in role. Then we used a variation of an electronic discussion group by having a group of students write questions to an author, played by another student, who responded in role. Since they could see each others' responses, we achieved a fabulous in-role online discussion.

Now it turns out that a group of students actually e-mailed an author who has agreed to an e-mail interview, so the enactment technique has taken a turn toward total reality!

Great stuff. I think it works so well because it is so closely connected to reality, and because it treats characters as real people worthy of respect and attention—authors, too, only more so.

—Doug

CHAPTER 12

DISCUSSION DRAMAS AND FORMATIVE ASSESSMENT
Rehearsing and Developing Our Thinking

It's the end of our civil rights and social justice unit. I ask my students how the historical figures and characters about whom we've read might respond to our inquiry question: *How can we best protect and promote our civil rights?*

Carrie, the quietest girl in the class, raises her hand and in a near-whisper asks, "Why don't we discuss this in a Radio Show? So the characters can speak for themselves?" The rest of the class roars its approval.

I immediately step into role as a radio show host: "Welcome to WURA talk radio, 97.9 on your dial! Today we take up the question of what we can do to protect and promote our civil rights. I'd like to hear thoughts from people from throughout history and in literature. What are civil rights? Where do they come from?

What threatens them? But most of all, what can we do to protect them? The lines are open… and look at them light up!"

Joe is waving his hand in the corner. I go over to him, miming my use of a microphone. "Caller number one, what is your name, and where are you from?"

Joe jumps right in, "I'm Dr. Martin Luther King, Jr., from Birmingham, Alabama. I once had a dream that if all people work together we could all have our God-given rights. But I learned that if *all* people don't work together, everyone loses their freedom. And most people are too selfish to work together. They only want to look out for themselves and keep what they already have.… They don't realize that when they don't protect others' rights they put their own rights at risk!"

Carrie, who rarely talks in class, calls in and identifies herself as Annemarie from *Number the Stars.* She voices her agreement with Dr. King, and points out that all the Danes worked together to save their Jewish neighbors from persecution. But she disagrees with him that everyone has to work together. "The Nazis were working against us, but we learned if any small group will stick together you can make big progress. And like Dr. King, we learned that you can't fight violence with violence."

Other students call in, taking on various roles. Chief Joseph: "The fight for rights can cost you everything—and sometimes you lose. History isn't always progress." Harper Lee: "Sometimes you have to take small steps towards civil rights. We have to go step by step." Frederick Douglass calling back in a booming voice: "I don't have time for small steps! My people were enslaved and we took small steps!"

In role, the students agree and disagree on fine points of the discussion, using the experiences from stories and history to make their various cases and distinctions. The discussion dances along animatedly for 30 minutes without a break, with each student taking at least one turn, and each responding to another's comments. I occasionally ask for justifications or clarifications, but I pose few questions; the students are talking to each other.

Carrie calls in to the show three times, a phenomenal participation rate for her.

Afterward, she has this to say: "I don't like to talk in class. I get mad if a teacher tries to make me. But I don't mind talking in a drama. It's easier for me to do and it makes me think harder. In drama it seems like you want to be involved, and you always learn something new… and it feels safer to take risks."

Getting Beyond Surface Talk to Sustained Dialogue

Discussion dramas are enactments designed to support student talk, which is essential. James Britton once said that all learning floats on a sea of talk. Research on classroom talk shows not only the importance of talk to learning but also how little substantive talk actually occurs in classrooms, and how the students who need it the most get the least of it (Nystrand, et al., 1997). Instead of engaging in conversation and building understandings, teachers typically run recitations where only a few students participate by "filling in" the blanks of the teacher's prepared lecture. These researchers found that the students who engage in these kinds of "discussions" do not exhibit what they call "substantive engagement" with the issues, ideas, or strategies that would enable them to develop an independent capacity to engage with ideas. In other words, the majority of class discussions rarely feed or support more sophisticated thinking.

This is not the kind of talk that leads to learning or that helps students see from new perspectives or use new strategies to deal with challenging concepts. As one student during our Boys and Literacy study complained, "In school, all you ever do is play 'guess what the teacher already knows'" (Smith and Wilhelm, 2002). The boys saw most class discussion as a fake and hypocritical pursuit. They wanted instead to engage in "real learning," which one boy defined as: "Finding your own way. Trying stuff out until you get it. Voicing your own opinion. Defending your position using what you've learned. Listening to others. You know, trying things out. Considering. Trial and error." Unlike most classroom talk, pre-scripted and insipid as it is, this kind of exploratory conversation would indeed help students grow and is consistent with Vygotskian principles of teaching.

Benefits of Discussion Dramas

Any enactment can be considered a discussion drama if it provides the opportunity for sustained conversation around an issue, a chance to consider and engage alternative points of views, to take a tentative position, to articulate where one (in or out of role) currently stands and why.

Anchor Standards for Reading, 1–10
Language, 1–3
Speaking/Listening, 1–6
Writing, 7–9

Students use discussion enactments to facilitate understanding of text and its meaning, of authorial positions and generalizations. They

- speak, in role or as themselves, in a supportive context that encourages their response.

- rehearse and try out new ideas in a supportive atmosphere.

- consider the meaning of text and textual ideas in the context of their own lives.

- speak from the perspectives of others, such as contemporary or historical figures, authors, or characters who are fictional and imaginary.

- speak from the safety of role to insert new ideas into the conversation—ideas that may be unpopular, ideas of characters that have been discounted, or ideas that are not their own but may need to be considered. Since students are not speaking as themselves, they have more freedom to insert such ideas into the conversation.

- explore the perspectives of various characters or figures on particular issues.

- uptake, extend and/or contend with ideas that are new to them.

- make intertextual connections by speaking as a character or author from another text to comment on the text being discussed, or by commenting as a figure from another era or situation on the context under consideration.

- reflect on and explore the consequences of different kinds of positions and actions in the world.

In other words, these techniques ask students to engage with, reformulate, and transform understandings—to think and learn deeply and with engagement.

Encourage participation. Though I have often experienced the difficulties with classroom discussion reported in the research (such as the difficulty engaging students, involving everyone, drawing out substantive ideas and the like), I have found discussion dramas to provide a powerful antidote. Structured to encourage everyone's participation, they highlight that the conversation is about developing meaning often around very edgy and important topics with far-reaching real world consequences, voicing and trying out different points of view, contending with each other, with characters, and with authors. This is exciting and interesting stuff, the stuff of real conversation in communities of practice. It is very unlike the fake kinds of "recitation" typical of school.

Encourage new points of view. If you have a point of view that you want inserted into the conversation, but feel uncomfortable doing so, you can insert it as a character or as another person, not as yourself (even if it *is* your position!). Since characters in an enactment are responsible for their views and actions, but only as characters, you can do and say things, try things out and experiment with views and actions that you might feel uncomfortable testing in real life. Enactments provide a "liminal space" that provides a safe space for experimenting.

Talking Through Issues:
Discussion Drama in "The Fan Club"

During "The Fan Club" drama, I usually employ three different discussion dramas to facilitate students' talk. We do one before the reading so students can articulate their feelings and stake a position on the issue we are going to read about: harassment and civil rights abuses in school. This builds personal investment in the classroom inquiry about civil rights and lets students bring their personal knowledge to bear on the story. It also activates and builds their schematic knowledge about social justice and, therefore, sensitizes them to building or adapting that "schema," or pattern of knowledge about the topic.

Our second discourse drama occurs near the climax of the story to highlight the thematic statement being made by the story thus far. This allows the students to weigh in on that issue and alerts them to details that will sensitize them to the irony and surprise of the ending.

And, of course, discussion can be a powerful reflective device after reading, so we do a choral montage technique when the story is over so students can discuss what has happened from the perspective of the characters.

Before Reading: Continuum/Vote With Your Feet Enactment

Hotseat: Vote With Your Feet

I frontload the reading of "The Fan Club" by using a continuum enactment. It is important in a continuum to present the participants with an issue related to a text or topic, but around which there is some kind of true tension and disagreement. The continuum starts with the teacher (or a student) making a statement that the class responds to. Though they might write out their position first, they quickly form a continuum—a lineup—with the people who most strongly disagree with the statement standing far to the left and those most strongly agreeing on the far right. This requires students to discuss the issue with several other people so they can correctly situate themselves within the lineup. In cases where everyone agrees or disagrees there will still be a continuum as the strength of opinions will certainly vary.

Since the unit in which I use this story is about civil rights and social justice, I frame a question for the Continuum that relates to this topic. I might pose one of the following statements:

> Despite being called the land of the free, the United States is really a country full of prejudice and intolerance.

or

> The ordinary American citizen harbors many prejudices.

If I do not think there will be enough disagreement, I might strengthen the statement or bring it closer to home, as in this example:

> Dangerous and hurtful prejudice is expressed right in our classrooms, and many students are unaware of it.

If I wanted to focus more on the role of friendship in the story, I might use continuum statements like:

> Most people have only one or two good friends throughout their lives, and they are lucky if they do.

or

> Friends are often the ones who are the first to betray you or let you down.

It can also be quite effective to make continuum statements based on current events related to the topic. Every time I have done this unit with students, there were civil rights issues in the news that I could use for continuum dramas:

> Clarence Thomas should be endorsed as a Supreme Court Justice.

or

> We must undertake military action in Kosovo/Afghanistan/Iraq/Iran/ the Palestinian territories/wherever because it is our responsibility to protect the freedom of people everywhere from repressive regimes.

or

> The United States has caused itself many problems because we only act in self-interest and not in the interest of peoples whose lives our policies influence.

As always, it is important to start with Continuum statements that are close to student experience and then build to statements that may be further from their experience. Once students form their Continuum, they can be interviewed in a Radio Show or matched with a student from another part of the Continuum to discuss their differences.

During Reading: Radio Show

This is one of my very favorite enactment techniques. My students are all familiar with the conventions of talk radio and are eager to use and satirize these conventions to discuss issues that arise in our reading.

In "The Fan Club," we discuss Laura's assertion that "we are all prejudiced in quiet ways." Radio Show facilitates discussion and classroom debate.

Using issues from a reading, a class can debate character or authorial statements or views; jump in at a point when a character has a decision to make to determine what he or she should do; assess, attack, or defend character or authorial decisions; or give characters our advice. The Radio Show enactment can also be used to discuss issues that have come up in current events or the school environment. Here's how you might carry out a Radio Show:

Pose a Provocative Question

When I first use this technique with students, I introduce the topic. In this case, I'd ask: *What do you think of Laura's statement that we are all prejudiced in quiet ways? Is she right on, kind of right, or totally wrong? And why do you think so?*

Invite Brainstorming

Next, I ask small groups of students to brainstorm who might feel strongly about this issue and what they would say on the show. I remind them that they can call in to the show as themselves, as political figures, as characters from this story or others we have read. If I think the students need help, we briefly brainstorm together who would be interested in the topic and what they might have to say about it, and then students continue brainstorming on their own.

Students Choose Role

After short discussions in groups, I ask the students to write down what role they will take and what they will have to say about the issue from the perspective of that role. (This step usually isn't necessary after you have done Radio Show once). Of course, they are not committed to calling in from this role, but it does ensure they are prepared to participate. Often students change their position and role to respond to what someone else has said. This is a good thing.

Frame the Enactment

We pause in our reading after Laura's speech and do the preparatory activities listed above. Then I go into talk radio mode, framing the enactment and getting things going. I remind the students that they can be "victims or volunteers," in other words, they can call into the show by raising their hand, or I can call on them. Once things get rolling, there is no trouble soliciting callers because students get involved and want to respond to each other.

Play Radio Host

I start with my best radio voice, booming out: "Welcome to WURA talk radio, 97.9 on your dial, home of talk radio! Many of our listeners have been following the story of Laura, and you may have heard her speech on civil rights that was broadcast live right here on this station. In that talk, Laura asserted that 'we are all prejudiced in quiet ways.' That will be the topic of today's show. Listeners, what do you think about that? Are you prejudiced? Are those around you prejudiced? Is our very culture rife with prejudice? What do you think and why do you think it? Call in now and share your opinion."

Once a caller is on the line, I ask for her name and from where she is calling. I might ask if she is "a first-time caller, a long-time listener" or invoke other conventions of talk radio.

Challenge Callers

In my role as a talk radio show host, I might challenge or press the caller: "But why do you think that?" "What would you say to Caller Two, who disagrees with you?" "But what if…?" After his call, I might restate his position in more provocative terms or play devil's advocate. I'll do anything to get kids to defend their positions, or cite evidence, and to invite other points of view, to make connections to other life and literary situations. I certainly encourage disagreement by saying things like "Is there anyone out there who would disagree with that provocative view?"

This can be a tremendous amount of fun, and you always get more perspectives than in a typical discussion since students can insert and satirize positions that are not their own but with which they want the class to contend. Everyone becomes part of the meaning-making community.

Variations include getting the students to play the host, or to have a panel of experts discuss the issue and then take calls. Students can stage a full-blown radio news show with reports a la NPR or public service announcements about the issues.

Another variation is Town Meeting, which can be done via a radio show, or can be conducted like a real face-to-face town meeting. Students are confronted by the teacher, in role as a government leader, with a story-bound, current, historical, or technological decision to make. They can be presented with opportunities and issues, for example to make their town totally dependent on alternative energies, to go west along the Oregon Trail, or to engage in a sociological experiment. Pros and cons can be discussed in the radio show format.

In my part of the world, we do use town meetings to make decisions affecting the community. In some schools where I have worked, the day starts with a school, "house," community, or class meeting to raise and discuss issues facing the students. If your students aren't familiar with the format, they can watch town meetings on CNN. Just like Mantle-of-the-Expert enactments, town meetings can range from real to fictional. But even the fictional is an exploration of real issues and an "imaginative rehearsal for living."

After Reading: Choral Montage

Choral Montage

I often use choral montage after key points in a text to explore different points of view about what has happened or what may happen. With "The Fan Club," I work it in at the end of the story.

Frontload the Activity: Have Students Write and Exchange Notes

I ask half of the students to imagine they are Laura and to write a note to Rachel, explaining their actions, expressing their feelings, saying what's in their hearts. The other half of the students become Rachel and write about what she is feeling at this time in a note to Laura. (This is a kind of Correspondence Drama.)

When they are done writing, students exchange notes as characters, so each Laura would exchange with a Rachel. If there are an odd number of students, I will also write a note in role. They then read the note that was written to the character they are playing and circle the words or phrase that is most poignant, powerful, or moving to them. (When using this technique, I instruct students not to circle clichés like "I love you" or "I'm sorry" so that we have more substantive phrases.)

A variation here is to have the characters write back to each other, or meet and discuss the notes. (On several occasions, students have independently elected to write several notes back and forth in role, sometimes over the course of a few days!)

> Rachel,
> Why can't you understand your just not cool? I'm not going to sit around and let you ruin it for me. I've waited forever to be popular and I don't know if you'd understand this or not but you have to make sacrifises to be popular and you have to be popular to survive high school. I was offered an oppertunity which I'm smart enough not to turn down. Maybe we weren't ment to be friends. The whole nature, nerdy style might work for you but it doesn't work for me anymore. There's a time to grow, we're not little kids anymore. Times have changed. I'm sorry
> xoxo
> Laura
> P.S. I don't want to see you anymore.

After reading "The Fan Club," a student in role as Laura wrote this note to a student in role as Rachel. She circled the line she'll use in a Choral Montage.

Introduce the Activity

I tell the students we are going to create a kind of poem called a Choral Montage. Samuel Taylor Coleridge wrote that poems were the best words in the best order, and we have identified and circled the best words from each character's feelings. Now we need to put them in the best order.

I divide students into groups of eight or so and ask them to form a montage by putting their words and phrases in an order that will make a poem. Of course, lines can be revised to fit the coherence of the poem—in fact, some lines usually have to be. Some lines can be repeated or become a chorus or *ostinato,* repeated after each line or two lines. Sometimes students create a varying ostinato, changing a line slightly with each repetition to emphasize changing feelings or a realization that is coming to the characters, or to emphasize an author's theme.

Model the Activity

The first time we do this, I model the process by helping one group create their montage. After this, as with most enactments, the students can quickly organize and stage their own.

I model by having the group line up in a row. I ask who has a line that might begin a poem about the character's feelings. If more than one person volunteers, they all read their lines out loud and we choose one and justify our choice. (I remind them we can always change our minds.) The rest of the class serves as a forum to give advice about what to do and how to revise things to make the poem work.

Build the Montage

When we have the first line, I ask the student who read it out to go to the far left of the line. (Students in each subsequent line also stand in the order in which they will read. They can be moved around in a different order and explore the effect.) This is a kind of *human mystery pot*, a technique where you cut up all the constituent lines of a poem or short text and ask students to arrange the lines into the best possible order. Students see that there are many possibilities, and that each construction has a slightly or sometimes greatly different meaning. It also sensitizes students to text structure, transitions, and other elements, such as repetition and parallelism, that develop and reinforce coherence. Additionally, this process provides an opportunity to practice revision, as lines can be moved around and tried different ways very easily.

Anchor Standards for Reading, 1–7 Language, 3–5 Writing, 4, 5

I then ask for a line that builds on or speaks to the first line. Or I might ask for a line that might end the poem; once we have established that ending, we discuss how the poem must proceed to reach this end point. Sometimes groups disagree about what the characters would feel and they must hash that out before deciding how the poem should proceed. For example, students sometimes disagree about whether Laura will be sorry for her actions or whether she will endorse and justify them. Such a decision should rely on textual evidence, and there is evidence for both positions.

From there, the poem is built, line by line. Usually the montages proceed with one character speaking, then the other, but sometimes one character speaks four lines and is then responded to by the other character in four lines. But all this is up to the students.

Perform the Piece

When students are satisfied, I ask them to perform their poem by using big voices with inflection. I usually videotape the final efforts, and almost always some students change their lines in a final act of revision (remember, this is a good thing!) and ask to redo it (also a good thing, showing their commitment to revision and creating a well-crafted final product). In fact, choral montage is a way of making the whole revision process visible to students.

Students organize themselves into a Choral Montage based on lines from character letters they've received.

Choral Montage: Student Example

S8: Our montage is called "You Know You Can't Hide."

S1 (Rachel): I can't believe you did this to me. Betraying our years of friendship.

S2 (Laura): We may have been friends once. But now you make it impossible.

S3 (Rachel): Once you believed in beautiful things: justice and the beauty of butterfly wings.

S4 (Laura): I still believe, but I keep it inside. I keep it inside, so I can survive.

S5 (Rachel): You hurt me so badly. Only you could hurt me so much.

S6 (Laura): I know that I hurt you, but I hurt myself more.

S7 (Rachel): Why don't you admit who you really are? I believe in the real you.

S8 (Laura): What's happened to me? I used to like who I was and who you were.

S3 (Rachel—ostinato): Once you believed in beautiful things: justice and the beauty of butterfly wings.

S4 (Laura—ostinato variation): I still believe, but I keep it inside. I keep it inside though I know I can't hide.

Once students grasp the idea, they can easily create montages on their own. But again, adequate modeling and coaching must precede such independent work.

For variations, include more voices, such as characters like Terri or Bill, a parent, or a teacher. When there are more voices, montages can be done with bigger groups, or with groups of students reading the same line like sections of a choir. Invite students to write notes in-role exploring character reactions immediately after the humiliation of Rachel and the reactions the characters might have a week afterward. We all know how our reactions to events change with time, and two montages could be created to compare the immediate with the more reflective views.

Montages don't always require the preparatory work of note writing. You can do a spontaneous montage by having students respond instinctively to an artifact or concept important to the story. For instance, have them use the prompt "Justice is…" and take turns filling in the blank. You could prompt them to react in terms of the story by responding to "Justice would be…" or to respond in terms of the world outside the story, articulating "imaginings," different personal or cultural constructs around the theme. These could then be used for further discussion, and different views could be contrasted and discussed. This kind of work makes for an "**instant montage**," though these, of course, could also be shaped later by grouping certain lines together, adding or revising lines, and so forth.

In a **voice collage** variation, all of the students become a character, like Rachel, Laura, or a parent, and stand in a circle. Each student responds in turn, or is tapped-in by the teacher who asks, "Will you tell me what is in your heart right now?" or "What are your concerns?" "What do you think must be done?"

Voice Collage: Student Example

Listen as a group of five students goes around a circle twice, responding to two prompts—one general and one related to the story:

> **Justice is…**
> When you get your own back.
> When you do unto others what they do to you.
> When the punishment fits the crime.
> When revenge is perfect and sweet.
> When the bad person's conscience won't let her sleep.

> **Justice would be….**
> If the Fan Club dumped Laura.
> If no one in school would speak to her.
> If Rachel won the lottery and Laura was poor.
> If Rachel got a college scholarship in science.
> If everyone knew what Laura did.

Like a Quakers Meeting, the teacher could ask students to respond to the prompt in or out of role whenever they feel ready, whenever the time is right. I usually ask that each student speak once, and say that some may respond more than once (but not more than three or four times!). I usually try to refrain from participating, though I may do so to shape the piece. Sometimes I record these so we can talk later about why we said what we did and discuss the coherence and meaning of what we have created.

Students could also write or read aloud diary entries to create raw material for a montage, or as a discourse technique on its own. Spoken diaries can be prompted: "Imagine what you are writing in your diary this night." Students can be tapped-in or use Voice Collage to speak their diary entries aloud (cf. Morgan and Saxton, 1987).

Continuum Variations

Stimulating Statements. I have also used continuum enactments while teaching science by making statements such as "Uniform motion does not exist," "Electricity is a wave," and "Chemicals like dioxin should never be created because they cannot degrade and end up in the environment forever."

Of course, students have to know enough to have an opinion, so before I used statements like these, we had done several experiments and some reading, or I had provided the statement and asked students to do some research.

Despite our work together on the first statement (which showed that uniform motion does exist, meaning that an object can travel at the same speed over time), most students still clung to their prior misconceptions. In the continuum, the students clustered around the two ends with only a few unsure students in the middle. So I added a Radio Show and layered it with Mantle of the Expert by announcing that WURA radio was on site at the local physics convention where the topic of uniform motion was being debated. I then asked a group of physicists (the cluster of boys at the far left end of the continuum) why they believed uniform motion did not exist. They responded with a series of philosophical statements about inertia. "Everything in the world is either speeding up or slowing down. Nothing is static. Nothing stays the same," said one boy.

At the other end, I interviewed a group of girls. "And here is an opposing group of physicists who maintain that uniform motion does exist. Why do you say so?" The girls immediately jumped in by talking about the experiments we had done with balls and ramps. "When we timed a ball at the top of the ramp for one meter and at the bottom for one meter, the times were the same, therefore uniform motion exists!" "Our empirical research proves it!" said one girl quite smugly!

By the time they were done speaking, the boys at the other end had broken ranks, either moving to the opposite end of the continuum or by setting up the experiment described by the girls!

Again, statements may have to be revised to prompt opinion and disagreement. Sometimes these enactments go quickly, and you can do several in a short time. The important thing is the talk that creates the continuum and that talk results from staking positions on the continuum. How do you justify where you are? Why are you so sure? On what do you base your opinion? What kind of evidence and evidentiary reasoning is most powerful?

Fold-Overs/Match-Ups. Talk can be facilitated by "folding over" the line and asking students to discuss their positions. When I do this, I break the line in half and match the students up with each other, so that students who moderately agree should be discussing the issue with those who most strongly disagree, and those who most strongly agree with someone who moderately disagrees. Their job is to try to convince each other to change their view and position.

Continuum Plus. Information or conditions can be added and then students can show how they change their opinion and position by moving or staying put on the continuum. For example, students could be asked to form a continuum based on the statement: "All people have the right to privacy." After students form their line, the statement could be revised to: "We must give up our right to privacy in times of war or terrorist threat," or perhaps, "We must give up some of our rights to secure greater rights." This, in turn, could be revised to: "The government has a right to all our personal information; if we have nothing to hide we have nothing to fear." At this point, students could be interviewed or write about why they positioned themselves as they did, and why they changed or maintained their position with the introduction of new information.

Repeated Continua. A follow up to the continuum is to read about the issue and to engage in other enactments that confront or confirm various positions. The continuum can then be reenacted later, and people can be interviewed about their change in position.

In-Role Continuum. Continuum can also be done in role. In the "Space Trader" enactment (Wilhelm and Edmiston, 1998), we cast students as senators and asked them to make a decision as to whether we should trade prisoners for the gold and environmental solutions offered by the aliens. On the continuum almost all of them agreed. So we then had the students become the prisoners and enacted how they came to be in prison, their various relationships, and the various possibilities of their future with the aliens. Finally, students became senators again and redid the continuum. This time, all of the students disagreed.

Such a continuum can be done to explore how various historical figures or literary characters or authors would weigh in on particular issues. How would Dr. King respond to the statements about our right to privacy? How would our national security chief or Ghandi?

Other Variations of Discussion Techniques

TV Coverage. As with Radio Show, students create their own TV coverage of events from the text or topic being studied. Elements could include news, features, commentaries, analysis, and so forth. Some of the techniques that work well with such enactments are voiceovers, in which tableaux are commented upon like a reporter, or summing up, in which the teacher or a student sums up what has happened so far in a text, the unit study, or the enactment. In the process, he or she sums up what has been learned and what positions and understandings have been reached: "What we know so far is…" "The point we have reached could be summarized as …" Of course, it can also reach into the future: "The problems facing us now are…" "What remains to be seen is…" Universalizing is a kind of summing up that focuses on deeper meanings. It connects the textual experience to other events and life situations, for example, "Dr. King's experiences are similar to Rachel's in these ways…" Universalizing helps students "identify with a wider range of other human beings throughout time." (Wagner, 1976)

Teacher in Role/
Talk Show/
Forum Drama

Talk Show. Students enjoy discussing texts or issues in a talk show format, often spoofing popular shows from TV. I usually ask that students in the audience write questions on cards, and sometimes I stipulate that the questions be particular types, for example, think-and-search inference questions. Students can read aloud their own questions or pass them in so that an emcee can choose the ones to read aloud.

Quiz Show. Quiz shows are excellent ways to stimulate kids to articulate both summaries and inferences about stories. *Who Wants to Be a Millionaire? The Weakest Link*, and any other show are great models. I prompt students to ask three level questions that are alternatively factual, inferential and critical/applicative questions or as a variation: plot-level, deep meaning, and feeling-level questions.

Trading Rumors. Students trade rumors either in or out of role, making inferences that explain certain actions, making predictions about future action, building understanding about character. Rumors can be traded in pairs or triads and then shared in a circle or in a large group. Reasons to disbelieve or endorse the rumors can be shared.

Memory Circle. Either in or out of role, students share memories of a character, or about a time period, event, and so forth. It can be used before reading to frontload background information, during reading as students summarize textual events and/or make inferences about what has happened to characters before the story started, or after reading as people who were affected looking back.

Walkarounds/Poster Sessions. In Walkarounds, each student or group of students asks a question, proposes an inquiry topic to pursue, or makes a comment/judgment about the text or topic being studied and prints it on a piece of posterboard or newsprint sheet. The students can illustrate as they desire, but they should leave most of the sheet blank. These sheets are then passed to another group or posted around the classroom, and other students must write a comment or response on it. One person from each group stays with their poster so that conversations can be pursued about the point of view or about a request for information. That student can then be relieved by another member of the group.

Visitor comments may be possible answers to the question or ways to explore and address the question. In the case of inquiry questions, the responses are suggested resources, people to interview, books to read, movies to watch, or other kinds of suggestions that will help the students with their inquiry. To the comments or evaluations, visiting students could agree or disagree with a comment, or make some other kind of insightful comment about the point of view expressed. When the class is done, there should be a transcript of ideas recorded on each poster sheet that includes a comment from every classmate (or group of classmates). Naturally, students will talk to each other as they mill around, but they must record a summary of their views or suggestions on the poster of each group so there is a record of their contributions. Students can be asked to sign or initial their comments on each sheet.

Forum. There are many different kinds of forum enactments. Forums require that there is a dialogue between the participants creating a scene/tableaux/montage and the observers who watch and give advice. The participant and observer are two stances of a reader, since readers both enter into and immerse themselves in story worlds, and detach themselves to reflect on the experience of that story world in various ways (Langer, 1995). The forum shows that the engaged reader is both inside and outside of the text, both experiencing it and spectating on her experience. One kind of forum that I use quite often is the unfinished scenario in which the teacher provides a group of students with a short role-play that is left unfinished and encourages the rest of the class to become involved in the discussion with characters about their possible choices. Or students can be challenged to write their own short role-play that invites other perspectives to join in, as in the following example. All forums are a kind of interactive theater where the audience or those on the outside are invited inside in some way to participate, shape, advise, and respond.

Another kind of forum is where one group of students is creating a tableau, montage, or any other kind of performance and the rest of the students are engaged as directors, producers, or other experts giving them advice or suggestions about how to proceed. In an Inner Circle/Outer Circle forum, those in the outer circle observe what is going on in the inner circle as they pursue an enactment or some other kind of task. The outer circle can then do any of the following:

- See and identify something interesting, reporting what it observed.
- Place something in the scene.
- Give lines of dialogue.
- Provide an epigraph or label.
- Suggest a new direction for the scene.
- Replace an actor.
- Add an actor.
- Explain a change and how it changes meaning.

Forum Theater Activity to Explore Censorship
Guidelines for Students

Create a role-play that will highlight the various perspectives at work in the following scenarios. You will present the beginning of your role-play to the class, and we will then join in as other characters to add details, discuss motivations, and talk about the issues involved. Make sure your introduction lays out the issues and invites the rest of us to enter into your conversation from various roles.

1. A parents' group brings concerns about *Huckleberry Finn* being read in school to the English Department. The book, they argue, uses racist language and therefore encourages racism. They want the book to be eliminated from the curriculum.

2. A community panel objects to a Stephen King book, *Rose Madder*, which is in the middle and high school library. They want the book to be removed. They are also concerned about other Stephen King books, and about certain series books like *The Hunger Games* and *Harry Potter*. The panel members are concerned primarily about violence, but also about the use of the supernatural.

3. A group of teachers is worried about unrestricted Internet access at the school. They feel that this access causes students to waste considerable time, and they know that students are accessing specious kinds of information, if not pornography. They want Internet policies put in place, and some also want student access to the Internet stopped.

4. The faculty is concerned about a new schoolwide free-reading program. In particular, high school students have been selecting books like the *Fear Street* series. Though students have been pointed toward more "literary" texts, these are the kinds of books most students have gravitated toward.

5. A teacher has been put on leave for teaching *The Witch of Blackbird Pond*, a past Newbery Medal winner. A parents' group, supported by funding and materials from a think tank group, is waging a campaign called: "Immoral Teachers Teaching Immorality—Get Out of Our Schools!" They call an open community meeting. You are there.

(Scenes could be revised to reflect any kind of issue such as scientific issues of evolution or political issues like freedom of information.)

- Give other suggestions.
- Analyze the activities.
- Converse with the inner circle, interviewing members about what they have done, in or out of role.

This technique is similar to the Fishbowl, in which the inner circle is in the "bowl" being observed by those in the outer circle. Those on the outside can simply learn from the inner circle or jump into the fishbowl to help out. Later they can comment on the action or respond to it in some way. The inner circle takes the initiative and the outer circle participates, shapes, or responds in some way to what they do.

Another version of Inner Circle/Outer Circle includes getting the two sets of students to play different roles and talk (each student in the Outer Circle plays the same character, and those in the inner circle play that character's former self, current self or future self, as one character to another, as advisor and character, character and author, and so on.

Guided Imagery/In the Mind's Eye. This is a good technique for assisting kids with visualization. Sometimes it helps for students to close their eyes. The teacher may prompt with a description from a story or with a question and will then ask students to build on that, speaking out what is in their mind's eye—whatever it is they see, feel, hear, or sense. A teacher working with *Roll of Thunder, Hear My Cry* might say, "We arrive at the Logan's home just as they are sitting down for Christmas dinner. What do we see?" Students can then respond in turn. "How do the Logans respond to us?" Students respond. "How do we feel about how they treat us?"

The students can then compare their visualizations and predictions with the scene where Jeremy Simms comes to visit them. The technique also works to flesh out textual detail when the author has left it to our imagination. Some students also need extra help to create the story world and their place in it, and this technique supports that.

Four Corners. This fabulous technique is similar to **Continuum** and **Vote With Your Feet** enactments in that students stake their position physically. Students respond to questions or perspectives, staking their position by placing themselves in the part of the room that shows their response. This can be done as characters, authors, or as one's self. One corner of the room is for Totally Agree, another for Mildly or Somewhat Agree, another for Somewhat Disagree, and one for Totally Disagree. Sometimes I post visuals such as a smiley face, a somewhat smiling face, and so on in the different corners of the room.

I was recently working in the Chicago Public Schools with Yolanda Williams, a remarkable teacher. She was working on a unit on bullying and had prepared a series of statements that she felt her students would disagree about. She also wrote some that were contradictory so kids would have to move around with different statements:

Cool kids don't trick on other kids.

Some people deserve to be teased—it's for their own good.

Kids cannot be held responsible to the same degree as adults.

It is your responsibility to argue or fight for your rights when they are under attack.

There is no bullying in our school.

Ignoring bullies is the most effective way to deal with them.

Fair is the same as equal.

As Yolanda read out the statements, students had to put themselves in the corner that designated their response. Then they were asked to justify their answer, or to pair up with a person from another perspective to discuss why their views differed. As they read stories about bullying, Yolanda cast students in the roles of different characters and authors and asked them to respond to the same comments by using Four Corners. The students had to explain, in role, how they knew their character belonged where they were.

In another class, students were studying immigration, and the teacher used the same technique to get them to respond to related issues like: Non-citizens should have the same rights as citizens to education, fair trials, work, and education; We have a responsibility to care for anybody who is in our country; People who have not entered this country legally should be made to leave; People who are living in America should learn English.

Since the school was culturally diverse, many strong opinions were stated. During their unit, students eventually devised family scrapbooks for characters who had immigrated to America, created a documentary about the problems of immigrants in Chicago, created their own citizenship test that they thought reflected true American values, and some students even undertook social action projects, by helping people prepare for citizenship tests, tutoring people in English, forming a community welcoming committee, and many other projects.

These strategies led to real-world decision-making and action. And that, in the final analysis, is the point of all enactment strategies—to assist more powerful reading and enable more democratic living.

Moving Toward Understanding and Use: Drama and Formative Assessment

One of many insights I've learned over the years from George Hillocks and his research is this: if we are interested in promoting our students' engagement and learning, then we are wise to spend most of our time and energy planning creative lessons and interacting with students rather than focusing on grading. In his important assessment research, George found that most assessment does not contribute at all to student learning, nor to student improvement on future assignments. When assessment does make a positive difference, two essential elements are typically in place: 1) teachers provide assessment at the point of need and in a context of use; and 2) students apply the feedback immediately to the task at hand.

In other words, if we are interested in our students' learning and not wasting our own limited time and energy, then we will provide formative assessments *in the process* of teaching and learning *that we can use to plan* our next lesson, and students can use to *immediately* revise their thinking and work. All assessment and feedback will directly lead towards deeper understanding and greater facility with actual application. Formative assessment helps both teachers and students learn towards these ends. Understandably, then, we should spend more time on formative assessment than on the summative assessments that occur after the process of learning is complete. Teachers use summative assessment to assign grades, and the data is clear: this act does not contribute to student understanding or use.

Action Strategies as Gut Checks and Quizzes

So, imagine that I want to know whether my students have read and understood the last reading assignment. I could give a quiz, which would take ten minutes of class time. Plus, unless I managed to construct a very thoughtful examination (which takes even more time and energy), a run-of-the-mill quiz typically provides limited information—and I have to spend even more time grading it. *Or,* I could ask students in their learning groups to become a newscast team. I could invite them to number off by fours. Student 1 could assume the role of newscaster reporting on the lead story from last night's reading. Student 2 could play the role of composing interview questions for the major character from the reading. Student 3 might become the major character and write answers to the questions Student 2 composes. Student 4 serving as a feature reporter might connect the text to an interesting current event or issue, or to our inquiry. (Of course you can assign any roles you want. I've had sports reporters who look for a sports or competition connections of some kind, weather reporters who report on the effect of weather or setting on what has happened, either literally or metaphorically.) The students could write out scripts that demonstrated understanding of the text and its connection to our inquiry and to the world as I walked through the class and observed. I this way, I could quickly ascertain who had done the reading and what was understood.

Mark leads a discussion in role. The students around him act as his brain, advising him on how to respond to the class.

Student discussion and collaboration is encouraged—both actions support students' learning and mine. Listening in provides a source of data I need to inform my teaching. If I want, I can have my students actually perform their newscast to a partner group, and jigsaw or feature an especially good one that will be presented to the whole class. I can do this in approximately twenty minutes. This process might take a bit longer than administering a quiz, but students are doing all the work, and the work is not simply recall, but involves the meaningful construction of collaborating, inferring, seeing connections, reflecting on meaning, representing what they have learned, playing the mantle of the expert and taking on the discourse of reporters, and much, much more. And I don't have to grade any papers. My time and energy is preserved for lesson planning that might actually contribute to my students learning.

Action strategies of all kinds can work in this way as quick gut checks: we can ask students to hotseat a character and provide an alter ego or inner voice to report on what was most important to a particular character in an assigned reading. We will quickly learn whether they understand the literal information in the text, as well as whether they can infer from this, see patterns, make real world connections, and much more.

Working through the mantle of the expert, students have multiple opportunities to "show their smarts" on the literal, inferential and critical/applicative levels: imagine a lesson involving geography where students are asked to play travel agents promoting a setting for eco-tourism, or ecological experts considering a proposal to drill an oil well or open a mine in a particular location. For a lesson involving civics, students could play the role of elected officials or staff responding to some kind of dilemma or proposal that would require them to make use of their reading. For a reading involving history, students might perform as sculptors creating tableaux of important scenes or portraying the meaning of events, or artists creating memorials, displays, or museum exhibits of any kind.

For this kind of formative assessment work, I particularly like forum dramas where students have to present and then respond in-role to questions from the class. I also like "Rewind" or "What If?" dramas where we rewind a scene to the beginning and introduce changes in situation or conditions and ask the role players to revise what would happen as a result. This kind of work puts kids on the spot, and asks them to think spontaneously, creatively and in patterns, extrapolating and interpolating what they have learned in new ways. They are making meaning with central concepts and procedures from the unit instead of just reporting out on factual recall.

We can also ask students to invent their own drama presentations that demonstrate knowledge of the reading and what it means or how meanings might be applied. Obviously, the possibilities for these quick-hit enactments are endless.

Using them not only gives you as a teacher a sense of what students understand now and could understand next, but these techniques also engage the students, are fun, further their learning, and can revitalize the learning process by emphasizing the purpose of the learning, placeholding what has been learned, and providing avenues for discussing it. Such work is also clearly a part of an overall process and works toward a culminating presentation, particularly if that presentation involves the kind of work students are doing in the "gut checks."

Responding to and Writing About Drama Work

You can use drama activities in any course to explore course content, or social connections, or cultural issues from a multi-disciplinary perspective. You can incorporate informal in-role reflective writing activities into or after any kind of drama work to encourage students to generate a record of their thoughts for sharing with others. One such tool for doing this kind of writing is a "critical response protocol" (adapted here from Beach, et al 2010), which invites a slow reflectivity and encourages the essential first steps for critical meaning-making, reflection, and meta-cognitive awareness. You might use this protocol to encourage students to write in-role or as themselves in response to the drama work they experienced in class.

- What did you notice in the text/drama work? What roles or lenses (e.g., a gender lens as a male or female, a power lens tuning you in to power relationships, a cultural lens, religious lens, etc.) do you use that helped you notice this?

- What does what you noticed remind you of? What personal or global connections to our inquiry unit or other readings can you make?

- How does what you noticed make you feel?

- What questions does the drama work/presentation raise for you?

- What facets of the context/setting are you tuning in to (e.g., the larger historical and cultural elements and issues, the more regional elements and issues, or the very specific local elements and issues)? Which ones are you ignoring? Why?

- Try on a role/lens that is not typical for you and revisit the first five questions to explore how your response changes from this new position.

- What have you learned from your reading and response? Factually, by inferring/ pattern-seeing, by critiquing and looking for applications?

- In what ways do you accept, question, or resist what you have learned? What role/ lens are you using that lead to this response? What if you were using a different role/lens?

- What do you want to learn more about? How might taking on different lenses/role positions help you to learn this?

- How could you go about pursuing future learning?

Action Strategies as Teacher Research

Whenever we set up situations where we can learn from our students about what they know and what they can do so that we will know how to teach them more effectively in the next lesson, we are engaged in the process of reflective teaching and teacher research. Whenever we try something new with our students to see what will happen, and then try to extract the principles of whatever success or shortfall ensues so that we can become more consciously competent, we are engaged in action research. When we use drama as a method of formative assessment, our students will be actively engaged in demonstrating their learning at the same time that they will be revising, extending, representing and sharing it.

When we use action strategies as formative assessment, seeing what we can learn from what they do and how they do it, we are engaged in learning from our students how best to teach them. This process refocuses us on the WHO—those specific human beings we are teaching—and on the HOW of their qualitatively lived through-learning-experience—the processes and the feelings they have about what they are learning, what they accept and resist, what they understand and don't quite understand. All of this is done in a liminal space so articulating problems and questions is safe and encouraged. All of this is very good stuff indeed, and makes our teaching as well as our assessments fun, humane, and inherently supportive of our students' learning—just as it should be.

Voices From the Field

Jeff:

I have been using continuum dramas for a long time in my Advanced Biology class. We dissect rabbits each year as part of a unit on anatomy and physiology. We begin by doing an "opinionaire" about our beliefs on animal rights and other experimentation issues. I ask kids to line up on the continuum about each issue, and I encourage discussion as this helps students position themselves. Students must then make a case for their position on the continuum. If other students are convinced or persuaded in some way, they can move.

Having been given the opportunity to clarify and share their views, and to consider opposing ones, students are then allowed to opt out of dissection and do an alternative project.

Though I have done this for years, I want to thank you for the idea of incorporating the Talk Show interview format into it. Layering this on to the continuum helped the kids develop more thoughtful responses and gave more direction to what was sometimes a hectic activity. It allowed me to slow things down and tease out differences of opinion, to challenge and intervene as a teacher. I made sure that every student expressed and *justified* her views on at least one of the issues. And I must say there was a lot of laughter, and a good time was had by all.

—Dennis

Closing Reflections

I've just returned from my latest trip to Australia, where I had the privilege of working with some Aboriginal students and their teachers in their homelands. The students were absolutely beautiful children, who were taught in both their home language and English. One day I worked with a group of third through sixth graders. I asked them to tell me a traditional story, and after discussing it amongst themselves, they jointly told the story of the two crocodile sisters. These shape-shifters caused many problems for humankind. One day, one sister became a crocodile and had great fun repeatedly scaring her sister, who eventually figured out the trick. The sisters decided to become crocodiles permanently so they could eat whatever they wanted and rule the waterways. This caused mankind to make many adaptations when fishing or using the estuaries, actions like putting strings on the water or beating the water before going into it to get a fish trap.

When the storytelling was done, we created visual tableaux to create a slide show of the story. I then asked the students to brainstorm the possible topics and associated lessons from the story.

I was astonished with their capacity to identify topics and themes—something that is often very challenging for much older students to do. They came up with several answers: Topic: Appropriate teasing. Theme: Don't scare somebody too much or keep teasing them over and over! Topic: Misuse of power. Theme: Don't use your power to scare or eat people! Topic: Warnings. Theme: You've got to pay attention. Like where there are crocs around, you better be really careful and not sit on the river bank, especially if you are a little kid!

The teachers and I concluded the lesson by asking the students to take the themes they had identified and show a two-sided tableau of a best/worst scenario: What good things would happen if you follow the lesson; what bad things might happen if you do not. Small groups energetically organized their tableaux and rehearsed them before feeling ready to present them to the group. When they did, there was much laughter and clapping.

Toward the end of the lesson, I asked the students if they could apply the thematic lessons they had learned to other areas of their lives. They turned inside to their small groups, sitting on the floor, and energetically discussed connections from lessons about teasing, power, and cautionary action to their own lived experience, or foreseeable experience. They then presented these in mantle-of-the-expert monologues.

These are very complex processes of understanding, and the students made use of substantive concepts as they engaged in these processes. And they pursued the various aspects of the drama work with what can only be called great engagement and joy. Is this not what we want for all of our own students? The final takeaway: Action Strategies make this kind of substantive and joyful work available to us all. Let's take up the challenge of using them!

Bibliography

Works Cited

Bakhtin, M. M. (1981). *The dialogic imagination*. Translated by Michael Holquist. Austin: University of Texas Press.

Bandura. A. (1998). Perceived self-efficacy in cognitive development and functioning. *Educational Psychologist*, 28, 117–148.

Beach, R., Campano, G., Edmiston, B. & Borgman, M. (2010). Literacy tools in the classroom: *Teaching through critical inquiry, grades 5–12*. New York: Teachers College Press.

Begley, S. (2008). *Train your brain, change your mind: How a new science reveals our extraordinary potential to transform ourselves*. New York: Ballantine Books.

Bloom, B. (1976). *Human characteristics and school learning*. New York: McGraw-Hill.

Bloom, B. (Ed.) (1985). *Developing talent in young people*. New York: Ballantine Books.

Blythe, Tina & Associates (1998). *The teaching for understanding guide*. San Francisco: Jossey-Bass.

Bolter, J. D. (1991). *Writing space*. Mahwah, NJ: Erlbaum.

Bordan, S. (1970). *Plays as teaching tools in the elementary school*. New York: Parker.

Bronowski , J. (1976). *The ascent of man*. New York: Little Brown and Company.

Brown, J., Collins, A., & DuGuid, P. (1989). Situated cognition and the culture of learning. *Educational Researcher (18)* 32–42.

Brown, S. (2009). *Play: How it shapes the brain*. New York: Penguin.

Bruner, J. (1986). *Actual minds, possible worlds*. Cambridge, MA: Harvard University Press.

Buehl, D. (2001). *Classroom strategies for interactive learning*. Newark, DE: International Reading Association.

Coles, G. (1998). *Reading lessons: The debate about literacy*. New York: Wang and Hill.

Csikszentmihalyi, M. (1990). *Flow: The psychology of optimal experience*. New York: Harper and Row.

Csikszentmihalyi, M., Rathunde, K., & Whalen, S. (1993). *Talented teenagers: The roots of success and failure*. Cambridge, England: Cambridge University Press.

Damasio, A. (2008). *The brain that changes itself*. New York: Pantheon.

Dewey, J. (1916). *Democracy and education*. New York: The Free Press.

Dewey, M. (1994). *Combining literature with drama*. (ERIC document Reproduction Service No. 376 508).

Doidge, N. (2007). *The brain that changes itself*. New York: Penguin.

Edmiston, B., & Wilhelm, J. (1998). Repositioning views/reviewing positions: Notes for action researchers and reflective drama practitioners. *Educational drama and language arts: What research shows*, Edited by B. J. Wagner. Portsmouth, NH: Heinemann.

Eisner, E. (1999). *The kind of schools we need*. Portsmouth, NH: Heinemann.

Fredricksen, J., Wilhelm, J., & Smith, M. (2012). *Tell me a story: Teaching the reading and writing of narrative*. Portsmouth, NH: Heinemann.

Greene, M. (1995). *Releasing the imagination: Essays on education, the arts, and social change*. San Francisco: Jossey-Bass.

Halliday, M. (1978). *Language as social semiotic*. Baltimore, MD: University Park Press.

Heath, S., & McLaughlin, B. (1993). *Identity and inner-city youth: Beyond ethnicity and gender*. New York: Teachers College Press.

Heathcote, D. (1978). Of these seeds becoming: Drama in education. *Educational Drama for Today's Schools*. Edited by R.B. Shuman. London: Scarecrow Press.

Heathcote, D. (1982). *Heathcote at the National: Drama teacher—facilitator or manipulator?* Edited by T. Good. Banbury, Oxfordshire: Kemble Press.

Heathcote, D., Johnson, L., & O'Neill, C. (eds.) (1984). *Dorothy Heathcote: Collected writings on education and drama*. London: Hutchinson.

Heathcote, D., & Bolton, G. (1995). *Drama for learning: Dorothy Heathcote's mantle of the expert approach for teaching drama*. Portsmouth, NH: Heinemann.

Hillocks, G., & Smith, M. (1995). *Teaching writing as reflective practice*. New York: Teachers College Press.

Hillocks, G. (1999). *Ways of thinking, ways of teaching*. New York: Teachers College Press.

Housum-Stevens, J. (1998). Performance possibilities: Curating a museum. *Voices from the Middle* (6)2, 19-26.

Iser, W. (1978). *The act of reading: A theory of aesthetic response*. Baltimore, MD: Johns Hopkins University Press.

Kahn, E., Walter, C., & Johannessen, L. 1984. *Writing about literature*. Urbana, IL: NCTE.

Kathriner, D. (2007). Educational relevance: Can technology make a difference? *English Leadership Quarterly 29*. 4 (Apr 2007): 6-8.

Langer, J. (1995). *Envisioning literature: Literary understanding and literature instruction*. New York: Teachers College Press.

Lave, J. & Wenger, E. (1991). *Situated learning: Legitimate peripheral participation*. New York: Cambridge University Press.

May, F. (1990). *Reading as communication: An interactive approach*. Columbus, OH: Merrill.

McMaster, J. (1998). "Doing" literature: Using drama to build literacy. *The Reading Teacher (51)7*, 574–584.

Meek, M. (1983). *Achieving literacy: Longitudinal studies of adolescents learning to read*. New York: Routledge and Kegan Paul.

Mercer, N. (1995). *The guided construction of knowledge*. Avon, UK: Multilingual Matters.

Moffett, J. & Wagner, B. (1983). *Student-centered language arts and reading, K–13*. New York: Houghton-Mifflin.

Morgan, N. & Saxton, J. (1987). *Teaching drama*. London: Hutchison.

Nystrand. M. (1997). *Opening dialogue: Understanding the dynamics of language and learning in the English classroom*. New York: Teachers College Press.

O'Neill, C. (1995). *Drama worlds*. Portsmouth, NH: Heinemann.

O'Neill, C., & Lambert, A. (1982). *Drama structures: A practical handbook for teachers*. Portsmouth, NH: Heinemann.

O'Neill, C., Lambert, A., et al. (1976). *Drama guidelines. London*: Heinemann Educational Books.

Pajares, F. (1996). Self-efficacy beliefs in academic settings. *Review of Educational Research*, 66, 543–578.

Palmer, P. (2007). *The courage to teach*. San Francisco: Jossey-Bass.

Papert, S. (1996). *The connected family*. New York: Cox.

Peterson, R., & Eeds, M. (1990/2007). *Grand conversations: Literature groups in action*. New York: Scholastic.

Pope, R. (1994). *Textual intervention*. London: Routledge/Kegan Paul.

Rabinowitz, P., & Smith, M. W. (1998). *Authorizing readers: Resistance and respect in the teaching of literature*. New York: Teachers College Press.

Ross, E. and Roe, B. (1978). Creative drama builds proficiency in reading. In N. H. Brizendine & J. L. Thomas (eds.), *Learning through dramatics: Ideas for teachers and librarians*, pp. 52–57. Phoenix, AZ: Oryx.

Shickedanz, J. (1978). You be the doctor and I'll be sick. In N. H. Brizendine & J. L. Thomas (eds.), *Learning through dramatics: Ideas for teachers and librarians*, pp. 44–51. Phoenix, AZ: Oryx.

Siks, G. (1983). *Drama with children*. New York: Harper and Row.

Smagorinsky, P., McCann, T., & Kern, S. (1987). *Explorations*. Champaign, IL: NCTE.

Smith, M. & Wilhelm, J. (2002). *Reading don't fix no Chevys: The role of literacy in the lives of young men*. Portsmouth, NH: Heinemann.

Smith, M., Wilhelm, J., & Fredricksen, J. (2012). *Oh yeah? Teaching the reading and writing of argument*. Portsmouth, NH: Heinemann.

Smith, M., & Wilhelm, J. (2006). *Going with the flow*. Portsmouth, NH: Heinemann.

Smith, M., & Wilhelm, J. (2009). *Fresh takes on teaching the literary elements*. New York: Scholastic.

Valde, G. & Kornetsky, L. (2002). Transformative learning. *NEA Higher Education Advocate (19)3*, pp. 5–7.

Verwys, B., Haberling, J. & White, B. (2000). Cultivating concern for characters. Paper presented at the annual meeting of the National Council of Teachers of English. Milwaukee, WI. November.

Vygotsky, L. (1978). *Mind in society: The development of higher psychological processes*. Cambridge, MA: Harvard University Press.

Wagner, B. J. (1976). *Dorothy Heathcote: Drama as a learning medium*. Washington, DC: National Education Association.

Wagner, B. J. (1998). *Educational drama and language arts: What research shows*. Portsmouth, NH: Heinemann.

Wilhelm, J. (2001). *Improving comprehension with think-aloud strategies: Modeling what good readers do*. New York: Scholastic.

Wilhelm, J. (2004/2012). *Enriching comprehension with visualization*. New York: Scholastic.

Wilhelm, J. (2007). *Engaging readers and writers with inquiry*. New York: Scholastic.

Wilhelm, J. (1997/2008). *You gotta BE the book: Teaching engaged and reflective reading with adolescents*. New York: Teachers College Press.

Wilhelm, J., Baker, T., & Dube, J. (2001). *Strategic reading: Guiding students to lifelong literacy*. Portsmouth, NH: Heinemann.

Wilhelm, J., & Edmiston, B. (1998). *Imagining to learn: Inquiry, ethics, and integration through drama*. Portsmouth, NH: Heinemann.

Wilhelm, J., & Friedemann, P. (1998). *Hyperlearning: Where projects, inquiry, and technology meet*. York, ME: Stenhouse Publishers.

Wilhelm, J., & Novak, B. 2011. *Teaching literacy for love and wisdom*. New York: Teachers College.

Wilhelm, J., Smith, M., & Fredricksen, J. (2012). *Get it done! Teaching the reading and writing of informational text*. Portsmouth, NH: Heinemann.

Wilhelm, J., Wilhelm, P., & Boas, E. (2009). *Inquiring minds learn to read and write*. Oakville, ONT: Rubicon.

Yaffe, S. (1989). Drama as a teaching tool. *Educational Leadership*, 46, 29–32.

Index